COLLECTING, RESTORING AND DRIVING

CLASSIC CARS

'I would certainly recommend it to anyone who is tempted to get involved with a classic car'

The Daily Telegraph

COLLECTING, RESTORING AND DRIVING
CLASSIC CARS

GRAHAM ROBSON

PATRICK STEPHENS
Wellingborough, Northamptonshire

First published in 1987

British Library Cataloguing in Publication
Data

Robson, Graham
   Collecting, restoring and driving classic
   cars.
   1. Automobiles—History
   I. Title
   629.2'222'09   TL15

   ISBN 0-85059-918-0

Patrick Stephens Limited is part of the
Thorsons Publishing Group, Denington
Estate, Wellingborough, Northamptonshire,
NN8 2RQ, England

Printed in Great Britain at
The Bath Press, Avon

10 9 8 7 6 5 4 3 2

Front cover: Top *Battle of Britain — the
1960s-style Aston Martin DBS faces up to
the 1970s-style BMW 3.0CSL. Both are
140mph cars.* **Bottom left** *If you own a
suitable classic car, why not enter in a
suitable competitive event? This was pre-event
scrutineering for the 1986 Mille Miglia
retrospective.* **Bottom right** *Everyone's
favourite from Porsche? This is a Type 356
Coupé of the 1960s, which immediately pre-
dates the famous 911 family.*

Back cover: Top left *If the classic you buy
is in awful condition, you might need a
completely new body shell building as part of
the restoration.* **Top right** *One of the most
brutally impressive back views in the
motoring business — the Lamborghini
Countach in its definitive QV guise.* **Bottom**
*For many years the Chevrolet Corvette was
the only two-seater sports car built in North
America. This is a 1955 model.*

Colour photographs (including cover)
from *Classic and Sportscar, Autocar* and
Mick Walsh, with thanks to Haymarket
Publishing Limited.

Contents

Introduction

Interest in fascinating old cars—classic cars—has grown enormously in recent years. One-make clubs have sprung up, magazines have been established, and dozens of marque histories have been published. Yet there are still many people who find the whole business of classic cars and classic motoring very confusing.

I hope this book will act as a thorough introduction, and guide, to what is a fascinating subject. Everyone knows what a classic car is—or do they? Everyone knows where and how to buy one—or do they? Everyone knows all about restoration—or do they? Everyone, surely, knows which are the best classic cars, and which are not—or do they? Perhaps, after reading this book, all will have become clear.

This book is not at all an elitist book, for it is not written for the classic car expert, or for the rich dilettante who is looking for a fresh way to invest his money. It is written for those of us who would like to buy an extra car, to use it for fun, and to indulge in a hobby. For that reason I have tried not to spend ages drooling over Ferraris, Bentleys and Porsches—there really is an easier introduction to classic motoring than paying the price of a small house for one motor car...

Incidentally, after reading this book the reader will probably realize why a simple definition of 'the classic car' is so difficult to write. The term covers, thank goodness, a multitude of cars, a multitude of prices and a number of activities. It also means that the reader is quite likely to have his or her own ideas, and that he (or she!) might eventually come to disagree with some of my opinions. But then, that is the joy of the classic car movement—its variety, its potential and its ability to accommodate all sorts of cars and people.

Happy motoring!

GRAHAM ROBSON

Chapter 1

Classic cars—background and definitions

Some time ago I took part in a spirited debate at the National Motor Museum, in which the motion being argued was, 'That this house believes that the term "Classic Car" is meaningless'. Even though the initial civilized proceedings soon degenerated into a good-natured ding-dong between a series of 'vintage' die-hards and those of a more modern persuasion, it was quite clear that there was a problem. Just what *is* a classic car?

At first, the thrust of that debate was that about half the audience believed in the worth of 'vintage' Morris 'Bullnose', Bentley and Rolls-Royce machines, to the exclusion of almost every other type, whereas the rest of us were enthusing about E-Type Jaguars, Ferrari Dinos and Chevrolet Corvettes, but it soon became clear that there was an enormous area of misunderstanding, or confusion, in the hall.

The pre-1930 enthusiasts scoffed at the very idea of a Morris Minor Convertible, or an MG MGB GT, ever being considered a 'classic', or even worth preserving, whereas those in opposition were quite willing to agree that a late 1920s Lagonda, for instance, was not only 'vintage' but 'classic' as well. 'Vintage' members of the audience, however, often had worried expressions, and after most of the major speeches had been made, one of them stood up, took a deep breath, congratulated all and sundry on their efforts, and suddenly said:

'It's all been very interesting, but how do you define what *is* a classic car?'

Then, as now, this is one of the most difficult tasks that a motoring enthusiast like myself has to face, for there is no simple answer to the question. Everyone has his own ideas, and one pundit's definition may be scorned by a rival; that, indeed, is one of the enduring delights of the classic car movement. On the one hand, *everyone* seems to agree that cars like the Porsche 911, Aston Martin DB2/4, Lotus Europa and Alfa Romeo Guilietta Sprint GT are classics; on the other, great argument surrounds the inclusion of cars like the Ford Cortina 1600E, the Volvo saloons, the Ford Mustangs, and the BMC Mini-Cooper S.

Right. It's deep breath time, and I can avoid the issue no longer. Let's

Above *The Lotus Europa Twin-Cam, a very collectable British car.*

Below *Any sporting 1960s-type Alfa Romeo — this is a GT1300 Junior — is collectable.*

A trio of Porsche 911s including the Carrera Targa and Turbo models — now, as probably for ever, true classic cars.

start with the dictionary definition. 'Classic', according to the Oxford Dictionary of Current English, is: 'Of the first class, of allowed excellence'. Better, even, 'in the classic style' is defined as: 'simple, harmonious, proportioned, and finished'. Something that is 'classical' is said to define a standard, and to be first class.

Note, please, that dates have not been mentioned—and *this* is the aspect of the whole business of classic cars which irritates the traditionalists, who believe in 'veterans', or 'vintage cars', and the like. According to them, a car *must* be rigidly categorized if it is to qualify.

That is nonsense, of course, and the point is quickly made by turning their own definitions back at them. How can a car be classic, they say, if it can be anything from ten to eighty years old? To which an obvious reply would be: just because it was built between 1919 and 1930, how can a car like the Model T Ford, the cheap-and-cheerful Austin Seven, or the lumpy Morris 'Empire' Oxford, qualify for vintage status?

The classic car really invented itself as the so-called classic car movement developed in the 1970s, not because it was a commercially led, or promoted, craze, but because some sort of definition was needed. Until the 1930s there were no definitions—cars were merely new, old or worn out. Then in 1934 the Vintage Sports Car Club was founded on the premise that no worthwhile cars had been built since 1930. The phrase 'vintage car' was applied indiscriminately to any car built in the years 1919 to 1930 inclusive, and soon everyone seemed to know what was intended. It wasn't long, however, before the same Club agreed that some fine cars, perhaps, had been built after 1930, so the phrase 'post-vintage thoroughbred' came into general use.

In the meantime other definitions had been applied, if only to make certain cars, and motoring periods, respectable and understandable. The title 'veteran' was applied to any car built before the end of 1904, while 'Edwardian' was applied to cars of the 1905-1918 period. (Incidentally, the fact that the Edward referred to—King Edward VII—had died in 1910, and that he had no jurisdiction over other car-making nations like France, Germany and Italy never deterred the definition-makers from building barriers!)

Now it all begins to get confusing again. Over in the United States, in the 1950s, the Classic Car Club of America also decided that modern cars were not worth owning, decided that certain older machines *were* worthy of recognition, and defined a 'classic' as one built between 1925 and 1948!

All of this, however, left hundreds of thousands of fine cars ignored, and without a group title to their name. Those built after 1930 were not eligible to be called 'vintage' (even though they might have been designed or even originally built before then!), and they could not be called 'thoroughbred' unless the VSCC graciously gave them that title; they could not be American 'classic' unless they were built at the right

In the 1960s, a modern sports coupé like this Triumph GT6 could not be categorized, but now it is certainly acknowledged as a classic car.

The Alvis TC21/100 Coupé was as nicely built, and as graceful, as any vintage car, but it was not until the 1970s that there was a category — the 'classic' category — into which it could be slotted.

time, and only then if the rather exclusive CCCA would accept them. All of this left the Porsche 356, Triumph TR2, Jaguar XK120 and Morgan 4/4 owners in limbo, but fortunately for them the world of motoring began to change and give them all a new lease of life, reputation and value.

Way back in the 1930s the Vintage Sports Car Club's founders had seen that cars' essential charm and individuality were gradually being squeezed out of their characters as mass-production techniques swept across the world of motoring—and harking back to the delights of 'vintage' motoring was the result. The miracle, for motoring enthusiasts, is that there was *still* a great deal of character in most cars as late as the 1960s. By that time, however, the 'Detroitization' of the world's motor industry was under way, the world's legislators were beginning to demand universal standards of visibility, crash protection and anti-emission engine capability, with the result that more and more new cars came to look the same, sound the same and feel the same as their competitors.

Almost inevitably, this aroused motorists to complain. The opening words of the companion volume to this book (*Collecting, Restoring and Riding Classic Motor Cycles*, also published by Patrick Stephens Ltd) aptly sum up what followed:

> There seems to be an almost innate propensity in human beings to bemoan their present state of existence and harp back to the days when everyone was materially poorer but somehow far happier. 'The good old days' viewed through rose-tinted glasses also make us insist that standards have fallen dramatically, and 'they don't make 'em like that any more' is not an uncommon claim.

The Bentley S3 Continental, with saloon car styling by H.J. Mulliner, was a fine car by any standards.

The problem, quite simply, was that the choice of different types of car was disappearing fast, road congestion was increasing rapidly, as were the rules and restrictions surrounding the cars, and there simply wasn't as much enjoyment as before, either in the shopping around for a car or in the motoring which resulted.

Faced with the choice of running a Cortina that looked like a Victor, an Avenger which looked like an Escort, a Volvo that looked like a Peugeot or a Fiesta that looked like a Polo, and not getting *any* fun out of any of them, a lot of car owners began to rebel. It was at this time that the phrase 'grey porridge', if not actually original, came to be applied to the dozens of cars which seemed to have been designed by a computer to be as ordinary, and boring, as possible.

As in so many others walks of life, the result was that drivers began to look elsewhere for their fun. To some people this meant a move into motor sport, but to many it meant looking back to the cars which *were* fun to own, and which were avilable in large numbers, all over the place.

The growth of what we now know as the 'classic car' movement began before the end of the 1960s, but it was not until the early 1970s that a new wave of specialists emerged to look after the much-loved older cars, and the first books and magazines came on to the scene to cater for this new interest. Until that time the only successful British magazines catering for older cars were *Motor Sport* and *Veteran and Vintage*, both of which concentrated their efforts on 'vintage' machines of the pre-1930 period. I well recall being involved in the discussions in 1973 which led to the formation of the first 'new' magazine, *Thoroughbred & Classic Cars*, for it was obvious to all of us that there was yawning gap to be covered.

The rest, as they say, is history. *Thoroughbred & Classic Cars* was an even greater success than its sponsors had expected, similar magazines were founded in other publishing houses, and the number of books devoted to so-called classic cars increased considerably. Sales of 'traditional' publications slumped as those of the new wave forged ahead.

The 'classic' cars which evolved in this period were not defined by a committee, not restricted by date, and certainly not blackballed because of any rules concerning numbers built, country of origin, or details of their running gear. A car quite simply *became* a classic car if enough people insisted that it was one.

Dozens of famous cars, hitherto unclassified, were immediately swept into the net. If you had any Ferrari, Rolls-Royce, Porsche, Jaguar or MG, for instance, you knew right away that you had a classic. On the other hand if you owned a Ford Prefect, an Austin A99 or a Vauxhall Velox, you knew that there was no chance of recognition by your peers.

The fascination at this period lay in seeing which cars emerged as deserving classic status. Most genuine sports cars and sports saloons, of course, had to be recognized as such, as did almost every genuine Supercar; it was the theoretically unlikely cars which gained a reputation which surprised everyone.

The classic case—I apologize for the pun—was the post-war Morris Minor, and this was soon joined by machinery like the Land Rover, the rotary-engined NSU Ro80, the Lancia Fulvia Coupés and the Ford Escort RS models. On the other hand, no amount of energetic lobbying could

MG's Y-Series saloon was introduced in 1947, and was built until 1953. These cars were never very fast, but had a great deal of character.

The BMW 2800CS Coupé had a six-cylinder overhead-cam engine, sleek styling and a 130 mph top speed. Even though rusting is a serious problem in old age, the cars have a steady following.

convince people that cars which were merely strange, or unsuccessful, or merely obsolete should qualify, which put paid to the claims of cars like the Nash Metropolitan or the Chevrolet Corvair. Neither did the existence of a large and vociferous one-make club necessarily mean anything— and I, for one, refuse to see classic status conferred on cars like the Austin A30 or the Farina-styled MK Magnette Mk III!

For a car to qualify as classic, however unofficially, it needed a great deal of character, a definite personality (however quirky) and that indefinable quality which took it well out of the mass of also-ran machinery. Looked at in that way, it was easy to see that there were millions of cars designed only to take passengers from point to point, without pretension and flair, and there were others in which the same journey could be a pleasure, a special occasion, a Main Event.

To be classic, a car had to stand out in a crowd, it had to hold a special appeal for a number of people, and it had to make its owners proud to own it. Interestingly enough, a car didn't have to have special engineering, performance or styling to be a classic machine; if it did, you could immediately rule out the MG TC, the Citroen 2CV and the VW Beetle respectively, and that would never do!

Further, if a car has the sort of appeal which could not possibly be blended from a book of specifications or a list of figures, it may become a classic. On the other hand, almost anything conceived by the massed ranks of product planners, cost accountants and marketing executives is bound to fail. Whatever the original price tag when new, for a car to qualify as a classic it could never be ordinary, never totally predictable, and never boring to own and drive.

Once the whole idea of classic cars and classic motoring had settled down, it was fascinating to see what type of car was recognized, and where it had been manufactured. Very few, it seemed, had originally been conceived in North America (where the product planners dominated the engineers), and few came from Scandinavia or Germany, where logic and a certain stolid national characteristic shone through in the sort of cars being built. The vast majority of classics seemed to be European, with the accent on Latin machinery and on anything with an

A car like the Ford Lotus-Cortina of 1963-66 could never have been evolved by a product planning committee. It was the result of the enterprise of two men — Colin Chapman of Lotus and Walter Hayes of Ford.

individual, sporting flavour. It was mostly in countries like Great Britain, France and Italy that the love of such cars flourished, and where there were still enough entrepreneurs ready to take risks and indulge their designers and stylists. Interestingly enough, most of the cars built seemed to be sold in North America, where the market was huge and the prosperity self-evident.

As the 1970s closed, however, the problem was that the number of people interested in classic cars, and looking to own one, continued to grow, while the number of cars stayed virtually the same. At the same time, more and more specialists came into existence, and standards of maintenance and restoration rose markedly. What followed was inevitable, as any student of economics would confirm: an increase in demand, compared with a static supply, led to a sharp increase in prices. Terms like 'modern classic' or 'instant classic' were invented to describe new models which might eventually qualify when their breeding and pedigree settled down, but this could not halt the rise in its tracks. By about 1979, with world inflation raging away and people not liking to keep money in the bank for too long, the whole business had become overheated. One result was that the rubbish and the undistinguished 'grey porridge', began to sell at levels far above their value, but there was then a sharp slump, and it was not until the mid 1980s that asking prices reached consistent new values.

Nevertheless, after ten years or more it was clear that the classic car movement was *not* merely a passing craze, and the interest in such machines continues to grow, and mature, as the 1980s progress. There is, however, much more to owning and running a classic car than merely signing the cheque when you buy it—and that is what this book is all about.

Chapter 2

Buying your bargain—where, why and how

We have all heard those fairy tales of entrepreneurs who went out and bought a barnful of old cars in the 1960s, stored them for a decade, sold them at a huge profit, and used the money to pose around in a Ferrari or a Rolls-Royce ever afterwards. But in most cases these *are* fairy tales: behind that glossy collector's piece is usually a great deal of money or hard labour.

Everyone who is itching to get his hands on a distinctive car for the first time has heard encouraging tales from friends and acquaintances. But in every good book of quotations there is one very appropriate saying from William Congreve: 'Marry'd in haste, we may repent at leisure'—change 'Marry' to 'Buy' and you have a summary of the perils of rushing in to buy your first classic car.

It is much easier (and perhaps more expensive) to make a big mistake in buying a classic than it is when buying a conventional recent model; my first advice to anyone ready to buy an older car on impulse is—don't! Sit down at home instead and work out why you want such a car, and what you want to use it for.

I bought my first classic car because (a) it was very cheap and (b) it was there. People I already knew who were on the fringes of the classic business assured me that I could not go wrong, and that it would surely appreciate and make money for me. High hopes. . . A month later I knew that I had done the wrong thing, and I wasn't going to enjoy owning it after all. For the next few years it stood, neglected, in a corner of my driveway, and when I came to advertize it for sale there wasn't a single enquiry. In the end I had to give it away. Mine was a case study in doing it all wrong, and I was *very* cautious next time around. Now, how to do it right?

Let us assume that you have no practical experience of classic cars except as an observer and an enthusiast. Don't feel ashamed about this, because you are in the silent (and maybe rather wistful) majority. Most young people, after all, start their car-owning career by buying something cheap, cheerful and old; they don't actually graduate to new car owner-ship for some years. The lucky ones then either make enough money to

Some cars, like the lovely Jaguar E-Type, already sell for a great deal of money and their values will increase in years to come.

buy better, rather distinctive, new cars, or a grateful company buys one for them. There may be no opportunity, or money, along the way for them to consider buying a classic.

The first question to be settled is: why do you want to buy a classic car? Do you want one as a restoration project, as a potential investment, as a working car to use every day, or just as a toy? Or are you merely attracted to the idea because it looks glamorous?

If you fall into the last category then you have a problem, and you could finish up spending—and losing—a lot of money. I wouldn't want you to dabble, get your financial fingers burned and retire hurt through lack of experience, so read on and learn some more before taking the plunge.

If you are attracted by the idea of making a lot of money out of classic cars, then my late-1980s advice is—forget it! The value of almost any car which qualifies as a classic leapt upwards in the 1970s, but by the end of that decade sanity had returned in almost every case, and prices had fallen back. Rare cars continue to be valuable, but mundane, more easily available machines have settled down again to more realistic levels. Look at the number of cars going through a specialist auction and being 'bought in' (which means 'unsold' in auctionspeak) if you need proof.

Nowadays, big profits are only made on a very restricted number of truly important cars, and you can be sure that most of these are already in the hands of people who made the same decision as you years ago. Certain dealers advertising exotic cars at exotic prices only pay the rent by selling a *very* few cars every year!

For sure, there are several famous breeds of car—the Lancia Stratos, the

Even though you might like the idea of owning a Rolls-Royce, remember that running costs, and restoration costs, will be very high.

Jaguar E-Type and the Ferrari 246GT Dino are three perfect examples—where notional values continue to increase as enthusiasts come to realize that they are unique pieces of machinery. On the other hand, cars like the Porsche 911 and the MG MGB are not making their owners much money right now.

A classic car as a toy? Why not? After all, they do say that the only difference between the men and the boys is the size of their toys. It follows, as with all other toys, that you intend to use it purely for pleasure, as a pastimé, and that if it breaks or displeases you, you will discard it and buy another one. Congratulations. You obviously have a lot more money than me.

Seriously, though, using a classic car as a toy is one of the purest ways of getting involved in the movement, for above all such a machine should be a source of pleasure. Many people don't want such a car to use all the time, and they haven't the expertise or the desire to go in for a lot of restoration. It costs more in the first place to buy the sort of well-preserved car that needs little cosseting and maintenance, but it may be worth it. It is a great pleasure to own an attractive car that can be used at weekends, holidays, or only when the sun is shining, and which can then be locked away when the family Cavalier or Sierra will do the work-aday runs instead.

Make no mistake about the cost of running a classic car as a toy, however. *Everything*, even a Rolls-Royce car or a Stradivarius violin, wears out in the end if it is used intensively, so as the years roll by you need to be prepared to spend quite a lot of money with specialists and

Above *The 1930s SS100 (foreground) is worth a lot more money than the modern XJ-S Cabriolet, but it isn't as practical for everyday use. Think carefully before buying a classic to use all the time.*

Below *By all means buy a historic Mini-Minor (like this 1959 model), but don't expect it to be suitable for regular long-distance driving.*

professional restorers if you are not able to tackle the rectification work yourself. Don't pay a lot of money for an expensive toy on the basis that it ought to be a better long-term proposition than something less costly. It simply isn't so. . . .

So you need a car to use very day, and you are considering a classic for that purpose? *Every* day—when there is snow on the ground? When it is foggy? When there is a rail strike and the journey to work is traffic-jammed? When the temperature soars into the 90s? Are you sure?

If you are considering using a classic car for this purpose—a car which, by definition, means something with an interesting character, but of a certain age—you should be very analytical of your actual needs. The idea of taking a sexy-looking convertible to the office on a fine morning is one thing, but would you like the same car to be right for the same journey on a February night when all the traffic lights have failed, when you need a draught-proof interior, and when you need the ventilation system actually to be working?

If you don't mind wearing out one of the world's finer cars in a couple of years, spending a fortune on it to restore it to original condition and buying another classic to use in the meantime, then perhaps you *could* use one every day. Consider, however, that yesterday's cars, no matter what make and what period, were by no means as well made as today's, and certainly not as reliable.

Yes, I know, we've all heard the old hands say that 'they don't make 'em like they used to'—which is an absolutely meaningless remark in almost every way. Cars like vintage Bentleys might have been built like battleships, and they were very suitable indeed for the near-deserted roads of the 1920s, but in modern conditions, with *twenty times* the traffic on British roads, they are a slow, underbraked and ungainly embarrassment.

Most more recent cars, even some of the most famous models, have their faults, and none of them cope well with late-1980s conditions. There are two USA-originated stories which paint a tell-tale picture: one rich Texan once boasted to his neighbour that he always owned *two* VW Beetles in the summer months: 'I use one at time, and I park the other in the freezer to keep it cool. . . '; and there was the standing joke that you always needed to own two new Jaguars in the mid-1970s so that one could be used to provide spare parts for the other when it broke down.

In my opinion, a classic car is only suitable for everyday use today if it was designed for the same sort of everyday use when it was new. Which means that if 'everyday' to you means scudding up and down motorways, then a Ferrari might indeed do the trick, and that if 'everyday' means organizing a school run, going shopping and leaving the car overnight, then a Morris Minor or a VW Beetle might be just right. But don't expect any sympathy if you use an 850 cc Mini for the motorway driving and a Lamborghini to take the kids to school. . .

Special-purpose cars like the Ford RS200 are fine for fast, long-distance journeys (I know, I run one!), but don't use it to go shopping.

It is easier to give advice about buying a run-down car as a restoration project. By all means do this, but before you sign the cheque, please be sure that (a) you can afford to pay all the bills and (b) you have the patience to withstand the inevitable delays, frustrations, mess and sheer upset that a dismantled car will cause. Right away, too, you should decide whether you can do the job yourself or whether you are going to have to have everything contracted out, at great expense; I cover this in more detail in Chapter 4.

I hope this doesn't sound too simplistic, but you will make sure, won't you, that the car you have in mind actually *can* be restored, and that parts prices are believable? It's no good for instance, buying a rare vintage car as a basket case if it lacks a chassis frame or an engine—you're not likely to be able to find spares in stock at the local dealership. Did you know, for instance, tht if you need a new cylinder block for a six-cylinder Riley, it has to be specially cast, from new patterns, at enormous cost? Or that newly-cast cylinder heads for a pre-war Rolls-Royce cost at least as much as a new Metro?

Anyone who is planning to get into the restoration business for the first time should be advised to tackle something as simple and straightforward as possible; there is plenty of time to get into the world-wide search for parts, literature or expertise when you already have one successful

If you go out shopping for a car to restore, be sure that it is complete, and has not been partially cannibalized for spares. Is it, in truth, 'ripe for restoration'?

rebuild under your belt. In other words, tackle the reconstruction of a Triumph TR before you even look at a Pegaso, an Austin A35 before a Rolls-Royce Silver Shadow, or a 'Bullnose' Morris Oxford before an eight-cylinder Alfa Romeo.

Beware of those winsome adverts which mention an 'abandoned restoration project', for there is usually an expensive horror story behind the scenes. In many cases the current owner has become discouraged by the growing problem of rebuilding this car, and this is often because something vital isn't available. Beware, in any case, of those adverts which speak of 'ripe for restoration' (which means rusted away), or anything with the phrase 'partially dismantled' in it (probably meaning that part of the car is stored somewhere else, forgotten, or just plain missing). In cases such as that, make very sure that you *are* buying a car, and not merely a collection of unrelated parts which vaguely resembles a car—don't worry, that sort of thing has happened in the past!

Above all, don't consider buying a classic car which needs to be restored if you are short of time. One way or another, a successful restoration cannot be hurried; a rush job can be done—in a rush—but you will invariably find that much of the work has to be done again in a few years time.

Now, how should you set about choosing, and buying, a classic car for

Above *Pick your first restoration project carefully — this separate-chassis MGA, for instance, might be more straightforward than a later monocoque MGB.*

Right *Would you like to be depressed about the values of present-day collectable cars? This was one of the* The Autocar's *advertising pages in 1936 when the 'classics' were only a few years old!*

the very first time? No matter how much money you have to spend, the first thing I would advise is that you should restrain your enthusiasm, try to be logical, and spend time deciding what you need. There is going to be a great deal of difference between the car you desperately yearn after and the car that actually makes sense to you. It doesn't matter how old we get, the glitter always makes the first impression—but unless the practicalities mean nothing to us we should always try to avoid accepting first impressions. I'm sorry to have to break your heart at this early stage, but if you're going to rush out and buy a Bentley Continental when an XK140 would be more suitable, or a Corvette instead of a frog-eye Sprite without thinking of the consequences, you are not thinking straight. If I can rephrase his colourful language to suit this book, that famous London motor trading character, the late Cliff Davis, once said that he sold lots of American cars to 'middle-aged men who were flattering their manhood'—and a lot of that sort of thing goes on. Shame on you. Better, perhaps, to go back to the beginning of this chapter and start again!

If you have a great deal of money, or have absolutely no intention of working on the car yourself, and if you are going to treat the whole thing as a good giggle, an indulgence, and a gigantic pose, then go ahead and

90 THE AUTOCAR. ADVERTISEMENTS. OCTOBER 9TH. 1936.

Specially Selected

1936 **FORD** 22 h.p. 4-door Touring Saloon £150
1936 **VAUXHALL** 14 Sln. de Lx., new cond. £150
1935 **RILEY** 1½-litre Kestrel, like new £175
1935/6 **TALBOT** 14 Fldg.-Head 4-str. Coupe £250
1934/5 **CHRYSLER** Airflow Sln., prac. new £135
1935 **CHEVROLET** Master Saloon £125
1935 **S.S.** Airline 20 Sln., extras, as new £175
1934/5 **MORRIS** 15/6 Saloon de Luxe £85
1935 **CITROEN** 2nd Ser. Super Mod. 12 Sln. £110
1933 **TALBOT** 95 M.W. Saloon de Luxe £130
1935 **HUMBER** 80 Special 4-light Saloon £200
1933 **W. HORNET** Saloon de Luxe £50
1934/5 **TERRAPLANE** 4-door Saloon £110
1934/5 **RAILTON** Open Sports 4-seater £195
1934 **RAILTON** 4-door Sports Saloon £150
1935 **VAUXHALL** 20/60 Saloon £135
1932/3 **INVICTA** 100 m.p.h. 4-str. Sports £250
1936 **A.C.** 16 h.p. 4-str. Coupe, new £375
1936 Ser. **MORRIS** 12 de Luxe Saloon £140
1936 **HILLMAN** Minx de Luxe Sln., super £135
1936 **AUSTIN** 10 Saloon de Luxe £125
1935 **SINGER** 9 Le Mans Coupe £105
1936 **MARENDAZ** £475 Spts. 4-str. £250
1934/5 **DELAGE** Straight 8 Sports Saloon £450
1935 **FORD** V.8 4-door Saloon £110
1935 **FORD** V.8 Coupe-Cabriolet, grey £110
1935 **MORRIS** 20 Saloon de Luxe £130
1935/6 **WOLSELEY** 14 New Series Saloon £130
1934 **WOLSELEY** Hornet de Luxe Saloon £70
1933 **STANDARD** Big 12 Saloon £65
1933 **HUMBER** 16 Saloon de Luxe £115

DENMANS LONG ACRE, LONDON, W.C.2
TE . BAR 9135. Pte. Exch. (Nr. Leicester Sq. Stn.)

VALE
FOR SPORTS CARS AND SPEED

BENTLEY, 1930/1, 4½-litre supercharged, fitted with Vanden Plas body, finished in international green. The car has been maintained regardless of cost by Bentleys who will give any intending purchaser a report on the motor. Capable of speeds considerably in excess of 100 m.p.h. with phenomenal acceleration. Extras too numerous to embody in an advertisement £350

FRAZER NASH. Completely rebuilt and reconditioned in these works and first registered in 1936. Chromium plated throughout. Fold flat screen. Cellulosed British racing green. Absolutely as new. Taxed £125

BENTLEY, 3-litre red label, twin carburetters, Vanden Plas 4-seater. Large F.W.B., finished in black and chrom., in superb order throughout. Capable of 85 m.p.h., 20–25 m.p.g., uses no oil, excellent weather protection £55

LEA FRANCIS Sports 4-seater 1930/1. A fine example of this well-known marque. Recently overhauled throughout the chassis and repainted black and red. Large ribbed F.W.B., 70 m.p.h., 30 m.p.g., tyres as new, excellent weather protection £35

RILEY 9 1928 2-seater. Extremely good chassis, sound and in all respects capable of sustaining a high cruising speed with extreme economy. A fast, reliable motor car at the very reasonable price of £27 10

Another £30

Many engines and chassis frames suitable for Special building in stock. Open Week-ends. Sundays 10-1.

VALE ENGINEERING CO., Ltd.
171, Elgin Terrace, MAIDA VALE, W.9.
Maida Vale 2231-2.

AMERICAN CAR CO.

The American Car Company offer a few guaranteed Cars from Stock.

1935 **RAILTON** 28.8 Sports Tourer, colour dark blue, amazing performance, immaculate condition, economical, cost approx. £600. Bargain Price £235
1935/6 **TERRAPLANE** 21.6, 4-dr. Sal., l'ther uphol., as new £175
1935/6 **TERRAPLANE** 21.6, Sports Tourer, col. Red, very attractive only 4,000 miles, in use only 3 months, Bargain £225
1935 series **TERRAPLANE** 21.6 4-dr. Sal. de Luxe, in showroom condition, gift £135
1934/5 **TERRAPLANE** 16.9 D/H Coupe, attractive Beige £140
1934 Series **TERRAPLANE** 16.9 Saloon, S/R wide track, perfect £75
1933 **TERRAPLANE** 16.9 Sports Saloon, clearance price £39.10
1935 **STUDEBAKER** 25.6 4-dr. Sal., immaculate condition, splendid car, bargain £165
1935 **CHEVROLET** 4-dr. Saloon, 26.3, nice car £115
1935 **FORD** V.8 30 h.p. D/H Coupe, perfect £120
1931 **CHRYSLER** 77 4-some D/H Coupe £45
1931 **CHRYSLER** 66 4-dr. Saloon, sound £25
1930 **HUDSON** 24.2 4-dr. Saloon, clearance £15
1933 **S.S.I.** 16 h.p. Coupe, brand new tyres, engine rebored, taxed year, bargain £79.10

Terms. Part Exchange.

272/4, Vauxhall Bridge Road, Victoria S.W.1
Victoria 2665-6. **One minute Victoria Station.**

SPEED MODELS LTD.
R. C. MURTON-NEALE
FOR GUARANTEED SPORTS CARS

- **SQUIRE** 1935 Special Racing 2-seater, 1936 racing engine, full road equipment, E.N.V. preselector gears, 10–110 in top in touring trim £375
- **BENTLEY** 1929 4½-litre Le Mans, green and chromium, hour-glass pistons, very fast, taxed year £195
- **M.G.** 1933 J2 (Oct.) Midget, specially tuned, new bearings, oil consumption negligible, ivory and green £75
- **FORD 8** 1936 de Luxe, sun roof, leather upholstery, green, small mileage £75
- **M.G. MAGNA** 1932 Sports 4-seater, black and red, new tyres, exceptionally good condition, choice of two £65
- **ALVIS** 12/50 1928 Super Sports Beetle Back 2-seater, outside exhaust, black and red, just rebored, crankshaft reground, new bearings, brakes relined £55

AND MANY OTHERS.
Best Cash Prices Given for Sports Cars.

PEMBRIDGE MEWS, PEMBRIDGE VILLAS, NOTTING HILL GATE, W.11.
Open Sundays 11-1. **Bayswater 5144-5**

A.C. HOGG LTD.
NEW AND USED SPORTS CAR SPECIALISTS

75 M.P.H.
1934 "J" type **M.G.** 2-seater. Taxed for the year. Fitted with good tyres and hosts of extra instruments. A really good example of this breed £87 10

85 M.P.H.
1934 "L" type **M.G.** Magna. This car has been fitted with a new black and special crank and will rev. at 7,200, and is probably one of the snappiest makes on the road to-day. Oversize stop Michelin tyres. Good all-weather equipment £95

85 M.P.H.
HOTCHKISS Super sports cut away side 4-seater. Good tyres and equipment. Beautiful condition. Real speed model. £82 10

90 M.P.H.
LAGONDA 1932 low chassis super sports model, good tyres, taxed, P.100 headlights, hosts of extras, really magnificent condition. Cellulosed black with red wheels £165

90 M.P.H.
BUGATTI 1½-litre Grand Prix Special rebuilt by famous racing engineer last year. New body. Racing wheels, all road equipment £195

Sports Cars urgently wanted for cash.
The New 4-cylinder 4-wheel MORGAN in Stock.
171, GREAT PORTLAND ST.
Tel.: WELBECK 1367.

R.S.M. [Automobiles] Ltd

1936 (registered June) **AUBURN** Super-charged Phaeton, finished Grey with Blue leather; fitted with radio; taxed to end of year; 3,000 miles; in absolutely new condition. **£585**

26, BRUTON STREET, BERKELEY SQUARE, W.1.
TELEPHONE MAYFAIR 0283/4.

LEX GARAGES LTD.
LEX-CONDITIONED CARS
12 MONTHS FREE SERVICE

THE EXCEPTIONAL CONDITION OF THESE SELECTED USED CARS MAKES THEM WELL WORTH YOUR INSPECTION.

1936 Triumph Gloria Vitesse 16 h.p. Special Sports Saloon. Black red upholstery. One owner. 8,000 miles. Cost £415 £255
1936 Triumph as above. Cream. 5,000 miles only. As brand new £255
1934 Daimler 15 h.p. Saloon de Luxe. One owner. Completely reconditioned £165
1934 Railtons, Series I and Series II Sports Saloons and Tourers from £155
1934 M.G. Magnette N-type Sports Tourer, in brand new condition £125
1936 Morris 12 h.p. Series II Saloon de Luxe. Black red. Low mileage £125
1936 Morris 10 h.p. Series II Saloon de Luxe. Black green. One owner £119
1936 Austin Seven Nippy Sports two-seater. 6,000 miles. Extras £105
1934 Armstrong 12 h.p. Saloon de Luxe. Doctor's car. Exceptional £95

PART EXCHANGES. DEFERRED PAYMENTS.
USED CAR DEPOT KENSINGTON PLACE, CAMPDEN HILL, NOTTING HILL GATE, W.8. PARK 8061.

BENTLEY BARGAINS

1930 Speed 6 **BENTLEY** Special Streamline Coupe by Gurney Nutting. Specially built to the order of a world-famous racing motorist. Recently overhauled and fitted numerous extras. Indistinguishable from new. Exceptional bargain at... £345

ALSO

1930 (September) 4½ litre **BENTLEY** Vanden Plas tourer. New tyres. D.W.S. Jacks. As new throughout £265

AND

1929 4½ litre **BENTLEY** Sun Saloon. Recent overhaul cost £100. Receipts available... £215

Many other secondhand bargains in all makes.

FRANCE, RADFORD & Co., Ltd.
46, ALFRED PLACE, South Kensington Station, S.W.7. Kensington 6642/3.

S. J.
BENGE ABBOTT & Co.
'Phone: Ealing 2442.

1936 **OLDSMOBILE** 6-cyl. Drop-head Foursome Coupé, black/brown hide, 4,000 miles only, taxed, cost £485, will accept £365
1934 **ALVIS** Speed 20 Vanden Plas 4-str., in superb condition, one owner, bargain £275
1935 series **TERRAPLANE** 16.9 Drop-head Coupé, black/brown hide £149
1934 (June) **TERRAPLANE** 8-cyl. Special C/B Sports 4-str. Tourer, cream/green, 85 m.p.h., perfect condition, any trial, taxed, yr. £119
1935 **AERO MINX** Cresta Sln., in perfect cond. throughout, finished black/silver, grey hide, low mileage, any trial £139
1932 **HUMBER** 16/60 Sports 4-dr. Sun Sln., finished in black with fawn hide upholstery, 22,000 miles, in absolutely unmarked cond. £65
1936 (late) **AUSTIN** 10 Sherborne Sln., maroon and black, mileage 4,000. This car is definitely as new £125
1935 (July) **AUSTIN** 7 Ruby Sln. de Luxe, green, green hide, 10,000 miles, super cond. £75
1934 **MORRIS** Family 8 Sln., blue/blue hide, mileage 9,000, indistinguishable from new—only wants seeing £75

51, THE MALL, EALING, W.5.

The Advertisement Index is on the page facing inside back cover. F50 buy the car of your dreams, and to hell with the inconvenience. Even then, you should take the trouble to read what follows.

There are millions of classic cars out there and most of them are for sale if the right sort of money is offered. The first thing you have to accept is that the vast majority of them are no use to you whatsoever. Logically, therefore, you have to settle down, riffle through some of the specialist magazines, sift through your own mind and experiences and decide on the type of car you are going to buy. Not the actual make, model and derivative at this stage, but the basic type of machinery. No-one—pundit, friend, journalist or know-all—should be allowed to deflect you from your preference.

As I have already made clear in the opening chapter, a classic car can be very old indeed (an early 1900s Mercedes, why not?) or less than five years old (what price a Ford RS200?), so the first thing you have to do is to plump for a particular motoring period. The choice is made easier when you realize that the vast majority of all accepted 'classics' have been built since 1945, and that every surviving car that was built before 1939 brings a parts and service expertise problem with it. Nevertheless, if you come from a motoring family which always seems to have favoured post-vintage thoroughbreds, or one where an E-Type is as essential to the garage as a toaster to the kitchen, who am I to deflect you?

You must, however, be comfortable with the period of motoring chosen. Personally (and I hope I am allowed to give an opinion) I would not want to have to struggle with anything older than a 1930s car, but on the other hand I know many charming enthusiasts to whom pressed steel panelling, coil ignition and closed coachwork with heaters is a sign of modern decadence. Somehow or other you must relate to the type and the ambience of the motoring offered before you take delivery, for you can't change the car's character afterwards, and you may find it difficult to change your own instead.

Once you have settled on a motoring period the time has come to narrow the target even further. Do you want an open sports car or a saloon, a small family car or a stately limousine? Do you want to 'Buy British' or choose a foreign car? You *must* make this decision right away, otherwise to browse through the 'For Sale' adverts can be a lengthy and unsettling business.

Now we're getting somewhere, and you should soon be able to home in on a preferred make, or perhaps even a preferred model, of car. If you decide to go for something truly rare, expensive and exotic (how many Ferrari Americas or Aston Martin DB4GTs are on sale at any one time, for instance?), nothing is going to deflect you from this choice, but in almost every other case you will sort out a choice of cars.

Purely as an example, therefore, let me assume that you have your heart set on buying a Jaguar. If you are lusting for an E-Type, this still gives you plenty of choice, but you should never be too rigid in your

What sort of classic car appeals to you? Young or old, modern design or archaic, closed or open? This 1950s Morgan 4/4 might satisfy one kind of enthusiast, but would disappoint another. Think carefully before buying.

desires. For instance, even though it was the least developed of all the types there is a great demand for the original flat-floor 3.8-litre model, which means that prices have gone through the roof; do you really want to follow the lemmings, when the truth is that *later* 3.8s were better cars in every way? In fact, unless you have very fixed ideas, perhaps you should still keep an open mind until you have looked at several cars, and decide whether to buy a six-cylinder or vee-12 example.

Now is the time to start looking round for the car of your dreams. First, however, here is one of the Golden Rules: *Always* resist the temptation to buy the first car you see. If you are flushed with enthusiasm (or cash!) you may want to put money down on the very first example, but this is usually a mistake. You must take time, make comparisons, weigh values and play the field before making a decision. Always remember that the vendor is very anxious to sell, but that it costs you nothing to string him along for a while. The value of a car doesn't increase overnight, or in a couple of weeks—and if the vendor says it has, then you shouldn't be dealing with him anyway.

The obvious places to search include the classified and display advertising columns of the reputable classic car magazines (which, in the UK, include the best-selling monthlies *Classic & Sportscar, Classic Cars, Practical Classics* and *Motor Sport*), the motor trade which specializes in classic cars, the one-make clubs, classic car auctions and the 'friend around the corner'. There are advantages and disadvantages in each area.

Jaguar S Type 3.8 auto, 58,000 miles and second car for spares £950. Tel: Horndean 592050.

Coupé Jaguar XJ12 1978. Indigo, 46,000 miles, GM box chrome wheels. Regretfully retirement forces sale. One previous director owner, immaculate condition, new tyres etc. JDC member. £5,600. Tel: Haywards Heath 0444 453524.

420 Saloon automatic, 1967, silver grey with dark blue leather, mechanically good but no M.O.T. £375 ono. Tel: S. Fisher, evenings only 041 423 4804.

XK120 Roadster 1950. Full mechanical and body restored and rebuilt, current M.O.T., needs some trimming to finish. £10,750. Tel: 061 485 4769.

1966 S Type Jaguar 3.4 auto for restoration. Full length Webasto sun roof fitted. Fully renovated woodwork. £300 or might break for spares. Delivery possible. Tel: Ken 051-931 2408.

XJ Coupé completely restored using zinc plated panels. Resprayed gleaming silver, many extras, chrome wheels. Stunning vehicle, no work to do. Auto 70,000 miles, manual conversion available. £3,500. Tel: 0705 379980 evenings.

Jaguar XJ6 3.4 Automatic 1977. Silver, black vinyl roof, black leather trims, 53,000 miles. Three new tyres and exhaust. Steering rack renewed, general condition very good. Slight damage to front of vehicle, ideal for restoration. £600. JDC member. Tel: Windsor 866574.

Cheap XJ12 beautiful biscuit coloured interior in very good condition, two new tyres, gen. 53,000 miles, engine and gearbox (auto) work perfectly, elec windows, air conditioning, tints, tow bar, but sadly rusty body panels, some not too bad. Fuel injected 1987 car, will sell for £425 ono or swap for Mk 8/9 for same value. Tel: Stuart 061 864 2906.

Mk II with 3.8 Litre engine. Rebuilt August '84 to partial Coombs spec. 9:1 comp. pistons competition clutch. Hardly used since. Good interior, tyres, wire wheels, louvred bonnet, manual/overdrive, elec fan. Believed low mileage — genuine (speedo reading 28,000) most things work as they did when new. Chassis and body recently rigorously checked and repaired as necessary. Very solid basis for concours preparation. Anti-theft etched glass, motorway fog lamps, new M.O.T. £2,750 ono. Tel: Windsor 865819.

1965 Daimler 250 auto, spares or renovation. Offers. Tel: Oxford 59688.

3.8 FHC 1963 E Type. Carmen red, restored to original specifications, beautiful condition. £6,500. Mark 2 3.8 — Mark 7, 8 or 9 taken part exchange. Larger Jaguar needed. Tel: 01-641 0073.

XJ12 Non Runner due to dropped valve, engine head stuck. Dark blue, N Reg (valuable for spares) only 1250. Tel: 01-402 7628.

Jaguar XJ6 1983 4.2 Rare 5 speed manual, one owner, FSH, Panasonic radio/tape, bargain £6,995. Tel: 0924 253853.

E Type 1972 2 + 2 V12 Signal red, black interior. Excellent all round condition, personal plate, 47,000 miles. £6,500. Tel: Chester 0244 22183 day, 535741 evenings.

1968 Daimler 2.5 V8 Dark blue, automatic, wire wheels, 80,000 miles. £2,200. Immaculate condition inside and out. Tel: 01-672 5283.

E Type 1970 FHC Yellow, LHD, unused six years, sold as is, buyer collects. £5,000. Tel: 0305 832473.

1939 Jaguar 1½ Litre Drop head requires total restoration but all complete. £3,000. Tel: 0536 85926 after 7 pm.

Daimler Sovereign 4.2 Automatic Series III, October 1979, BRG, Beige leather interior, vinyl roof, usual Daimler features plus alarm, 54,700 miles. £2,500. Tel: 01-776 1205 West Wickham.

XJ6 Coupé. Special number plate WJL 330. National stereo cassette/radio. XJS wheels, just repainted in original pristine white paint with black vinyl roof. 38,000 mile engine, modified stainless steel exhaust. Available with or without modified 3 carburettor manifold, making this a very quick beautiful vehicle. £3,250 or ... Tel: 01-951 1252.

1969 Jaguar 420G Auto. Black with red leather. Full history, 3 owners from new. Electric windows, stainless exhaust, new tyres, Waxoyled, body and interior restored, brakes overhauled, first class mechanical condition. A superb example of an appreciating classic. JDC member. Tel: 0323 832147 (Eastbourne).

XJS 5.3 S Reg. Silver, black leather upholstery. Recent GM400 gearbox 8,000 miles ago with warantee. Recent alloys and tyres, neat, tidy well maintained car. £4,200 ono. Tel: 0272 833708.

Manual XJS, 1977/R, 55,000 miles, FSH, mechanically and bodily excellent, immaculate interior, XJS/HE wheels, one fastidious JDC owner for last six years. £5,500. No offers. Tel: Slough 0753 48370.

Daimler 2.5/V8 1965. Under 90,000 miles with an M.O.T. until December. A lot of work has been done, but there is still a bit to do! Nevertheless a road worthy car but must sell soon so £485 ono. Tel: Andy on Boston 0205 69920.

1979 Series II XJ6 4.2 Auto, good runner but body needs slight attention. Nine months M.O.T., three months tax. Any reasonable offer considered. Tel: Derby 0332 515675 after 5 pm for details.

Daimler V12 Coupé 1977. White, blue leather, M.O.T./tax. Sunroof/stereo. Excellent example. £4,000 ono. JDC member. Tel: Edinburgh 031 343 3683.

E Type V12 1973 FHC. Sand, green. Manual, 54,000 miles, superb condition, new clutch, fuel pump, battery, electronic ignition. £6,450. Tel: Leicester 0533 881022.

420G. Registration number JBH 420G, chocolate brown/parchment. 55,000 miles, long M.O.T. Tel: Dr Fry 02217 2265.

Coupé Daimler V12 1978. Genuine 28,000 miles, documented service history, GM gearbox, chrome wheels, superb condition. £6,500. Tel: Southern Motors 0428 713511.   **(T)**

420G. 76,000 miles, 1969, M.O.T., red with white wall tyres, full length sun roof, tow bar, stereo radio cassette, electric tinted windows, electric aerial. Complete new exhaust system, rear suspension and brakes, two fuel pumps, jacking points, inner and outer sills, roof lining and sun roof, servo and master cylinder, water pump, engine overhaul. No rust, A1 mechanics, bills and service history, some spares. Colour photo of this car on page 35 of January 86 Jaguar Driver. £1,995. Tel: 04022 26633.

E Type V12 Roadster 1973. 5,700 miles, manual, immaculate original condition. Olde English White with black trim. Forthcoming addition to family forces sale. £15,000. Tel: 048 641 2340 (Surrey).

3.8 S 1965. This vehicle which is manual with overdrive and finished in Carmen red with c/w wheels has been the subject of a complete overhaul to the highest specification and has only completed 3,000 miles since. Tel: Chorley Wood 3533 for details.

SS90 Restored in 1979, asking £39,500. Contact David Barber on 0379 741361.

Coupé V12 1977 6/6 white with black vinyl roof. Remetalled/leaded, resprayed, with beautiful green plush leather interior, elec tinted windows, elec f/f sunroof, air conditioning, all in good working order. Excellent oil pressure, rem/mirrs, radio, chrome wheels, 10 months M.O.T., 4 months tax, stunning performance. Not concours but a very nice example of only 400 manufactured. Genuine reason for sale. £2,100 ono. Tel: 061 797 2638.

3.4 S Type 1968, Manual, o/d, wire wheels, British Racing Green, excellent condition, reluctant sale but must sell. £2,200 ono. Tel: 01-231 0149.

Jaguar 3.8 Mark II 1965. Body stripped to bare metal. All rust removed, resprayed Olde English White, new interior trim, red leather seats. Engine and gearbox overhauled, four new tyres, 12 months M.O.T. Bills for £7,500 accept £6,000. Tel: 01-941 4128 (Kingston area).

Daimler XJ12 Series I 1973. Squadron blue, beige leather interior. Extensively rebuilt by enthusiast. New front wings, nearly new tyres, 12 months M.O.T. £1,200 ono. Tel: 01-941 4128 (Kingston area).

Mk II Jaguar 240 manual, o/d. Reg OCJ 2259. Wire wheels, Blaupunkt stereo, mechanically very good. MOT, tax, workshop manual + owners handbooks. £2,000 ono. Tel: Cheltenham 0242 820475, evenings 603139. Ask for Paul.

XJ12 1972 Series I. Reg No. VRG 5K, superb condition, 79,000 miles, short wheelbase (rare type). Auto, chrome pressed wheels, leather, stereo, elec windows, new M.O.T. long tax, eligible for classic insurance (£85/yr. full comp.) Maintained by JDC mechanic, seen at Scottish JDC meets, very fast 4-seater. Regency red/biscuit int. £1,900 ono. Tel: Aberdeen 0224 883854 days, 580384 eves.

Jaguar V12 E Type 5.3 Roadster. Automatic, 56,000 miles, maintained regardless of cost. Superb condition throughout, history/bills. JDC member. Tel: 01-845 9617.

One-make clubs usually have thriving magazines, where most of the best types of car are bought and sold. This is part of a typical Jaguar magazine's monthly offering.

The 'friend around the corner' may, indeed, have a car which you desire, and you may have known it for a long period, but if you buy it without even researching the alternatives then you are breaking that Golden Rule. There is also the possibility of an embarrassing discussion over price, and perhaps an even more embarrassing aftermath if you discover hidden horror stories when you get it home, or it suffers an expensive breakdown within days of the cheque being signed. Because I would never be hard-nosed enough to be a motor trader, the 'friend round the corner' alternative is not for me. Is it for you?

If you set out to buy a car at an auction, please remember that the atmosphere of such occasions, especially if there are some glamorous, high-value machines coming under the hammer, can be a heady inducement to lose all caution. You could finish up contracting to spend a lot more money than you had bargained for—and auctioneers are not likely to accept any lame excuses about 'second thoughts' or 'misunderstandings'. Remember, too, that cars sold at auction come with no sort of

Classic car auctions have a heady atmosphere — my advice is to attend a few without trying to buy a car before you get serious about classic car purchase.

Some classic cars are bought and sold by franchise holders who still stock the new models. Lex Mead, at Maidenhead, had this interesting selection of Rolls-Royce and Bentley models in 1982, when their main business was in new Silver Spirits.

warranty, and that you only have chance for a static inspection (test drives are usually not on offer) before bidding.

My own observation of auctions is that some cars are there because their owners expect inflated prices to be achieved, some are genuine, good-value machines, and some are only there because their owners simply have not been able to sell them by conventional means. It is also worth remembering that the auctioneer is not doing this job for love—it is in his interests to drive up the prices as high as possible so that his company's commission increases at the same time. All in all, unless the car you want is individually well known and you are quite prepared to pay whatever it takes to become the owner, you should keep away from an auction.

Buying through the motor trade is more predictable though, once again, don't forget that every garage is in business to make a profit, and you are hardly likely to find a bargain in a glossy showroom. More than ten years ago, nascent classics were often sold at low prices, but there has been an expansion in know-how and historical knowledge since then, and that doesn't happen any more. Dealing with a long-established trader means that you can be assured of a straightforward, if not necessarily financially advantageous, deal. On the other hand, if you deal with a business whose premises seem to be a delapidated Nissen hut on the corner of a pig farm or a housing estate, take everything with great caution!

The legal advantage of buying through the motor trade is that you have some protection under the Trade Descriptions Act and the Sale of Goods Act. The one means that goods must actually be as described, while the other states that the goods must be fit for the purpose for which they are sold. The practical advantages include the possibility of greater choice (the 'dealers' mafia' system means that even if one dealer doesn't have the car you want, he might know another trader who does. . . .), and usually the option of buying the car on extended purchase terms. An active dealer specializing in one type of car, too, might be able to find you the car you need, even if he doesn't have one in stock at the time.

There is a famous military dictum which states that 'Time spent on reconnaissance is never wasted'—and this certainly applies when you are

'Collectors' cars' are often offered for sale in national newspapers; this is a Sunday Times *page from March 1987. What a variety!*

COLLECTORS CARS

ASTON MARTIN VOLANTE

Electric power hood, finished in bright red with magnolia hide trim. 1985 registered. Only 9,000 miles. £58,500.

Tel: 061 449 8808 (Day)
or 066 33 3944 (Evenings)

DE-SOTO Roadster. 1929 with rumble seat. Full restoration 1980. Yellow/black. Gd cond £8,750. Also un-reg Triumph Stag auto in Old English White/ tan upholstery, stored 10 years. Offers over £13,000. 0706 220793 Office /224827 Home.

MERCEDES 280 SL: 1969, auto. power steering. Hard/ soft top. metallic dark blue/ beige interior. History, excellent condition, current MOT. £7,750. Tel: 01-229 4621 After 5.00 pm

AUSTIN Westminster 6/110. Registered in 1965. Black. Genuine 6,000 miles. Chauffeur driven. Completely original. Offers over £1,500. Tel. 0685 814216

JAGUAR MARK 10 - 4.2 Auto. 1966. 48,000mls. colour British Racing Green with Green interior. Very good condition. Tel: 0526 860622.

MORRIS 1000 SALOON 1970. Good condition. Reconditioned engine. MOT June 1987. Offers around £1000. Tel. 078 16 73412.

CORTINA 1973 1600 L. 21,450 mls only from new. Magnificently preserved throughout. £1,000. Bournemouth 516944

1954 FRAZER NASH Lemans Coupe. One of eight built. exc restored cond. Tel 0757 638713.T.

MORRIS 1000 TRAVELLER 1971. 2 owner car in fine original condition. Tax, new MOT. £1,350 ono 0953 83244.

TRIUMPH SPITFIRE 1977. yellow with overdrive. 20,000 miles from new, immaculate. £4,250. Tel: 01 223 1501.

JAGUAR XK 150 1958 practically completely restored. £10,000 Tel Hatfield 07072 61334

KARMANN GHIA for sale. 1972 Very good condition. £3,400 Ring: 01 249 3646.

MORRIS MINOR Reg:1248 HK 1957. 4 door. taxed & MOT'd. £1,000 ono. 0375 381338.

B.M.W. 3.0 CSi 1975. Not concours but nearly. Just resprayed fjord blue. velour interior. new wings & exhaust. full Webasto. All bills since new. Lovely car. £4,950. Tel. Bath (0225) 837256 (eves/weekends) or 339633 (office).

MGB V8 Roadster 1974. engine and mechanics faultless. maintained regardless of cost. Body work superb. in original maroon with new leather seats amd maroon piping. Superb example of a rare collectors car. £6,500. Tel 0303 30508

SUNBEAM TALBOT (1951). convertible. MOT'd 1 year. Totally restored. Offers over £4,000. Tel. 031 667 2223 eves and w/e's only.

BMW 2002. Cabriolet. 1973. Mid grey. Alloys. Fully reconditioned. Superb. MOT and tax. £2,950. Tel 0858 32552.

CHRISTOPHER REEVE reluctantly offers for sale his super TR6 at £4,750. Serious offers only to 01 894 5937.

BMW M1 (1981) Cert. 13,000 kms white. superb investment. POA Sytner BMW 0602 582831

HUMBER 16/50 1929 Saloon. Sunroof. Black on mole. MOT. Superb. £6,250. Tel. 0385 64334.

ROVER 80. Good condition. Original valve radio. tool kit etc. One year's MOT. £900. Tel 01 699 0085.

SILVER CLOUD III (64) Garnet. beige leather. only 66,000 miles £26,950. Sytner BMW 0602 582831.

69 280 SL Pagoda. certified 12,000 mls. concourse. £21,950. Sytner BMW (0602) 582831.

ASTON MARTIN DV6 and A.M. Vantage. Full details on request. Tel: 0256 57557/20806

ASTON MARTIN DB4. Good condition throughout. Full history. £9,500. Weekdays 458 9272

ASTON MARTIN D.B.4 good condition throughout. Full history. £9,500 weekdays 458 9272

ASTON MARTIN D.B.4 good condition throughout. Full history. £9,500 weekdays 458 9272

ELAN 2+2. 150 S. 1974. Blue. Only 16,000 miles. £7,995. Tel 0234 51054.

TRIUMPH STAG immaculately restored. man/OD. alloy wheels. £3,500. 0227 70607 T

AUSTIN 16/6 1932 Saloon. Must be seen. £6,950. Also 1964 Hillman Super Minx Convertible. 20,000 miles. £2,950. Tel. (0622) 861789.

ALPA SPYDER Duetto Convertible. very rare. 1967. 1600 cc. 5 speed. new hood. recent MOT. £3,495. 0752 667451. T

COLLECTORS CARS WANTED

HAMBLE require classic British & Continental sporting cars. Jaguar, TR, Healey. Sunbeam, Alfa Romeo. MG etc. For best price phone 0703 453757. Collection nationwide.

VANDEN PLAS Princess 11/1300. Must be good cond. Top prices paid. 0273 570050

preparing to buy a car. The more time you spend looking around, and the more cars you look at before buying, the better and more logical will be your choice in the end. Whether you are looking for a rare exotic or one of the most popular classics, the most likely place to find one advertised is in the 'small ads' columns of either the classic magazines, the Sunday newspapers (in Britain, the *Sunday Times* has a large selection) or the one-make magazines. On the basis that you are going to be patient, this is probably the most fruitful source of all.

Unless you respond to a classified advert which turns out to be a screen for an established motor trader (you would be surprised how often this happens), you will probably find a seller who is a genuine private owner like yourself. He will probably know more about his car than a motor trader could ever do, will often have a collection of spares and literature to sell with his beloved car, and will usually be anxious to make a straightforward and honest deal.

Private sellers have been told over and over again never to part with a car against a cheque, or without verifying a buyer's honesty and credit-worthiness—though in many cases that isn't easy to ascertain. As a buyer, you can only expect a straightforward deal with a private owner if you are straight with him. This means that you must sort out a formal deal before leaving him, and that you should give him time to have your cheque cleared before you take delivery of the vehicle. At this time he must certainly hand over all the vehicle's documents, and you must be sure that he has legal title to sell you the car in the first place. Other authors have glibly suggested that you should offer a banker's draft, or cash, instead of a cheque, which is a lot more difficult than it sounds. And suppose you are proposing to pay more than £20,000 for a Rolls-Royce or a Ferrari—have you ever *seen* so much money, in one place, in bank notes? You need a very understanding bank manager before you can waltz into your local branch and withdraw so much cash! Mind you, if you *can* produce so much cash in front of the seller, it's amazing how often you might be able to bargain down the price significantly. In the same way that a starving man salivates at the sight of a steak, folding money sometimes has a miraculous effect on a vendor. . . .

In my view, the ideal way to find and buy the car of your dreams is to plan well ahead and join the best and most practical one-make car club connected with this model. Learn as much about the cars as possible, read all about them and, above all, listen to the most experienced members of the club. Then, when you think you have the full picture, set out to buy a car from one of the members. The large one-make clubs (in the UK, the Jaguar Drivers' Club, the MG Owners' Club and the Ford RS Owners' Club are all excellent examples) all have thriving magazines which feature columns of small ads every month.

Now for some of us this may be the most difficult part of all. Except when you are buying a car through an auction, you can always assume

British classic sports cars at their best — an MG MGB faces up to a Sunbeam Alpine.

Left *The 'gull-wing' Mercedes-Benz 300SL of 1954-57 was one of the most sensational new cars of its day.*

Below left *One of the most desirable American cars, a 1947-model Lincoln Continental Mk 1.*

Right *If a classic car has a competitions history, so much the better — this is a well-known 'ex-works' BMC Mini-Cooper S.*

Below *If a sports car is too fast for you, why not dabble in Second World War militaria?*

Two 1970s European cars whose classic reputation is rising are the Citroën SM (left) and the Alfa Romeo Montreal (right).

Inset All the glitter and high tension of an auction — this is Christie's exclusive Mercedes-Benz sale of 1986.

Perhaps the ideal way to get into classic car motoring, and purchase, is through a one-make club. The Courier *is the monthly publication of the fast-growing Triumph Sports Six club, which caters for all the 'separate chassis' Herald/Vitesse family of cars.*

that the advertised price is merely the asking price. Which means that if you are persistent enough, persuasive enough, and very hard-nosed about doing the deal, then you should be able to haggle away with the vendor to arrive at a more equitable bargain.

But what is the right price for a particular car? There is, after all, no Glass's Guide or 'little book' to tell the trade how much to ask for a 1965 MGB, a 1972 Ford Mustang or a 1935 3½-litre Bentley. This is where your own experience—and, presumably, that of the vendor—comes in. Over a period of time the price level for a particular car becomes known, and you can pick this up by looking at the prices achieved in auctions, by the advertised prices in the motoring press, and by simply asking other people (if they will tell you!) what they paid. A cautious 'look, but don't touch' approach ought to pay off. It is all too easy for the novice to see a very glossy car advertised for a very glossy price, and assume that it must be worth the money. Don't believe this. As a guide, the highest asking prices are in the motor trade, the next highest are in the classified adverts and the most sensible prices are quoted in the one-make club columns. Attempts to 'talk up' the value of a particular breed of car have often been made, but like most other attempts to corner the market in a given commodity, these usually fail, and a generally accepted price level appears.

There is no doubt that some cars sell for silly money these days, just because their reputation has become legendary—and because they are scarce. We all know of the Ford GT40s which were worth less than £5,000 in 1970 but which sell for well over £150,000 today. Even so, it's difficult to see why a car so numerous as the Austin-Healey 3000 (or that obvious case, the Jaguar E-Type) has reached such high classic values when there are so many of them still in existence.

You might not like this, but you can't fight against it. You will get nowhere by assessing the value of a mint condition Morris Minor Convertible at £500 if excellently preserved examples of such cars are selling for £2,500 in the market place. No-one is going to sell you one at £500, so you must re-align your sights and your expectations.

So, now you have a good idea of the car you want to buy. What should you look for when you inspect a possible purchase? This deserves a complete section to itself.

Chapter 3

What to look for when buying

There is a right, and a wrong, way to go out shopping for a classic car. I have already listed the various places in which you might locate the car of your dreams. Now—how can you be sure that a particular car is right for you?

First and foremost, when you have settled on the car you should try to learn all about the model *before* you start looking out for one, and before you even reply to the first advertisement. This is going to cost some money—maybe even a substantial sum of money—but it is usually a good investment in the long term.

Start by joining the appropriate one-make club, whose members usually know as much about 'their' cars as anyone else in the business. Unfortunately, there is a 'Catch 22' situation here as far as certain clubs are concerned—you're not allowed to join the club unless you own one of 'their' cars, and you don't want to buy one of their cars until you have joined the club! The only short-term solution is to have a friend who is already in the club, and use him as your source of reference and research.

There, or elsewhere, get on with reading (and, if possible, acquiring) all the original archive material and catalogues available about the car in which you are interested. This should include technical descriptions and road tests, which were published in authoritative motoring magazines like *The Autocar* and *The Motor*. This will help you to learn all about the car's original specification, its performance and fuel efficiency, and its general capabilities *at the time it was new and up-to-date*. By careful study of the catalogues and contemporary adverts, you will learn to pick a 'Special Equipment' from a 'De Luxe', or an early from a late model. You will also get a good idea of the factory options which might still be found on a classic these days, about the various colour schemes and about the various sub-derivatives. By getting right back to the source, too, you can get the facts, rather than the folk stories which have been handed down from storyteller to storyteller.

Photographs of the cars from the factories, as built, are valuable sources of reference, particularly when you are carrying out a difficult restoration, but you should beware of inconsistencies. Many a classic car was given

THE AUTOCAR, DECEMBER 9, 1949   1381

Although the H. J. Mulliner sedanca is a four-light style, with pivoting ventilator panels additional to the drop glasses in each door, it is primarily intended for chauffeur driving. A glass division behind the non-adjustable driving seat is electrically operated.

No. 1393: ROLLS-ROYCE SILVER WRAITH SEDANCA DE VILLE

DATA FOR THE DRIVER

ROLLS-ROYCE SILVER WRAITH

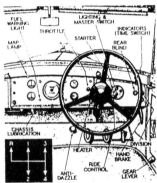

The *Autocar* ROAD TESTS

PRICE, with sedanca de ville body, £3,875, plus £2,154 5s 6d British purchase tax. Total (in Great Britain), £6,029 5s 6d.

RATING : 29.4 h.p., 6 cylinders, overhead inlet, side exhaust valves, 89 × 114 mm, 4,256 c.c.

COMPRESSION RATIO : 6.4 to 1. 23 m.p.h. per 1,000 r.p.m. on top gear.

TYRE SIZE : 6.50 × 17in on bolt-on steel wheels with discs. LIGHTING SET : 12-volt. WEIGHT : 42 cwt 1 qr 0 lb (4,732 lb). LB. per C.C. : 1.11.

TANK CAPACITY : 18 Imperial gallons : approximate fuel consumption range, 15-17 m.p.g. (18.8-16.6 litres per 100 km).

TURNING CIRCLE : (L) 44ft 11in ; (R) 46ft 5in. MINIMUM GROUND CLEARANCE : 8.125in.

MAIN DIMENSIONS : Wheelbase, 10ft 7in. Track, 4ft 10½in (front) ; 5ft 0in (rear). Overall length, 17ft 2in ; width, 6ft 1in ; height, 5ft 11in.

ACCELERATION

Overall gear ratios	*From steady m.p.h. of*		
	10 to 30	20 to 40	30 to 50
	sec	sec	sec
3.727 to 1 ..	13.5	12.4	13.0
5.001 to 1 ..	9.5	9.1	10.0
7.520 to 1 ..	6.0	6.6	—
11.113 to 1 ..	—	—	—

From rest through gears to :—

	sec			sec
30 m.p.h.	7.9	60 m.p.h.	24.0
50 m.p.h.	17.2	70 m.p.h.	37.4

Steering wheel movement from lock to lock : 3½ turns.

Speedometer correction by Electric

Speedometer :—

Car Speed-ometer	Electric Speed-ometer m.p.h.	Car Speed-ometer	Electric Speed-ometer m.p.h.
10	8.5	50	48.25
20	18	60	59
30	28.25	70	69.5
40	38		

Speeds attainable on gears (by Electric Speedometer)

		M.p.h. (normal and max)	K.p.h. (normal and max)
1st	..	14—24	22.5 — 38.6
2nd	..	31—44	49.8 — 70.8
3rd	..	56—68	90.1 —109.4

WEATHER : Rain, cold ; fresh wind.
Acceleration figures are the means of several runs in opposite directions.

Described in " The Autocar" of April 5, 1946.

IN a world of shattered monetary values and yet much-improved cars, the Rolls-Royce still stands alone. Perhaps the most striking general thought in considering this supreme machine today is that it has a name more universally known, more universally honoured, as a symbol of quality than that of any other manufactured product. That may sound a proud boast, which can be put forward on behalf of a British car. If it can be justified, and there is little doubt that it can, it is because the name stands so extraordinarily high in relation to cars, and without need to call upon the powerful aid of the reputation of the Rolls-Royce aircraft engines.

An opportunity to renew acquaintance with the current Silver Wraith, which with the recently introduced Silver Dawn, of shorter wheelbase and for export only, represents the post-war cars bearing the Rolls-Royce name, has enabled the practical reasons for this tremendous reputation to be re-examined on the road. A natural question asks what it is about a car that should make it cost between £3,500 and £4,000, according to body style, in its country of origin ; and what a reflection it is upon the times that on the actual model that has been tested now, the sedanca

de ville, the home market purchase tax paid to the Government is more than the chassis price.

Detailed answers to that question are of book length rather than within the scope of a Road Test. A great part of the considered reply lies in the past, bearing in mind the research and development and painstaking, restless progress that have gone to develop the Rolls-Royce car seen today. This is not, however, to imply that the design has stood still, for independent suspension was adopted for its predecessor, the Wraith, as long ago as 1938, and even outwardly the present engine and its auxiliaries show a considerable change from that pre-war forerunner, whilst on the export-only car mentioned previously the modern feature of a steering column gear change is available.

The charm, the appeal, the true practical worth of this car among other cars has nothing to do with the highest performance capable of being derived from 4¼ litres of six-cylinder engine designed and built in the Rolls-Royce manner, a phrase meaning so much, but, as so often has been said, the way in which the car behaves and handles and its day in, day out consistency. The Silver Wraith, with a sedanca body, intended primarily for chauffeur driving, looks a

Above *An autojumble is often a useful source not only of spare parts but also of information, brochures and catalogues of the car which you intend to buy.*

Left *Read as much original material as possible about the car which interests you before you go out to buy one. That way, you will immediately know whether the car is still in original condition.*

detail styling or equipment changes between the date it was first revealed and the date when deliveries commenced—the mythical MGB two-spoke steering wheel of 1962 is one perfect example of this! Many of the one-make clubs have a stock of such photographs which can be consulted but not borrowed, and many of them have an archivist who has enough experience to separate right from wrong. *Never* trust pictures of a car taken in later years, or in restored condition, and *never* trust the opinion of another owner unles he can back it up with documentary evidence.

In a few cases, factories retain an interest in their obsolete models— especially if these have an established reputation which is good for the company's modern image—and even keep a small historical department. Not many corporations, however, are as well served as the old 'British Leyland' combine, whose British Motor Industry Heritage Trust is a magnificent example of benevolent preservation.

All the large autojumbles tend to have traders' stands specializing in makers' catalogues and old motoring magazines with descriptions and road tests. These traders are in business to make money and to satisfy their customers, so don't be shy—if you can't see what you need, ask them for exactly what you want. Most of these traders can only show a fraction of their stock at an autojumble, and have to leave a lot back at home—so if you can't immediately see it, don't despair. . . .

If you live within reach of a comprehensively-stocked motor museum or reference library, the staff will probably allow you to consult their material. The National Motor Museum's Reference Library at Beaulieu, for instance, has a very experienced staff, and there seems to be accurate source material on *everything*—in Michelin guide terms, it is 'worth a detour'.

One easy way to short-cut this research process is to invest in the many 'one-make' books published about most cars. In the UK, Brooklands Books publish hundreds of slim volumes which are, effectively, reprints of original descriptions and tests—buying these might save you a lot of rummaging time at autojumbles! Most popular makes and models of cars are now well covered by books—some fat and some slim, some serious and some light-hearted, most being either straight marque histories or individual model stories. Have a look at the Appendix to this book, which lists the most important titles. Which are the best ones? I mustn't ventilate my own prejudices here (modesty forbids. . .); let's just say that the one-make clubs have a very clear idea of the most valuable volumes covering their own particular cars.

If you are already a classic car fan, it may be assumed that your house is already overflowing with motoring magazines of all types, and especially those which specialize in the classic car scene. Apart from the fact that these are all so enjoyable to read, I would always recommend an enthusiast to have a complete run of one of the magazines (complete with Indices, if he can find them), for their pages regularly turn up astonishing amounts of information, from so many different sources. Not only do the magazines cover the careers of important makes and models at great length (*Classic & Sportscar*, for instance, runs a popular 'Profile' series every month), but they often run special features about the personalities behind the most famous cars, about preservation and restoration and surveys of the auctions scene. Some of them carry surveys of classic car values, but as these go out of date in a matter of months they are not very valuable for archive purposes.

Once you have a good working knowledge of the car of your choice, it is time to start looking round, to be ready to 'go shopping'. However, for the well organized classic car enthusiast it is decision time again. Ask yourself, do you want to buy a car which is:
(a) Beautifully restored or preserved, for concours only?
(b) A well loved but essentially 'working' classic?
(c) A badly neglected machine which needs a complete rebuild?
(d) A 'basket case' which needs recreating?
The answer will determine where and how you will search for a car.

In the case of the 'basket case' (or what our American friends some-times candidly call a 'parts car'—which means that it is not really worth

Above left *Perhaps this Austin Seven is not a 'basket case', but it's getting on that way. Could you tackle the comprehensive restoration which would be needed?*

Above right *Many a restorable car is to be found at the back of a breaker's yard, or in an orchard. But make no mistake, there will always be a lot more work than you expect. . .*

rebuilding!) you have my sympathy, and you are on your own, for I have only limited experience of the horrendous problems you are going to encounter.

Most people buy 'basket cases' to provide a few useful spare parts for another example of the same type, but if the basket contains the remains of a very rare and desirable car indeed, then I suppose a full re-creation is worth trying. In this case, and as already mentioned in the previous chapter, be sure that all the essential, and irreplaceable, components are present. This effectively means that you need everything to make a complete and driveable chassis; bodies can be recreated by one of a dozen craftsmen in any country—engine blocks and back axle casings cannot. Not, that is, without cheating, or using something similar, but not original, from another type of car.

Cars of this type are usually privately owned and found in the proverbial barn, abandoned garden shed, motor house or lock-up garage, and no, I haven't a clue as to how you put a value on the pile of bits.

Even though the classic car boom has now been with us for more than a decade, there are still thousands of very badly neglected machines out there looking for a good home. Many of them are still in sporadic use, but an equally large number are stored, perhaps snugly in garages, but more likely in an open driveway, garden, back lot, field or orchard. This type of car is often privately owned, but a proportion is to be found in rambling breakers' yards (and not yet piled one on top of the other, or partly stripped for spares), and even in the back lot of a large rural garage or transport business. Some have been turned up in lock-up garages, unearthed by executors trying to wind up the affairs of a deceased relative!

The interesting thing here is that while an older car is still unfashionable, the survivors tend to disappear from view, but the moment the demand perks up they begin to pop up all over the place. Where have all the Ford Pilots and Hillman Minxes gone? Be sure that if some group should decide to promote them as 'classics', a number will suddenly come onto the market. . . .

Some of these cars will have been stored for a long time—I don't mean months, but years, or even decades—which usually means that every possible sort of deterioration has set in by the time you see them. During World War Two, motoring magazines like *The Autocar* gave a great deal of advice about storage 'for the duration', and this included comments about sitting the chassis of the car on blocks so that the suspension and tyres were not permanently loaded, draining off the engine cooling water during the winter and (when the water was still in place!) occasionally starting up the engine to warm it through. Batteries had to be removed and given regular charge, and every attempt had to be made to keep out the damp.

This, of course, was only done by owners who firmly intended to use their precious machines again as soon as the emergency was over. Unfortunately, such attention to detail in storing a car is rarely completed today, and once the rust, and the damp, sets in, the car is well on the way to ruin. Unless you can be sure that the 'lovingly stored in heated motor house' story is true, you should *always* expect the worst when you follow up an advert.

Nevertheless, if the car is rare enough it is probably worth rescuing. Some years ago I visited an avid restorer of commercial vehicles who had just bought what appeared to be a connoisseur's collection of rusty panels and decaying mechanical components which were just recognizable as one of those 1930s-type short wheelbase charabancs.

'It looks awful,' I said. 'Why on earth did you bother?'

The restorer's eyes, though, were positively dancing:

'You don't understand, it doesn't matter about the rust. It's *all* there! That's what's important. If there was anything missing, I couldn't do the job. This will be easy enough!'

The moral of this story is that you can restore or reclaim *anything* if you have all the parts with which to do the job. In other words, if there are no missing pieces to the jigsaw, you can solve the puzzle. One of your aims when buying a derelict car should be to find one which is complete in all respects, even if some of its components or fittings don't work any more, or are in an awful condition. Of course, if that car is, say, a Chevrolet Corvette in the USA, or a Triumph TR6 in the UK, where the parts supply problem has been solved by enterprising remanufacture, you don't need to worry too much about missing bumpers, windscreens or instruments. But would you feel the same if you were sizing up an aged Volvo, Armstrong Siddeley or Cord?

It is at this stage of the inspection of a complete car that you should convince yourself that it is not only complete but original. Nothing is more frustrating in the end, and nothing so surely detracts from the value, as to find that parts of the car do not really belong there. This can encompass everything from, say, a steel-bodied car having glass-fibre 'after-market' wings or bonnet panel, to an MG MGA fitted with an MGB engine, or perhaps an Escort RS2000 fitted with a Sierra's five-speed gearbox. This might have been done with the best of intentions to keep an old car on the road, but it has, to be frank, helped create a 'mongrel'—and these are not very desirable.

Another aspect of originality which is not usually encountered with this sort of runner, but is much more regularly found with better preserved 'classics', is that the car may have been faked in some way, and this is where your research and reading into all aspects of these cars may pay dividends. We all know of desirable looking 'homologation-specials', like Mini-Cooper S and Lotus-Cortina models, which have been 'created' out of less exclusive components, and there are well authenticated cases of Porsche 911s of a certain desirable rarity being 'created' out of the more mundane variety.

When you set about buying a car that is, superficially at least, in fine shape, your task is easier. Once you have established that the vendor has the legal title to the car in question (a surprising number of cars are stolen first, then quickly sold off at apparently bargain prices—and it is easier to steal a classic car which doesn't have a steering column lock and almost certainly doesn't have an alarm system, than it is to steal the more modern variety), the next and very obvious question to ask a private owner (but not a motor trader) is: 'If this car is so desirable, why are you selling it?'

You have to start by assuming that the world is full of honest enthusiasts, and usually there will be a very good reason for the sale. In others cases it will have been replaced by another, and even more desirable, machine. In others, unhappily, the owner may have struck hard times, and may be having to sell his 'toy' to keep ahead of the bailiffs. Some owners sell because they have got thoroughly bored with their older cars, and some because they simply cannot afford to keep a dream car (like a Rolls-Royce or a Ferrari) in the manner to which it is accustomed. Others may have become discouraged by the regular attention, and expenditure, which has to be lavished on a car of this type; it's not that it isn't justified and they can't afford it, but that some people come to begrudge the effort.

(Which magazine writer was it who, in debunking the trendy food specialists who take ages to finish a dish, said: 'Life's too short to stuff a mushroom. . .'?)

If the reason for sale is more sinister—that a major part of the car, not immediately obvious, is about to burst asunder with hideously expensive consequences, or that vital spare parts have suddenly gone out of stock— then I hope your original research into these cars, and perhaps this particular car, will have forewarned you of the problem. In any case, let us hope that a thorough inspection will tell you all you need to know.

When you decide to look over a car, don't meet on neutral ground (such as a windy car park in the middle of town), but make an appointment to see it, preferably at the owner's own house. You learn a lot about the character of a motoring enthusiast by the size, equipment and state of his garage, and even by the general atmosphere of his home.

There are no exact rules which you can apply, but clearly you should worry about anyone who lives in a council house and has a Lamborghini for sale, or alternatively someone who lives in considerable style yet appears to be selling a mundane 1960s saloon because he says he is short of money. On the other hand, let's suppose you are going to look at a Porsche 911, and find the car living alongside one or two other classics of similar pedigree and value—in that case the whole deal might begin to 'smell' right, at once. I know this may sound a bit sneaky, but you might even use the 'friend of a friend' network to see what can be found out about the vendor, before you even meet him. It happens quite a lot in business—and if we are talking about a deal with a car valued at £10,000 or more, you would be foolish to ignore any scrap of useful information.

First impressions are very important, so you would be sure to see your prospective 'deal' (a) outside in the open air, and (b) in broad daylight. For all the obvious reasons (which include the basic fact that you are sure to miss something), don't even consider making a deal over a car that you

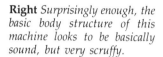

Left Perhaps this old Rover 110 is *worth restoring* — but at least you should see it in its abandoned state, in full daylight, before making any sort of decision.

Right Surprisingly enough, the basic body structure of this machine looks to be basically sound, but very scruffy.

can only see in the dark, in the cramped confines of a garage, surrounded by junk, and viewable only under harsh strip lighting.

Straight away, check that the car *is* what it is supposed to be (you might be surprised to learn that some owners don't know exactly what they have been hoarding for such a long time, and might not know the correct year of manufacture. . .), and make a visual check to see that it is complete in all respects.

If you are the type who wants his classic not only to look right but to *be* right, and to give you the satisfaction of knowing it, it is important that you look for details like a spare wheel, all the trim and carpets, the tool kit, and preferably even the appropriate literature as well. You should be able to pick up the most obviously jarring mistakes—odd tyre and wheel sizes, for instance, and unsuitable accessories—at a glance, but the rest will follow in a matter of minutes.

It actually puts you 'one up' over the vendor if you can refer to authentic documentation, road tests, catalogues and the like, when checking over a car. He will know immediately that you have done your homework, and that he must therefore be completely honest about the proposed deal.

In my opinion, every inspection of every classic car must begin with its structure, and in all these operations it is worth having a knowledgeable friend who owns one of these cars along with you as an expert witness. Body panels can be repaired or renewed, and major engine and transmission components can be rebuilt, but if the main chassis or, in the case of a unit-construction model, the monocoque, is damaged, badly corroded or otherwise defective, then the deal should be called off.

Get the car onto a ramp or over a pit and see that the 'chassis', whether separate or part of the body shell, is still strong, and still straight. I have seen expensive Jaguars, by the way, which betrayed the existence of a twisted chassis by the widely differing number of packing pieces under the various body mounting points; it's a thought worth applying to other separate-chassis cars, if you know where to look.

Now is the time to look for any signs of repaired accident damage in the chassis, or for signs that major sections have had to be replaced, either due to damage or due to the originals being corroded. Unexpected patch plates, or what looks like extra welding, should be treated with suspicion. At this stage you will certainly get frustrated by the presence of pounds and pounds of rubberized undersealing gunge which might have been applied with the best of intentions but which might now be hiding existing corrosion; this will not have stopped developing even though it has been covered up for ages! The one advantage of a car with a rather 'leaky' engine, by the way, is that the oil mist discharged from the engine bay often does a great preservation job on the underside of the car.

The stealthy use of a screwdriver (or not so stealthy, if you are confident enough!) as a probe is often valuable here—if a section is covered with the muck of ages, scrape some of it away to see what horror stories you expose underneath.

Such signs need not necessarily be a disappointment, just so long as the work has been carried out properly—but if the restoration is scruffy it might give a clue to the state of the rest of the car. Even though it is not yet time to test drive the car, you might want to have the car rolled backwards and forwards, or driven past you on a straight piece of road, as a double check that the chassis integrity has been preserved.

Time now to check out the front and rear suspensions, and of course the steering. If the car is old, it is almost certainly suffering from wear in some joint or another. Once again, I hope that your researches will have shown—for instance—whether it is the front suspension links, or their bushes and joints, which wear first, for the usual 'give it a hard shake, then listen for the noise' test doesn't always give you a complete story. (But you can almost guarantee getting an eyeful of grit. . . .)

If the owner objects to his car's suspension being vigorously bounced up and down, or the wheels being shaken from side to side, then he was something to hide, and you should tell him so. Unless you actually do anything silly enough to damage the suspension (and, if the car is properly designed, driving it across the infield of Donington Park, or into any concours parade ring, will do the job much more efficiently than you can!), he surely can't object.

Check that the car actually rides level (yet another reason why the inspection shoud take place out of doors, where you can get far enough away from it to gain a proper perspective), and if it does not, check up on that 'corner' of the car which is, literally and actually, letting the side down. With a simple-to-understand car this might be due to a leaf spring or a coil spring which has sagged with old age, but complicated cars like the modern big Citroens, the Rolls-Royce Silver Shadow family or any Mercedes-Benz car with air suspension, may have all manner of hydraulic

Above left *Some cars get into an awful state, and are patched up with glass-fibre or even less permanent repairs. Look around carefully when viewing a possible purchase.*

Above right *If the car has wire spoke wheels, the 'pinging' test with a screwdriver usually tells you if any of the spokes are loose or broken.*

or pneumatic problems to be solved. Leaky dampers are usually soggy dampers, by the way, so you should expect to have to renew these soon after you have bought the car.

Check for steering 'slop' in the conventional manner (this is where having an accomplice to hold on to one road wheel while you get the 'feel' of the steering wheel, will be invaluable), and for any signs of fluid leakage, especially if the car in question has power steering. A linkage which has been damaged in a shunt will neither feel right nor do its job properly; a bent track rod is usually obvious (except that some cars, the Sunbeam Tiger being a notable example, actually have bent rods by design!), but you might not be able to see that a steering arm is actually distorted. You can often deduce something from the wear pattern of the front tyres, and it will certainly be obvious on the test drive.

Now is the moment to jack up each corner in turn and spin the wheels, to check not only for free rotation and unexpected noises from the bearings, but also to see that the road wheels are still round and running true. Wire spoke wheels, in particular, may have become 'sloppy' with age and a lot of mileage; incidentally, lightly running a pencil around the spokes and listening for the consistency of the 'pinging' noises can tell you a lot.

At the same time you should inspect the brakes. Cable brakes (some foot brake linkages, and almost every handbrake in the world) may fray

Classic cars

Left *Cars which have been neglected or have stood out in the weather for ages tend to go rusty at body joints. This is the inner/outer wing joint which has almost collapsed into thin air.*

Below *This Riley is more than fifty years old, but still has a tidy, well-preserved, and original, instrument panel layout — except for one unexplained 'hole' ahead of the passenger's eyes.*

in old age, or their links and cranks get rusty, and sticky in action—if your friend sits in the driving seat and operates the controls while you look around, you might learn a lot.

Drum brakes tend to hide their secrets until you actually take them down after purchase, but the condition of an exposed disc usually tells you whether the system is in good shape or not. A rusty disc might mean that the car in question has not been used for some time, but on the other hand it may denote a caliper which has seized up and not allowed the pads to press together. Some Dunlop brakes used in 1960s Lancias had that rather disconcerting reputation.

Leaky, and rusty, hyraulic pipes could signal a danger spot—I ignored these signs on my first classic car, and fifty miles after I bought the car a brake line burst, and I scrabbled round the next roundabout only by hauling on the handbrake. . . .

Break off, now, to look over the body. First of all, look at it in good, strong, 'flat' light, so that any blemishes, dings and imperfections are obvious. Stand well back and look at it from as many angles as possible; don't be at all bashful about lying down on the ground, or about squinting along the line of panel. Doors which stick in their apertures, and panel gaps which are inconsistent from side to side, may all tell a story of distortion, or crash repairs not properly done. In the case of cars with wood-framed bodywork it might also indicate swollen, crumbled or otherwise decaying structural woodwork. Unless the car is being advertised as 'concours condition', don't expect to find it completely rust-free.

Where you can't see the actual panel work for mud and grime, and you need to reassure yourself, dig this away, but don't use the screwdriver trick where the paintwork could actually be damaged (or if the owner is looking!). Quite a number of cars have been 'restored' with non-standard body materials like glass-fibre panels and patches, and if you suspect that this has happened, the two obvious checks are the rap with a knuckle (glass fibre doesn't 'ring' like pressed steel) or the use of a small magnet.

A study of all the available literature and magazine surveys (we are really *much* better served, in this respect, than ever before) will have given you an idea of the 'what to look for' spots in the structure, and if your friend is also an owner of this type of car his advice and experience will be invaluable. Never forget to check up obvious mud and water traps (inside wheel arches, behind headlamp pods, boot floors, and spare wheel wells), and always remember that overflowing water from a cooling radiator, or acid from an electrical battery, are prime causes of corrosion in nearby panels.

Your inspection of the body interior will not only tell you if the fixtures and fittings are complete, but it will also give you an idea of how much the previous owner loved his car. Dirty, torn carpets and trim panels either tells you that he didn't care all that much, or that replacement items

Left *This Jaguar E-Type interior is in 'as new' condition, as many well-loved classics tend to be these days. There are, however, many places in which deterioration can set in — carpets, seats, trim panels, door mechanisms etc. Check them all before making an offer.*

Below right *This nasty Vauxhall Viva HA will never be a classic car, but the state of its facia and wiring is typical of so many badly run-down cars.*

Bottom right *This car is old and scruffy, but everything seems to be working, and all the accessories are present. Don't turn down a possible purchase of a lot of grime.*

are hard to find. Worse still, if the interior is damp, or there are actual wet patches soaking the carpets or underfelt, it not only tells you that the car has been neglected but that there might be leaks in the floor. Lifting the carpets can reveal all manner of problems in the floor pan area, but you ought to have picked these up already, by looking under the car while it was on the ramp.

Incidentally, if anything should move, or adjust, check that it still does so. Does the seat back recline properly? Does the rear quarter window crack open as advertised? Does the sun roof slide back? Does an adjustable steering column still slide in and out, or up and down? Don't even assume that the safety belts, if fitted, are operational until you have tried them. I am sure I do not have to remind you that a car needing new seats or the complete re-upholstering of existing seats, can be a very expensive proposition. And, purely because of its size and the awkward installation, a roof lining which needs renewal is a very awkward job indeed.

Now check out all the electrical circuits and the operation of every component. A car which has been stored for some time will either have a flat battery or no battery at all, but this doesn't mean that you should take the operation of the circuitry on trust. Don't believe even the most honest man who tells you that 'it was perfectly OK when I last used the car'. Rats and mice love to nibble at old-fashioned cloth-covered wiring (though they don't seem to like plastic-covered wiring very much!), and if the car you are inspecting has been sitting, neglected, for some time, it might have suffered in this way.

My advice, therefore, is that before buying any classic car, you should ascertain that every electrical fitting works as it should. Don't just test the horn, the lights and the engine High Tension systems, but the instruments, the heater, the electric windows (where fitted), the heated rear window and all the warning lights. For every item that doesn't work you have the problem of repairing or renewing, and *every* electrical malfunction is a potential fire hazard.

Next, it's time to check the engine. Even though many classic cars' engines are in a parlous state, it's worth remembering that engine spares, and rebuilding expertise, are usually the last of all to become unavailable. If the vendor tells you that the engine will not run, or makes a feeble excuse about its condition, you should assume that it is going to be expensive to restore it to health. I will assume that you have already considered the implications of an engine rebuild in your choice of car: examples of extremes would be the cheap and cheerful restoration of a Triumph TR2 or an MGB engine, and the horrendously expensive reconstruction of a vee-12 Ferrari, Porsche 911, or *any* Bugatti unit!

You can learn a lot about an engine, and about the car's owner, by the general state, internal and external, of the engine. It is *not* the mark of a novice for you to check the oil and water levels, and to ask to watch the movement of the radiator water (with filler cap removed) when the engine is ticking over; at this time, too, you can check that there is no tendency for oil and water to mix in all the wrong places.

If the engine bay is filthy, the oil in the sump is in a nasty condition, and you can see water and oil leaking from old gaskets or joints, then you can assume that the entire lump is ready to die at any moment. A vendor who has, at least, taken the trouble to spring-clean his car, tidy up the engine, change the vital fluids and make an attempt at balancing the carburation, might also have looked after his engine during ownership.

A test run will almost certainly show up any water and oil leaks which are present, and will tell you everything you need to know about the engine's power output and general health. At this stage, however, ask for the engine to be started up, allowed to idle, and then to be revved up, so that you can listen for unexpected noises, look for oil fumes pumping out of the breather, and observe the condition of the exhaust fumes.

Apart from looking carefully around the outside of the various casings for any signs of oil leaks or cracks or damage to the castings, there is not much more you can do to vet the transmission before test-driving the car. However, it is always worth rocking the appropriate wheels to and fro to test for 'slop' in the various transmission joints, and on cars with exposed drive shafts and joints, this is the appropriate moment to look at (and listen to) every joint, and its cover, to assess its integrity.

Unless the car in question is advertised as a non-runner, it would be the height of folly to buy *any* classic car without taking a test drive. That, by the way, should not be a ten-minute crawl around a housing estate at low speeds, but a good, general purpose run on the open road, preferably taking in one or two sizeable hills, firm braking and uneven surfaces. If the car is currently unlicensed, you will still be able to drive it if suitable trade plates are 'borrowed'.

The test drive will not only tell you if this car is actually going to fit your needs (and by 'fit', I don't merely mean whether you can get physically comfortable in it, but whether its character and performance are what you expected), but it will also give you time to assess the general health of the engine, the condition of the transmission, the general state of the suspensions, steering and dampers, and (on a wet day) the overall health of the body, its doors and seals.

Although the vendor will naturally want to start the test by driving his own car, don't allow him to do all the driving or you will learn next to nothing about the general feel of the car. A skilled driver, in any case, can disguise faulty synchromesh in the transmission, poor brakes, or less than ideal steering, and we wouldn't want you to be fooled, would we?

Unless you already know that the car is being sold as a non-runner, it

OK, this is a Pininfarina 'glamour' shot, but it should also remind you that salt corrosion is one of the most pernicious diseases a car can suffer. Has it lived close to the sea, or been driven regularly on salt-treated winter roads? If so, you should worry about the condition of the underside.

would be premature to make an offer to buy it until you have given it a thorough going over for general condition, checked its *bona fides* and driven it on the open road. If the car has been shown to you along with a stock of parts and literature, you should also have asked whether these are going to be a part of the deal or subject to separate negotiation. If, by this time, you also know whether or not it has a valid MoT certificate, has a current licence, or if not that it is nevertheless 'plugged in' to the DVLC's licensing computer at Swansea, you should be ready to start talking about the price.

Don't incidentally, believe that 'gentlemen never discuss money'—that's a fiction put about by those who find the subject embarrassing and rather distasteful; they might not *carry* money, but they certainly discuss it avidly, especially when they are connected with motor cars. It is a well-known ploy for some vendors to express embarrassment about money and asking prices as an attempt to clinch a deal at the figure they first thought of.

I have to confess that I would not be a successful motor trader because I am too anxious to see both sides of a deal and always want to arrive at an equitable solution. However, many vendors are much more flint-hearted than this, and they will certainly have started by putting a high price on the car which is for sale.

The problem is that the novice gets used to seeing a certain level of asking prices in magazine and newspaper advertising, and assumes that the cars actually sell at that level. Unless a car is very rare indeed, and is in great demand, this is rarely so. As I have already spelt out in the previous chapter, it is *always* worth haggling over the price, and once the vendor realizes (a) that you really do want to buy his car, and (b) you will certainly turn him down unless he agrees to negotiate, an acceptable deal is usually there to be struck.

So now the car of your dreams is actually yours. What do you do next?

Chapter 4

Restoration methods—when, where and how—kitchen table or cheque book?

For a real motoring enthusiast, buying a classic car which is new to him brings an immediate problem. Should he start to use it, and enjoy it, right away, or should be stow it carefully away and begin the renovation and restoration that almost every car needs? Where a truly delightful car is concerned, only a seasoned veteran in the classic car field can restrain himself from that quick blast out into the countryside.

That might be a very foolish impulse, and at the risk of being branded a spoilsport, I suggest that you work out your long-term plans for the new toy before you even take it round the block. Since it is quite likely that the car you buy has been stored for a long time, or driven into the ground before being sold off, you might do it irreparable harm by going fast at once.

I speak from bitter experience. In the late 1950s, before the definition of a 'classic car' had ever been mentioned, and when old cars were cheap, and quite undesirable, the very first car I ever bought was an MG TA. I bought it one afternoon, paid over my £250 with a trembling hand, and drove it away.

Within twenty-four hours I had taken it out onto the local arterial road to see 'what'll it do, mister. . .'—and ran the big end bearings in the old long-stroke engine! Since that particular engine did not have shells, and since the white metal had to be built up again, then skimmed down, I had a long wait before the TA was mine again. It was never the same after that, and within a year I had part-exchanged it for a near-new Austin A35. No, don't mock—at the time it was the logical thing to do, and nobody blamed me. And it taught me a lesson which I am now passing on to you.

Let's now return to your own particular case. Over and over again I should emphasize that buying a classic car is not like buying a new machine, or even a second-hand model, from a respected dealer. By definition, a classic car is usually 'of a certain age', and is sold 'as seen, tried and tested'. Since it is highly unlikely that the vendor, even if he is a well-respected dealer, will give you any form of warranty, you are at risk from the day that you take delivery of the vehicle. (I did once hear of a deal that was offered with the extra inducement of a '5-50' warranty and a broad smile. When the buyer asked what was meant, the vendor, said absolutely straightfaced: 'Five minutes and fifty yards. OK?')

In spite of the careful inspection and test which you gave the car before you bought it (see the previous chapter), once you have got it home, and there is no embarrassment in poking around in front of a previous owner's gaze, you should go right through the car and all the parts you took over with it. I had better prepare you for this right away—it will probably look more tatty, and seem to have more wrong with it, than you expected.

Now, if it is a runner, and has a valid MoT, you should aim to give it a thorough clean—chassis, running gear, bodywork and interior—so that you get an even better idea of the problem areas which will have to be dealt with before it is restored to a high standard. As it is possible (but, thank goodness, less likely these days then ten years ago) that the previous owner was a smoker, you might need to leave the car parked, with all the windows and doors open, for several days, and let a fresh breeze clear out those lasting smells; if you can keep an eye on your new toy (and on the weather!), stand the car outside for a time every day. There are aerosol sprays which hide, but cannot dispel, the smell of nicotine; all I can say is, the best of luck!

Even if the previous owner has assured you that the car was recently serviced, you should now give it a thorough service and spanner check, and if special facilities are needed to set up the engine ignition settings, invest in a visit to a suitably equipped garage or specialist. After this you should check, and if necessary adjust, important details like the steering and suspension settings. Set the headlamps to their optimum levels, recharge the battery, change the windscreen wipers if they are scuffing on the screen, top up the washer bottle, clean out the brakes, reset all the tyre pressures and change the oils and cooling water (don't forget the anti-freeze and/or the coolant inhibitor), in the same way as if you were wakening up the car after a winter's rest.

For your first appraisal run choose a relatively quiet route on a quiet day, and make the run, first in daylight, then in the evening. Give yourself, in other words, the best chance to concentrate on the car and its habits rather on the roads and the other traffic. Don't go out alone, but take a respected friend and colleague with you. A second opinion is always valuable if you start to pick up strange vibrations, noises or smells. In addition (but only if you trust him!), your friend could drive while you occupied the left-hand seat, which leaves you free to poke around and assess the car without having to concentrate on the driving.

If you are lucky enough to own a garage with a pit, or an hydraulic ramp, give the car an all-over inspection *immediately* you get back home, on top, inside the engine bay and underneath the chassis, while the running gear is still well warmed through. At this moment, but perhaps not even after a half-hour's rest, any leaks of oil and water will be immediately obvious.

If the classic car you buy looks as good as this, then you don't have to go through a restoration programme before putting it on the road. But will you take care of it?

If your classic car is a potentially valuable machine—by which I mean certainly one with a nominal value of more than £20,000, and possibly if it is 'only' worth £10,000—it is my view that it is worth investing in a 'second opinion' from the small band of qualified motor engineers who advertise their services for such a task. An independent observer like this will not have been emotionally involved in the purchase (there is nothing quite like signing a big cheque for making you believe the best about everything!), and he is also likely to have more experience in this specialized business.

As a result of those runs you should have a fairly good idea of the problems which will await your attention at the restoration stage. The two-up test drive method allows one person to make notes (either in writing or into a portable tape recorder) while the other person drives. Take the time to sit down calmly and write up your conclusions, and take the trouble to discuss these with an acquaintance who knows even more about such a car than you do.

On the assumption that your new classic car is a 'toy'—or, in marketingspeak, it is an 'optional purchase'—and that you already own a mundane, modern car to look after the commuting, the shopping trips, or the expeditions to see the mother-in-law, you have now arrived at Decision Time. Is the car sound enough for you to start using it immediately, even if only in your spare time, or should you really garage it and start doing some of the essential repairs and renovations?

If you decide that you can, indeed, run the car straight away, please don't abandon this chapter and flick straight ahead to chapter 5. Even if you have paid a great deal of money for a car in beautiful condition, you'll still need to consider *some* restoration, one day. On the other hand, if you decide to start work at once, you have to work out a few priorities.

The joy of running a car that is original, as opposed to restored, is that you somehow get more of the correct period 'feel' from it. Particularly if the car is sound, and not visibly falling to pieces around you, there is a certain satisfaction in running it, and enjoying it, in that condition. In any case, if you haven't spent a small fortune on tidying the body and respraying everything, you won't feel too diffident about getting into the hurly-burly of a one-make club's rally.

There is one definite practical advantage to running your new acquisition for a time before you take it off the road for a rebuild. The better you come to know it, the better you will get rid of those 'rose-tinted spectacles', and you will find out what is most urgently needed. As an example, you might have missed a water leak around a windscreen on the early trial runs, but this sort of problem will certainly make itself known after a time. You might not have discovered, say, a fuel supply problem which only appears when the tank is nearly empty. You might not have realized that your pride and joy overheats in traffic jams. After only a couple of runs you might, in other words, not know the car as well as you should.

There is, of course, a difference between restoration and maintenance, and you should come to terms with this right away. Maintenance involves keeping a good car in tip-top condition, by regular service, and by the regular changing of consumables like lubricants, brake materials, spark plugs and tyres. Restoration involves the renovation, or rebuilding, of important items which have worn out or rotted away.

If he or she has practical, under-cover garaging facilities, and enough mechanical knowledge to get by, almost any motoring enthusiast can look after the preventative maintenance of a classic car. It goes without saying that routine work on cars as different as Jaguar E-Types from the 1960s and MG Midgets of the 1930s can also be tackled by a competent garage, though unless you can provide the new parts and the lubrication schedules, the mechanics might be a bit puzzled at first!

Did I hear you say that the car you choose to buy will not need much important restoration work for years? Sorry, but it just isn't true. Come to terms with one fact straight away. No matter how perfect your classic car was when you first bought it, and no matter how much you paid for it, it is already beginning to wear out even before you get it home.

I will have more to say about regular maintenance in the next chapter, but at this point it is necessary to consider restoration in all its forms. As any seasoned classic car owner will tell you, no matter what the task involved, there is always a choice between the easy way and the more difficult alternative. The easy way to restore a car is to have it done by a professional, and the difficult way is to tackle it yourself. It goes without saying, too, that if you choose the 'professional' way it is going to cost you a great deal of money; if you decide to tackle the job at home, it is going to cost you a lot of everything else: time, personal inconvenience, a lot of aggravation, and maybe even some mental and physical pain. Limbs have been broken, and marriages have broken up, because of an owner's obsession with restoration projects. I'm not joking, I've seen it happen.

Before you even buy a car that is going to need restoring, therefore, sit down and think, very carefully, about what you are starting and what you are trying to achieve. Consider, too, the number of classified adverts you have seen for attractive-sounding cars which include the spine-chilling phrases 'abandoned restoration project', or 'partly restored, needs completion'. The fact is that it is desperately easy for an inexperienced classic car enthusiast to get out of his depth financially, to get depressed at his lack of facilities or mechanical ability, and to lose interest in the whole thing.

Unhappily, there is one breed of so-called 'enthusiast' who goes in for buying nicely kept classic cars and runs them for a year or two without carrying out any more work than is necessary to keep them road-legal, and in possession of the vital MoT certificate. This type is then likely to give his cars a glossy but superficial preparation job and try to sell them on to someone else who will be faced with an unsuspected build-up of neglected work. You're not going to be one of those—are you?

Let us suppose you have decided to buy a particular car, or type of car, and you know that it needs work to put it right. What then? The ruthlessly logical way to proceed is to decide whether you *want* to tackle the job yourself, and—be honest with yourself about this—how much of that job you are truly capable of doing properly. As a result of your careful inspections, the test drives and the second opinions that you have invited, you should have been able to make a list of the jobs which need doing.

Now list them again, not only in a sensible order of priorities (stopping the rust is *always* more urgent than finding a new trim panel, for instance, and finding a replacement gearbox is always more important that searching for a new bonnet mascot) but with a clear idea of what you are capable of doing, and what you will have to farm out to a specialist.

Quite simply, it is foolish to be over-optimistic about *anything*—you must never convince yourself that you can 'pick that up as you go along'. You can't, and you won't—you will finish up putting the job off, or bodging it up, and you will always regret it. In any case, there are many jobs (replating and heavy machining, for instance) which are quite out of the reach of the amateur; there is no other way to get these done than to pay for specialist help.

Unless you own a weatherproof garage or, at least, a car port with a modicum of shelter, it is foolish even to consider starting to restore a car at home. Not only do you need somewhere relatively pleasant to work, but you also need somewhere to store the components of the car as you take it to pieces. In my experience, a car which has been reduced to its component parts takes up at least three times as much room as a fully assembled one, and unless you have a huge house and a very understanding family, it really isn't reasonable to expect to store a lot of rusty, smelly hardware indoors. Ideally speaking, you need the space of a double garage just to house one car and the parts you are working on.

There is another obvious reason for keeping a car indoors or, at the very least, securely sheltered from the weather. If you leave it outdoors, not only is it vulnerable to every aspect of rain, fog, snow or industrial fall-out, but the restored parts will carry on busily rotting away while you work on the rest.

Maybe the concept of the 'heated motorhouse' went out with the early motoring tycoons, but any car of yours should certainly be housed in dry conditions. Although I know that some of Britain's best, and most cosseted, concours cars live in single garages without much space around them, your own ideal restoration building should have as much elbow room around the car as possible. If you have a double garage, that's excellent news—you can always park the modern 'shopping car' outside while restoration work is in progress. (I know of modern cars which have to live outside *all* the time for precisely that reason. . . .)

Unless you are a masochist and have indestructible limbs, I do not believe you can tackle a proper restoration job without a pit, or a ramp, of your own. A ramp is ideal but costs a great deal of money and takes

Below left *This well-equipped professional restoration workshop already seems to have run out of space! Try to have space around your car for storage of dismantled parts.*

Right *This is the sort of professional workshop facility that an amateur dreams about, but apart from the engine building stand, nothing shown here is too expensive for the average enthusiast to install.*

Below *Wheel ramps (and even these are not as robust as some) are essential if you have to lift the car to start poking around underneath. Do not rely on blocks of wood or piles of bricks.*

up a lot of space. You can often dig out a pit by yourself, though you ought to get a seasoned handyman to concrete or brick the sides when you have shaped it. In either case, make discreet enquiries to make sure that you are not about to break any local bye-laws by installing such things at your home.

As a rather poor substitute to getting at the underside of the car (there simply isn't as much space to move around) you might try using a pair of really sturdy wheel ramps to lift one end of the car, or the other. However, *never* rely on temporary methods of lifting a car. This could be extremely dangerous. The car's own jack, a trolley jack, blocks of wood, piles of planks and worst of all, piles of bricks, have all been known to collapse and crush an unfortunate amateur mechanic; it doesn't bear thinking about.

The ideal garage, too, must have an adequate electric power supply whose wiring and plugs are robust enough to deal with any of the demands made on them by various appliances. It should also be well lit, and of course you should have an ample-sized fire extinguisher. Don't just treat the extinguisher as an ornament, by the way—learn how to use it. It's amazing how many restoration accidents can lead to fire breaking out. Just think of it: petrol, paraffin or other cleaning fluids, cleaning rags, electrical sparking, flammable plastics and welding/brazing gear—it's an ideal situation for a fire to take hold.

I know this makes me sound like a degenerate old man, but I think that every serious restorer should have heating in his garage. Let's face it—you are going to spend hundreds of hours alone in that garage, with only the radio for company. Why be cold and miserable as well as lonely? Don't use paraffin stove heating unless you cannot install electric bar or fan heating instead—paraffin smells, and there is that ever-present fire risk again.

You will, presumably, have a wide selection of tools, even some of the special tools which are right for this car; congratulations. Far too many owners new to this business don't even check that 'their' car's bolt heads and 'their' sets of tools are compatible. Right from the start consult an Owner's Handbook or the Workshop Manual to see if you need to have tools and socket sets to suit Metric, Unified, BSF, Whitworth, or other nut and bolt sizes. In this case, remember that near enough is *not* good enough—the wrong sized spanners or sockets may be butchered by being asked to do the wrong job, and a spanner slipping at the wrong moment could damage something, or even you. It will look very professional indeed if your tools are either in a sturdy tool box, or stowed neatly on a peg board on one of the walls.

When an amateur tackles his first restoration, one of his most elementary mistakes is that he doesn't keep records. Not only does he tend to send things away to be reworked, and forget how long ago this was done, but he tends to dismantle parts of the car, put them in cardboard boxes, stow them away—and forget where they have gone. In your case I recommend that you keep a stout exercise book near the car in which you can make notes of everything—from the phone number of an important specialist to the torque setting of the cylinder head holding down studs—and that you label everything.

My experience is that biscuit tins, cardboard boxes, glass coffee jars, stick-on and tie-on labels are all invaluable for your purpose. Don't let anything be thrown out of the kitchen into the dustbin before you have eliminated it as useless for your hobby. If possible, use one container for one sub-assembly—all the rear brake parts in one box, all the instruments in another, all the gearbox parts in yet another. If there are cases where some things can be wrongly reassembled (safety belt mountings with spring washers and spacers are good examples), then store them in a loosely reassembled condition. If there is any doubt, always make notes and sketches.

I have always found that 'candid camera' snapshots are very useful, and not just to make you feel good when you consult 'Before' and 'After' shots when the restoration is complete. If you have a suitable camera with flash equipment and need to recall how a certain section of the car goes together, a picture will be a lot more informative than a sketch; the two of them together will be invaluable.

So now the car is stripped out. What next? If you have a ruthlessly logical approach to this hobby, a lot of spare time and cash and a great deal of space, then you can obviously get several major rebuilding jobs under way at one and the same time. In most cases, though, this would

This factory shot of a complex modern wiring loom being assembled shows why some restoration jobs should best be left to experts!

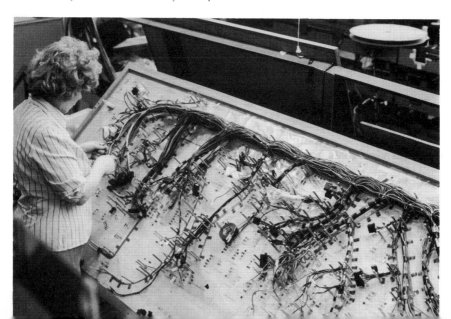

Above *To retrim a car, you need no expensive capital equipment but a great deal of patience and experience. Could you cope, or should the job go out to a professional?*

Below *This sort of detail repainting is certainly best left to a professional. The 'finishing touch' requires a very experienced and delicate hand.*

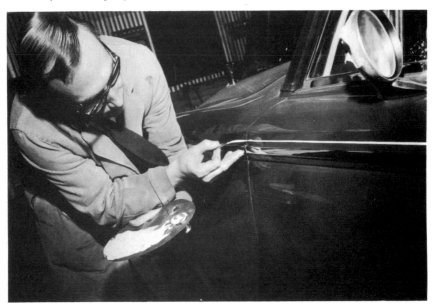

In the course of a restoration, you'll have recourse to autojumbles on many occasions. Collections like this are important, for they allow you to get hold of original components.

be foolish. Certainly, if some parts need to be sent away for replating, remachining or whatever, by all means do that at once, but don't dabble with several areas of restoration at the same time. It may take longer for the whole job to be completed, but I have always found it more sensible, and somehow more satisfying, to start, progress, and complete, one job before moving on to the next.

In the hope that you have an understanding family, I suggest that there are many jobs which can be completed indoors. I'm not suggesting, you understand, that you should rebuild the engine on the hearth rug while keeping an eye on the TV, but I do think that relatively small jobs which generate no muck could be tackled indoors on a large board. In any case, if you drop a screw from a speedometer head it will be easier to find it in the spare room than on the oily floor of a garage. . . .

I would now like to offer the alternative suggestion—that you should have most of the major jobs done by a specialist. On the understanding that you will have taken advice and found the right expert for each job (that doesn't mean the cheapest, by the way, but the one who will do the most thorough and complete job and—best of all—he will actually finish it when promised!), this might be a very wise decision.

The oily-handed traditionalists call this 'cheque book' restoration, but I see no harm in it. Many people love classic car motoring but are quite incapable of doing all the work themselves; why should they be denied

Left *With a separate chassis car, try to get the rolling chassis completed before you drop the body shell back into place — this is a Lotus Elan chassis in pristine condition.*

Below *When rebuilding an engine, it is important that you should not over-restore it. This Ford-Cosworth BDA unit of 1970 was in factory-fresh condition when photographed, so if you are rebuilding one, it never needs to look any more 'bulled' than this.*

Lamborghini's Miura was an enormously fast trend-setter and the world's first car to have a transversely-mounted vee-12 engine.

Below *The famous Datsun 240Z Coupé was Japan's first true collectable car.*

Above *Some one-make clubs make great efforts to attract interest at classic car shows.*

Above *There is so much interest in classic car shows that major exhibition halls are needed to house all the cars and the people.*

'Big Healeys' were built from 1952 to 1968 — this is a 1966-model 3000 Mk III.

the pleasure of ownership if they do not belong to that mafia of owner-mechanics?

In many cases, of course, you will have little alternative. I have yet to find a genuine private owner who can tackle the rebuilding of an overdrive or an automatic gearbox, and I doubt if many of them, as yet, would want to delve deeply into the mysteries of fuel injection or electronic engine management systems.

If you choose this route then you must be even more careful in planning the sequence of events. It would be silly, for instance to have the car's body shell completely restored and repainted before the chassis work, and the reinstallation of the engine and transmission, is complete. Similarly, do you really need to have the seats retrimmed before the body shell is ready?

The best way to have the job done is to discover how the car was assembled in the first place, and try to reassemble your restored car in the same way. In the case of cars with a separate chassis, it usually pays to get them back to the self-supporting 'rolling-chassis' stage before you even offer up the body shell. In the case of unit construction cars you should start from a painted trimmed shell before adding all the mechanical parts.

Unless you hand over the complete car to a specialist for restoration on his premises, you still have to act as your own progress-chaser and keep nagging away at everyone to get on with the job. Most of the specialists I know are splendid craftsmen, unsurpassed at their job, but a number of them do not treat jobs with any urgency.

(I'm reminded of the man who left his shoes at a shoe shop to be mended, then had the misfortune to be sent out of the country, urgently, on his firm's business. When he returned, three years later, he called in to collect them:

'Are my shoes ready?'

'Ready on Thursday!')

It's a cynical thing to have to say, but the best way to ensure that your job gets done is to keep on nagging. Visit the workshops regularly to see what is happening, and keep on telephoning to make enquiries. Of course, the ploy might misfire, but at least the specialist won't be able to forget that you are trying to do business with him, and he might actually give your job some priority, just to get rid of you. Then, of course, you could try delaying your payment for as long as he held you up. . . it's a thought!

Whichever way you decide to tackle the restoration, however, I think you should come to terms with these facts: it will take at least twice as long to get anything done as you originally thought, and it will certainly cost at least twice as much money.

Good luck!

Chapter 5

Running a classic car - pitfalls and priorities

I hope that in buying a classic car you are looking forward to driving it regularly, as a 'pleasure machine'. Of course that will mean different things to different owners. Some of you will want to drive the car every week, but others may only want to wheel it out in dry, warm weather. Unless, of course, you belong to that rather despicable breed of motorists who call themselves 'collectors', put their cars in store and treat them as a more interesting alternative to Krugerands, oil paintings or antique silver.

I have already touched on the subject of suitable cars for suitable purposes in earlier chapters, so at this point I only need to make one or two points.

Before even buying the car of your choice, I hope you have considered how often, and in what way, you will be using it. As extremes, you would surely not buy a Morris Minor if you wanted to make regular long-distance journeys in your classic car, and I doubt very much if you would find an AC Cobra, or a Morgan, suitable for traffic-jammed commuting.

Next, be sure that you have somewhere safe and secure to park it. The days when you could park a classic car in the street, in London or the provinces, have long gone, for there are now too many malicious, envious and plain dishonest people in the world to let it stay there for long. Even parking it in a lock-up garage some distance from home is no longer advisable.

My own advice (and yes, I *have* practised what I preach) is that the 'toy' should always take precedence over the regular day-to-day motor car. If you have a garage at home but are short of space, park the classic indoors and let your everyday car live outside in all weathers.

Look at it this way—if your 'ordinary' car is stolen, vandalized or ruined by an accident, or even by freak weather conditions, it can be repaired or replaced by another one; if your insurance cover is all-embracing, you might not even have to pay for this. On the other hand, if similar misfortunes happen to your well-beloved toy, it will cause you a lot of sadness, a lot of aggravation to 'make good', and it might cost you a great deal of money. Many insurance companies are notorious for disagreeing

It's a smart Riley RM Series saloon now, but don't leave it outside in all weathers to get wet or the rust will set in again.

with their customers over the value of an older car, and of course the whole question of what needs to be repaired, who should do it and how much might it cost falls right outside their 'usual' horizons.

Now, if you propose to run the car on a regular basis, let's begin at the beginning. You need to have a valid registration document, a certificate of insurance and of course an MoT certificate—and in each case you might run into problems getting one.

When you bought your classic car the previous owner should have handed over a registration document known as a V5, which is a computerized piece of paper issued by the DVLC in Swansea. For authenticity's sake, I hope that you were also given the old-style 'log book' with which the car was originally issued.

In other possible cases, where the car you buy has been off the road (and unlicensed) for some years, you might only be offered an old-style document, and in the worst possible case there might be no documentation of any type. The problem here is that you might find it tiresome to get the car registered again for road use, and—if this matters to you—it might be extremely difficult for an 'age-related' number to be secured.

There is an important difference between the two types of document.

This is an old-style vehicle 'log book' which has been rendered obsolete by the new DVLC documents. It might, however, be a nice souvenir and, if necessary, a help in getting your old number reactivated one day.

If the previous owner (or even the one before that) did all the right things before November 1983, the car's original registration number will have been entered into the DVLC's massive computer records, and a V5 record will be kept. If this deadline was missed, the original registration number was rendered void for that particular car. If the car was not actually currently taxed at the time the old-style documents were officially rendered obsolete, but the DVLC was told that it was still in existence, the number will still be retained.

No matter how keen you are to restore the original registration number to an old car whose 'identity' has not been entered in the DVLC computer, you might find it impossible to do so. In 1983 it was actually supposed to be impossible, but more recently the authorities have established a *modus vivendi* with classic car owners. To reactivate that old number you will have to prove to the DVLC that the car was built when you said it was (road tests, catalogues, authentic dateable photographs, original sales records and similar evidence are needed), perhaps get a letter of authentication from a learned body or one-make club and—most significant of all—prove that the original registration number is historically important. (If perhaps, you bought a wreck which subsequently proved to be a famous old competition car, you would naturally want to use the same number again, wouldn't you. . . ?)

After all this effort has been made, you *might* be allowed the original number, but don't bank on it. In the end, it all depends on the good nature of the licensing officer of the day.

The alternative is to accept what is called an 'age-related' registration number—one that was in a sequence at the time, and was due to be used, but *never* actually was used when your car was built. The problem here is that for, say a 1953 car you will be issued with an appropriate 1953 registration, but it will almost certainly not be from the county in which the car was registered in the first place!

The easy way out (and I have to say that I have *never* seen this done on a classic car) is to accept a registration plate with a 'Q' suffix, which means that as far as the authorities are concerned it is a car 'of unknown age or origin'.

The very expensive way out is to go into the market and buy a 'cherished number' for your car, perhaps one where the letters form your initials, or have some obvious relation to the car—SS for an SS-Jaguar, MG for an MG, or AC for an AC, for instance. I was lucky enough to buy two such numbers—AAG 4 and GR 90—in the 1960s when all it cost was £5 and a letter to the appropriate licensing authority. Like I fool I let them go when I sold the cars (a Mini and Cortina GT respectively) and I haven't seen them since. Nowadays, of course, the notional value of such numbers has risen to absurd levels, and I don't recommend them to a classic car enthusiast, even as an 'investment'.

Think carefully before you decide to license your new classic car all the year round. Do you actually intend to use it in January, when it is snowing, or in November, when it is clammy and foggy? Save a bit of money by only registering it for a shorter period—you will also find that this helps cut down on insurance costs as well.

It doesn't matter whether the car of your dreams is three years old or sixty years old—before you can get it licensed, and before you can take it out on the road, you must be in possession of a valid MoT test certificate of roadworthiness. According to the law, the inspectors can make no allowance for the age, or general debility, of the car you happen to love very dearly, so when the time comes for the annual inspection you must always make sure it is in the best possible condition.

Before even visiting the station, however, be sure that your car complies with the law—and remember that there are different laws for different ages of car in matters such as lighting layouts, safety belt fixings and usage, and related details.

The best one-make clubs have developed special insurance schemes for their members, backed by large and respctable insurance companies.

As an example, I would be the first to agree that a 1930s-style car with less than perfect Bendix brakes is far less likely to pass the brake tests than is an E-Type with four discs; the fact remains that you must make the installation as good as possible. The exhaust system must be in good shape whether you are running a T-Series MG or a Ferrari Dino.

Your classic car-owning friends will tell you where the most sympathetic MoT stations are located, and you would be well advised to patronize that particular one. Such a tester will probably have experience of other cars of the type which you take along, and this means that he will have a better 'feel' for what you think is an acceptable condition. A sensible tester will take the test—and your car—seriously, but will not make impossible demands, and if your car is sound you should have no problems.

Unless your classic car is a well-known saloon car type which is likely to be familiar to an insurance company, I would recommend you never try to insure it with the same company which insures your everyday cars. They will be as uneasy about the whole deal as you are yourself, and because such companies are not known for their philanthropy you are likely to end up paying too high a premium for the privilege of keeping it all 'in the family'.

With what I call a conventional insurance company, and conventional cover, you will always have difficulty in getting the company to understand your idea of a classic car's replacement value; the company will usually assume a much lower value than you do. If you are ever unfortunate enough to be involved in a major accident, the company is likely to take one look at the estimate for repairs and write off the car, even though you know the damage is repairable.

In recent years, as the classic following has grown, a number of knowledgeable and specialized insurance companies have developed special schemes, and I would recommend that you should search around for one of these. If you have joined the best one-make club which caters for your car you will almost certainly find that the officers have a knowledge of such schemes, and can recommend the most suitable for your needs. In some cases, insurance schemes have been developed for a particular club, and those clubs have found that their membership has increased considerably as a consequence.

A good insurance broker known to the appropriate one-make club will help you work everything out, but you should perhaps consider these points:

A special scheme will usually include an agreed value clause, and although this always meaning paying a substantial annual premium, it means that you can sleep soundly at nights without worrying about the replacement cost of your precious classic after theft or other terminal misfortune.

Several companies offer limited mileage schemes, whereby the cost of insurance is related to the use you give your car. These may be written for annual figures of, say, 1,000 miles or 3,000 miles, and are very valuable indeed for concours owners, or those lucky people with several classics to choose from. If you exceed that annual mileage, however, and you need to claim, there will be substantial penalties.

Reputable schemes should include a salvage clause, which means that you should get first option on buying back the remains of your car; this is valuable where you own an important or irreplaceable car and want to be able to recreate it again after disaster strikes.

Betterment clauses mean that an owner can get together with his insurers, on an agreed partial investment basis, to make the whole of the car better when only part of it has been damaged.

Be sure that you understand the policy's terms regarding the preservation of originality in repairs: if you have a 'thing' about keeping a car's original parts, will they agree to mend or straighten rather than replace?

Be sure, too, that the policy's terms cover storage, and that they cover the car against theft, damage or other loss when unlicensed or even partially dismantled.

Remember, however, that in the end you only get what you pay for. An insurance company's premium rates are governed by its claims experience, and that is calculated by computer or, worse, by an actuary (one of a band of professional men who have been described as 'computers without hearts'—in other words, emotion and sympathy don't rate very highly in their calculations).

I now come to giving a little advice on running the car, especially if you intend to drive it on a regular basis. I assume right from the start that you will understand that it was neither as well designed, nor as well-built, as today's mass-produced models, and that it needs sympathetic attention at all times.

Your classic car will need to be serviced, and have all its vital fluids changed, at the same intervals as those specified in the original handbook. Although modern lubricants, oils and fuels are all better than they were when the car was designed, don't assume that this allows you to impose modern service intervals on an older car.

One reason for specifying more frequent service intervals in the old days was the car used only the materials and the systems designs which were thought adequate at the time. So, as an example, a modern grease might help a suspension ball joint to keep its original shape for rather longer, but it will still not last as long as a 1980s-type part.

I don't intend the next paragraphs to be thought frivolous, for they are not. You might give a bit of thought to the clothes you are going to wear in your classic, and the protective items you might use on all but special occasions. Of course I'm not talking about the eccentrics who always drive an Edwardian car in Edwardian dress, or the cowboys who tend to wear crash helmets.

However, I think there is every justification for carrying a ground sheet and working overalls in the car, just in case of breakdowns. If the car's floor carpets are precious, or cannot be replaced to original pattern when they wear out, consider using rubber mats in the footwells, or even having spare sections of carpet laid over the originals. Is it too obvious to suggest that you should never drive the car in dirty or oily clothes, or that you should consider using seat covers for some journeys? And although I'm a dog lover myself, should Fido be encouraged to ride in the back of the classic without a rug or a sheet covering the seats?

In every case I am thinking of the fact that your classic car tends to keep on wearing out, and that you will have to keep on spending money to get it back into pristine condition. Why not retard the process as much as you possibly can?

As you and I get older it seems to take us a little longer to get up and about in the mornings, and I think you should assume that your ageing classic car also deserves a bit of cosseting. When you are going to use it,

There is nothing new about traffic jams for older cars (this was a scene at Rochester in Kent in late 1930s), but don't subject your precious classic to any more hard work than necessary.

don't plunge into the garage, fire it up and drive away at once. Start the engine gently and allow it to warm through for a few minutes before you drive away. Similarly, at the end of the run, make sure the car is garaged and happy and cosy with its surroundings before abandoning it for the night.

Incidentally, I know many enthusiastic owners who *never* come in from a wet run in their classic car without at least sponging and leathering it down at the end of the day. Many people, too, keep their car covered by a protective cloth so that dust cannot settle and to make sure that no cats, birds, mice or other creatures who make their home in a garage can pad about on the precious paintwork.

Unless your car is small and there is nowhere sensible to stow them, I would always recommend the carrying of an appropriate tool kit, a service manual and perhaps a small pack of 'emergency' spares. If you have to call out the AA man for an electrical repair and find that the only suitable coil or distributor is back in your garage, you will not only feel a fool, but your return might be delayed by several hours.

If you propose to use your classic car in modern, everyday traffic conditions, I suggest that you discover how suitable it is for those conditions.

Taking your classic car out to rallies, or other club gatherings, is one of the great pleasures of ownership. Guess the age of this Bugatti Owners' Club occasion?

Naturally, a sports car built, say, in the 1960s should be able to cope with anything thrown at it today, but will a machine from the pre-motorways, pre-disc brakes, pre-traffic jams era cope as well? Cars of pre-war design may be particularly ill-suited for modern conditions.

Consider, first, the question of engine cooling. Does your car relish crawling along in heavy traffic on a hot day? Is the cooling system adequate? Is there even a water pump in the circuit? One, or two, generations ago a car's radiator was often kept cool by the passage of ram air through it, on the assumption that there were few jams, and that nothing more extreme than British summertime temperatures would prevail; British designers were an insular lot in those days.

This isn't a joke—in the 1950s there were many authenticated cases of Jaguars overheating in New York or Los Angeles traffic because their radiators were simply not passing enough air to keep water temperatures in check.

If you encounter an overheating problem, and the cooling system is definitely in 'as designed' condition, you should certainly ignore all your better instincts about preserving originality and fit one of the most modern, slim-line, electric fans. Better to preserve the engine and to withstand comment about originality than to risk a major breakdown.

The same applies to running an older classic at sustained high speeds. Even though the UK motorway speed limit is 70 mph (112 km/h) (and you do observe the law, don't you. . . ?), this was up at the top cruising limit of many smaller, older cars, which might not relish being thrashed along at such speeds for minutes at a time. In the 1930s, after all, even Rolls-Royce felt they had to caution their customers about the possible problems of running cars at sustained high speeds on continental roads. And if Rolls-Royce actually spelled it out, you can be sure that other companies felt the same but could never bring themselves to admit that their cars were not perfect!

You should always come to terms with the practical limits of your car's roadholding, steering and brakes, especially when running in company with modern cars, and drive accordingly. If this means leaving a bit more time and space all around you, don't worry about it—if and when the unexpected happens, it is better to have a precious classic car in one piece than to have been unnecessarily brave up to the very last minute.

Above all I hope that you have bought a classic car to rekindle the enjoyment of motoring, and that you plan to use it with that in mind. If you classic car is your hobby, then go motoring for fun, and treat every journey as relaxation. But if you don't enjoy it all, and you worry about the machine every minute of the day, are you sure you have the right car for the right purpose?

In the next few chapters I will be listing some of my favourite classic cars—old, middle-aged and near-new. Each one of them is right for someone. Could it be you?

Chapter 6

Veteran and vintage cars—the earlier days

This is where I have to start laying my opinions on the line, and begin to choose a selection of the world's classic cars. In the first chapter I hope I made it clear that a classic car can be one built at any time from 1885 to the present day. On the other hand, it should also be clear that a car certainly does not qualify as 'classic' merely because it is very old.

Although I know that the massed ranks of the VSCC and the VCC will now be dissecting this chapter word for word and car by car, I should remind them, and the general reader, that it is usually agreed that the 'classic' period did not truly begin until the late 1920s or early 1930s. There's no doubt, however, that many cars 'of the first class, of allowed excellence' were produced before then, and even though it has all been written down before, I ought to spend a little time describing the birth and rapid development of the motor car, and picking out some of the outstanding makes and models which appeared in the first thirty years or so of its life.

Origins
Only recently, a thoughtful observer pointed out that the world had moved at the speed of the galloping horse from the dawn of creation until the end of the Napoleonic Wars, and that the mad rush of speed had all happened in the last 150 years. The first major breakthrough was the harnessing of steam power to locomotives on iron rails, but the second, undoubtedly, was the invention of the motor car.

Considering the limited (Victorian age) technology which could then be applied to boilers, pressure vessels and transmission systems, the railway locomotive was soon developed into a very fast machine indeed, but there was no way that this knowledge could successfully be applied to independent steered road vehicles. In the second half of the nineteenth century it was tried, of course, but the problems of size, weight and operating economy could not be solved.

The breakthrough came with Lenoir's modified gas engine, while Otto's four-stroke cycle took the concept a stage further and miniaturized it, but it was left to two German engineers operating independently of each other, Karl Benz and Gottlieb Daimler, to harness the new-fangled 'four-stroke' engine to 'horseless carriages' and produce the first motor cars.

You can discount all chauvinistic claims to have produced earlier cars which actually worked, for there is no historic evidence to support them, and early celebrations of the centenary can be ignored. Disagreement about the real birth of the car led to the British celebrating the occasion in 1985, and the West Germans, who should know, celebrating it in 1986!

As so often happens, the Americans didn't invent the motor car, but they certainly exploited it most successfully. In fact, although the motor car was invented in Germany, France was the first to set up a fledgling industry in the 1890s, and the Americans developed the concept into mass production at the beginning of this century.

Between about 1890 and 1914 an enormous number of entrepreneurs set up firms to try and make a fortune in building cars, but few actually achieved it. The charlatans (such as Britain's Harry Lawson and America's Edward Joel Pennington) made—and lost—a lot of money. The under-capitalized concerns made a few cars, then collapsed. Many of today's successful car makers, such as Peugeot, Fiat, Daimler-Benz, Cadillac, Renault, Ford and Rolls-Royce, were founded in these early years. On the other hand, some of the original dominant marques from France—De Dion Bouton, Darracq and Panhard among them—disappeared years ago.

In the years leading up to the First World War France's industry lost its lead, technically and commercially. By 1914 the USA built more cars than everyone else combined, Britain was second, while France, Germany and Italy lagged well behind. It is also interesting to note that there was no motor industry of any type in Japan, Scandinavia, Australia, South Africa, South America or Russia.

Four years of war from 1914 to 1918 saw German imperialism repulsed but, after the dust had settled and the rebuilding had begun, the world's motor industry was little changed. The USA's car makers were bigger and even more successful, British production boomed upwards, and the European countries were well behind.

A few statistics tell their own story. In 1922, Ford of the USA became the first company to build more than one million vehicles a year; they doubled this in 1923. General Motors' first 'million year' was in 1929. By comparison, Britain's peak 1920s production year was 1929, when the entire industry built only 182,347 cars. On the other hand, no fewer than 179 makes of car were exhibited at the London Motor Show of 1920.

It was in the 1920s that techniques of mass production were refined, prices were brought down and many companies who used craftsmen to build cars slowly, carefully, and rather expensively, were forced out of business. It was this quite unstoppable trend which changed the motor car from an indulgence for the well-to-do into one which could be sold to the millions, and which led to the definition of 'vintage' in later years and to the worship of cars of that period.

Not that all of them were good, by any means, and many were certainly not classic, but there were some outstanding marques, with outstanding models. Here is just a selection of those still seen, and sometimes sold, today:

Great Britain
The first British-built cars were Daimlers, assembled under licence from the German concern in 1896, but the first British-designed cars were the Lanchesters and Wolseleys which were developed in Birmingham at about the same time. Within ten years these marques had been joined by several others, most of which had been designed by companies previously noted for their pedal cycles; the most famous of these were Humber, Riley, Rover and Singer.

One marque, however, stood apart from this Midlands-based collection, not only geographically but in design: Rolls-Royce. By 1904, when he designed his first car, Henry Royce was well established in Manchester in the electrical engineering industry, and his partnership with the Hon. Charles Rolls not only helped provide the famous name, but also helped provide a selling network for these expensive new cars.

Right from the start, nothing but the best was good enough for Royce, so every Rolls-Royce chassis was not only beautifully designed and detailed but a classic of its day. Note that Rolls-Royce only supplied

Dramatic changes in car shapes occurred in a generation. Here is an Edwardian Austin of the 1900s lined up alongside a late-1930s example of the same marque.

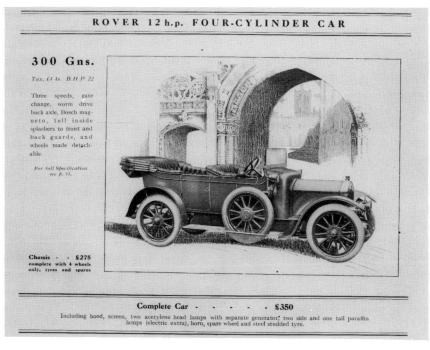

ROVER 12 h.p. FOUR-CYLINDER CAR

300 Gns.

Tax, £4 4s. B.H.P. 22

Three speeds, gate change, worm drive back axle, Bosch magneto, full inside splashers to front and back guards, and wheels made detachable.

For full Specification see p. 15.

Chassis - - £275 complete with 4 wheels only, tyres and spares

Complete Car - - - - - £350

Including hood, screen, two acetylene head lamps with separate generator, two side and one tail paraffin lamps (electric extra), horn, spare wheel and steel studded tyre.

Above *Rover of Coventry built up a fine reputation, especially with this car, the 12 hp model, introduced in 1912.*

Below *Riley's heyday was in the 1920s and 1930s. This is late-1920s 12 hp four-cylinder model at Connel Bridge in Scotland.*

rolling chassis up to 1939, leaving the building of bodywork to approved coachbuilders. First of all the models built in considerable numbers was the six-cylinder 40/50 hp model built from 1906 to 1925, which everyone now calls the Silver Ghost (a name which only properly belongs to the car, owned by Rolls-Royce, which had so much silver plating on its chassis, and to the extraordinary silence of its passage), and from 1922 there was the much smaller 20 hp, also a six-cylinder car, and the first from Rolls-Royce to have an overhead-valve engine. This was not as highly regarded at first by the purists. Later in the 1920s the 40/50 hp model was replaced by the New Phantom (retrospectively known as the Phantom I), which was effectively the old 40/50 hp model fitted with a new overhead valve engine, and was really only an interim model before the Phantom II of the 1930s.

By any standards, national, European, or worldwide, these Rolls-Royce cars were the models by which every other marque was judged. Even though devotees of Cadillac and Hispano-Suiza, in particular, wished that this was not so, this is how history now sees it.

In Britain, Daimler ran Rolls-Royce close, especially once they had established their patronage from the British royal family. By the mid 1900s all traces of German ancestry had gone, and the company's great days came in the 1910s and 1920s with a series of sleeve-valve engined models.

All Edwardian and 'vintage' Daimlers were fine cars, but the greatest of these was undoubtedly the Double Six type, in which the sleeve-valve principle was retained in a conventional chassis but the engine was a massive vee-12 unit. The first of these, introduced in 1926, was the '50', with a 50 hp, 7.2-litre engine, the chassis usually being topped by lofty but dignified limousine or landaulette coachwork. From 1927 it was also joined by the '30', which had a 3,744 cc engine. Because it was easy for these engines to sustain frost damage if the owner was careless in winter (third- and fourth-hand owners often were. . .), not many have survived to this day. A pity. . . .

The other truly 'big' name of the 1920s was certainly that of Bentley. Here was an independent company, founded by W.O. Bentley, which only sold cars for a decade, made a successful series of sports cars at Cricklewood, and whose reputation has lived for ever. One of Bentley's rivals once described them as 'the fastest lorries in the world', but since they also had a splendid competition record this could be put down to sour grapes. Every one of the 'pure' Bentley cars—3-litre, 4½-litre, Supercharged 4½-litre, 6½-litre and 8-litre—was a true classic. All had overhead cam, four-valves-per-cylinder engines, all had massive chassis and rugged construction, and there was the most amazing variety of body styles, for Bentley, like Rolls-Royce, did not build their own coachwork. A high proportion of those built have survived to this day, which says a lot for their durability.

The other makers of large, and rather sporting, cars of the period must

One of Britain's most famous 'vintage' marques was the Bentley, built from 1921 to 1931. Each of these cars is worth a great deal of money today.

include Lagonda and Sunbeam. Lagondas were built at Staines from 1906, but the first true sporting cars of this type originated with the 14/60 of 1925, which had an advanced twin high-cam four-cylinder engine, and this was soon supplemented by the 2-litre Speed Model of 1927. In the same period there was the overhead-valve six-cylinder 16/65 of 1926, which grew up into the 3-litre a couple of years later. All these cars had a similar character, typically British, with rugged construction, handsome but not sexily sleek coachwork, and all the charisma that a 'vintage' machine should exude. There would be even more exciting Lagondas in the 1930s.

All the Sunbeams of the period were built in Wolverhampton, and after the French engineer Louis Coatalen joined the firm in 1909 the cars began to look, and feel, more and more thoroughbred. In 1920 the company joined together with Talbot and Darracq to form the Anglo-French STD combine, which soon put its entire corporate financial structure in hock to finance a racing programme.

Most of the 1920s Sunbeam models were sturdy and refined but not very high performers, even though the more sporting 16 hp and 24 hp models had overhead-valve versions of the existing side-valve engines. Without a doubt, though, the most outstanding Sunbeam of the period was the 3-litre sports car of 1925-31, which not only had an impressive

AC cars of the 1920s were graced by a fine light-alloy six-cylinder engine. This car is starting out on the Monte Carlo rally of 1925.

twin-overhead-cam six-cylinder engine, but the very advanced feature of dry sump lubrication. Directly developed from the racing experience built up by Coatalen's design team, it was an expensive car—£1,125 in 1925, compared with the £1,225 price tag of a current Bentley 3-litre—though its supporters claimed that it was a better car. Few were made, and very few survive today.

Sunbeam's STD partner Talbot produced better and better cars once designer Georges Roesch was given his head. The first model to use his advanced, excellently detailed six-cylinder overhead-valve engine was the 14/45 of 1926, and this was soon followed by enlarged, 2¼-litre models called 75 and 90, which really belong to the next chapter.

At this stage we must remember that Vauxhall, who were bought up by General Motors in 1925, produced a series of fine sporting cars before that time, all inspired by designer Laurence Pomeroy (Senior). The original 3-litre Prince Henry sports car (which was named after the famous European reliability trial for which it was developed) arrived in 1910, and grew to 4 litres by 1913. At this point the famous 30/98 sports model was launched, and in its original E-Type form it had a 4½-litre side-valve four-cylinder engine, and was priced at £925. A 100 mph (160 km/h) top speed in stripped-for-racing form was guaranteed. Very few were built before war broke out, and the great days of the 30/98 came in the early 1920s, when it competed head-on against the Bentley 3-litre both in price and performance. From 1922 it became even better, for with an overhead-valve engine and 115 bhp it had the legs of the Bentley, but it was not until 1926 that front-wheel brakes became available. The last of all was built in 1927, there being around 600 30/98s of all types made.

There were several fine medium-sized sports cars of the period, many of which survive, in limited numbers, to this day. The most popular included the 2-litre AC models (which had a fine, overhead-camshaft, six-cylinder engine), the 1½-litre Alvis 12/50 models (particularly those with the fashionable 'duck-tail' two-seater coachwork), the two original Aston Martin model families, of which the 'Bertelli' 1½-litre cars of 1927 were by far the most interesting technically, and the Frazer Nash 'chain gang' sports cars which first went on sale in 1924, the nickname stemming from the fact that this design used a chain-drive transmission. Each marque was to become more effective, and more famous, in years to come.

There was also the splendid little Riley Nine family from Coventry, which was based around an excellent little twin high-camshaft four-cylinder engine. Although there was a wide choice of coachwork, most of which was made by the Riley company itself, the only actual sports car of this type produced was the diminutive Brooklands model, a hard-sprung, high-revving, little fire-breather which was much more at home on the race track than on the public highway.

There is a difference, however, between the classic car which can be enjoyed and used as a motor car, and that which is regularly polished, occasionally displayed, and more often treated as something of an icon. From the pre-1930 period of British machines there is no doubt that the three most popular 'usable' cars are the Austin Seven, the Morris 'Bullnose' and the early MG Midget.

The Austin Seven went on sale in 1923 as a minimum-size, minimum-spec., minimum-price four-seater which its designer, Sir Herbert Austin, intended to 'put the motor cycle and side car out of business'. In many ways its engineering was lamentably lacking, for the roadholding, braking and performance were all very restricted at first, as were the passenger space and the standard equipment. Even so, it was a simple 750 cc package which appealed to tens of thousands of 'marginal' motorists, and because it had an abundance of that indefinable feature—character—it was a great success. Prices sunk to little more than £100 for the cheapest Tourers, and a five-year-old car could be bought for little more than £10 or £20. It sold, and sold, until the late 1930s.

The Morris 'bullnose' set out to do the same thing as the Austin Seven but was always a considerably larger, and somewhat more costly, machine. Compared with the Austin, by the way, which was virtually manufactured 'in house' at Longbridge, the 'bullnose' was assembled at Cowley from a mass of bought-out components. Like the Austin Seven it was simple, rugged, practical, cheap to buy, and also full of character; the nickname came not only from the shape of its radiator, but from the badge on that radiator. There were Oxfords and Cowleys (with different size four-cylinder engines) in a variety of body styles, and hundreds survive in the late 1980s.

The other collectible 'Morris' of the vintage years is actually badged as

The Morris empire was founded on this simple little car, the famous 'bullnose' model of 1913, which ran successfully into the mid-1920s.

an MG, as that company was then personally owned by the founder of Morris Motors. The cheap and cheerful M-Series Midget, introduced in 1928, was really little more than a rebodied Morris Minor, and was struggling to achieve a top speed of 60 mph (96 km/h). Nevertheless it was a chunky and spirited little car, with a very advanced (for its day) overhead-camshaft engine, nice two-seater styling, and the first indications of that cheeky character which came to be known as the 'Abingdon touch'; there would be better, faster and prettier Midgets in the 1930s.

Other simple, rugged, reliable, pleasing British cars of the vintage period which still have their own following include the Bean built in Tipton, near Birmingham, with four-cylinder and six-cylinder engines; the 1.4-litre Coventry-Climax engined Clyno, produced a few miles away at Wolverhampton only in the 1920s (it was a real 'nine-year wonder' in that respect, for after the company hit financial trouble, it was never revived); and the HE produced at Reading (also a pure vintage product which disappeared in 1931).

A whole variety of practical Humber models was produced in Coventry, the smallest of which, the 8/18 (which eventually grew up into the 9/20) being one important size larger than the Austin Seven, and about as large as the Morris 'bullnose' models. Other well-liked Humbers included the 12/25 and 14/40 models, all having simple four-cylinder engines and a definite family likeness in the styling. Humber combined with Hillman in 1928, the Rootes family taking financial control shortly after this, and all individuality was soon lost in the 1930s.

Three other Midlands-based marques deserve a mention. In Coventry Rover made a name for themselves, first with the £350 Clegg-designed

The first-ever MG Midget was the M-Type of 1928 which used this chassis, a lightly-modified version of the new overhead-cam Morris Minor design.

Twelve introduced in 1912, and then with the quirky, air-cooled flat-twin Eight of 1920, which was only one step up from a cycle car, and was almost as frail at first. One of the most interesting Rovers of the 1920s was the 14/45 (later enlarged to become 16/50), which had an overhead-camshaft engine design, an opposed-valve layout with hemispherical cylinder heads, and featured cross pushrods from one side of the head to the other!

Also in Coventry, and Birmingham, was Singer, whose production rose so much in the 1920s that it became the third largest British maker behind Austin and Morris. Some of its cars were conventionally vintage in every way, but the most interesting were the Junior models, produced from 1927 with an 848 cc overhead-cam engine. This was the first of several such units whose complexity, and cost, must have contributed to Singer's financial problems in the next decade.

There were two different Wolseley periods, for the marque was Vickers-owned until 1926, when it collapsed into bankruptcy, and was controlled by William Morris (of Morris Motors fame) thereafter. Following their war time experience in building the technically advanced Hispano-Suiza aero-engines, Wolseley designed and produced similar overhead-cam motor car engines of their own. The most interesting Wolseleys of the 1920s were the Ten of the early 1920s and the large six-cylinder engined Silent Six and 21/60 straight-eight of the post-bankruptcy period. Wolseley's biggest contribution to classic motoring, though, was to design and produce the overhead-camshaft engines used by MG after 1928 and well into the 1930s.

Two other 'vintage' marques deserve mention for cars which were large, stately but decidedly, and proudly, British through and through. From Coventry there was Armstrong-Siddeley, a car created by the fusion of Armstrong-Whitworth and Siddeley-Deasy and made only as a sideline of a company which was much more interested in building aeroplanes and aero-engines. The big-engined cars (like the 30 hp 5-litre model built throughout the 1920s) were the most gracious of all and were distinguished by their massive vee-profile radiators. Armstrong-Siddeley's greatest technical innovation was the introduction of the Wilson-type pre-selector transmission in 1929.

Finally there was the Lanchester, which was Britain's longest-established independent car-making concern. The original Lanchester prototype had been built in 1895, but in the 1920s all its products were dignified, large engined machines of 3 litres or more which truly qualified as 'gentlemen's carriages' and were definitely in the Rolls-Royce category. The nobility and the squirearchy liked them almost as much as they liked their Daimlers. The Forty of 1919-28 was a splendid 6.2-litre overhead-cam engined 'six', and this was then replaced by an even better car, the straight-eight, 4.4-litre engined Thirty of 1928-33. Unhappily for Lanchester the company failed financially in 1931, was bought up by BSA to be combined with Daimler, and soon lost all its individuality.

Europe

In this section I must concentrate on those European cars which were actually imported to Great Britain in significant, if not large, numbers at the time they were current. As the percentage level of British imports was very low at the time, this limits the choice considerably, especially as companies like OM, Voisin and Isotta-Fraschini were barely represented here at all.

A small number of famous European 'veteran' cars occasionally change hands, but machines such as the early Benz, Daimler, Darracq, De Dion Bouton, Panhard and Peugeot cars are certainly not for everyday use. You'll see them every year on the London-Brighton run, and perhaps on other old car extravaganzas, but not in regular employment.

The most collectible European vintage cars, naturally enough, are the sports cars and Grand Tourers. Some of today's most famous names— Alfa Romeo, Lancia and Mercedes-Benz for example— were famous even then. Others, like Hispano-Suiza and Bugatti, had their heyday between the wars, then disappeared from view.

Let us start with Alfa Romeo, which typified everything splendid about Italian character and its attitude to motoring in general. There had been Alfas since 1910, but the first truly vintage model was the RL Series of 1923-27, of which the pointed-radiator RLSS sports car was the most charismatic of all. I need only say that the factory racing team's star driver was a young man called Enzo Ferrari, and the attraction is obvious!

This range was followed later in the decade by the 6C 1500, 6C 1750 and

6C 1900 family of 1927-33 designed by Vittorio Jano, where some cars had single-cam and some twin-cam heads, some had normally aspirated engines, and some were supercharged. All had beautiful and functional body styling, often by Zagato, which set standards copied by many other makers of the period. Such cars were rare in the UK, and costly too, but those of the 1930s would be even more hard to find.

There was little which was collectable from Fiat—their 'classic' period really lies in the 1950s and 1960s. The other famous sporting Italian marque was Lancia, a family-owned business which produced its first car in 1907 but whose first real technical breakthrough was the Lambda model, built throughout the 1920s. Cars of this family had an early type of monocoque construction where the frame also acted as the (sporting) body shell too, and the first of Lancia's uniquely laid-out narrow-angle vee-4 engines, originally 2.1, then 2.4 litres. Not only that but there was excellent roadholding, and the same sort of styling which distinguished Alfa Romeos built in the same era, along with sliding-pillar independent front suspension. Even though these cars were expensive—£775 in 1927, for instance—they were more agile, and more effective than most British types.

The best-known, and most popular, European sports car of the 1920s, of course, was the French Bugatti marque, where all the cars were produced at Molsheim, not far from the German border. Every model was personally designed by Ettore Bugatti and a small team of engineers; each model had overhead-camshaft valve gear and a simple chassis with rock-hard suspension. All were interesting, all had great pedigree (and a number of design idiosyncracies), but some were even better than others. One feature, for instance, was that a Bugatti either had a four-cylinder or an eight-cylinder engine—Ettore simply did not believe in six-cylinder units. They were all very expensive, and therefore exclusive—no-one bought a Bugatti unless he was already in the Bentley/Alfa Romeo category.

The first Bugatti family to reach the UK in any numbers was the Brescia and Modified Brescia, this being the 1½-litre model which introduced the characteristic horseshoe-shaped radiator to the British motoring public, and which was a very practical little car. In 'image' or 'glamour' terms, however, it was quite overshadowed by the new eight-cylinder engined family which followed.

The first of these was the Type 30 of 1922-26, which used the later familiar 'slab-shaped' engine of 2 litres, with three valves per cylinder and overhead-camshaft valve gear. This was soon followed by the Type 35 models, some of which were pure Grand Prix racing machines while others were sports cars. The Type 38 was a rather more refined derivative of the Type 35, and was a replacement for the Type 30.

The straight-eight engine, however, was an expensive proposition to maintain and service, so as a rather more practical proposition Bugatti

Each and every Bugatti, including this 1926 model driven by Cecil Bianchi, is a recognized 'vintage' car, and a classic.

then produced the Type 37 range, in which a 1½-litre four-cylinder unit was chosen instead of the 2-litre/2.3-litre 'eight'. Even so, it was still an exotic creation, not really suited to regular road use; that privilege was reserved for the 1½-litre four-cylinder Type 40 of 1926, which has some-times disparagingly been called 'Ettore's Morris Cowley'.

Another vintage Bugatti of the 1920s, built for normal road use, was the Type 43, which was a splendid 2.3-litre supercharged eight-cylinder car with a 100 mph (160 km/h) top speed (remarkable for this period, when the average 'family' car was happy with a 50 mph-plus (80 km/h) top speed). Arguably the best all-round Bugatti yet produced, it was neither the largest engined nor the most expensive—but I can hardly count the Type 41 Royale, of which only six were produced, and all are safely in rich hands!

Grand Tourers, in the grand manner, were all produced by Mercedes-Benz, Hispano-Suiza and Austro-Daimler, both before and after the First World War.

The Daimler-Benz merger, which produced the Mercedes-Benz marque, did not in fact occur until 1926, by which time both Daimler and Benz had produced some notable cars. The original four-cylinder Mercedes models, which originated in 1901, changed the whole concept of motor car design as we know it (they are extremely rare today), but these were chain-driven machines, and the first shaft-drive Mercedes cars did not follow until 1908.

There were several fine Benz models, but all except the racing cars were utterly conventional machines, rather overhsadowed by the magnificence of 1910s and 1920s Mercedes models. The most famous of all the vintage

Mercedes and Mercedes-Benz models, for sure, were the supercharged six-cylinder machines designed in 1924 by Dr Ferdinand Porsche. This range started with the 24/100/140 model, which had a light alloy cylinder block, an overhead-camshaft cylinder head layout and a supercharger which could be clutched into action when the driver pressed his throttle foot to the floorboards.

After the original there was the lighter, faster K-Type of 1926, which had a shorter wheelbase, 6.3 litres and up to 160 bhp, and that unmistakeable exposed exhaust system poking out of the side of the bonnet. From 1927 this model was supplanted by the S model (the British called this car the 36/220), with 180 bhp and a new lowered chassis frame. Next, in 1928, there was the SS (38/250 according to we British) with 7.0 litres and a nomenclature which really meant 'Supersports'. The final series-production car in this sequence was the SSK model (a title which the British accepted without demur), in which the wheelbase had been shortened yet again and in which for brief periods the engine could be persuaded to develop up to 300 bhp. (The SSKL was a limited-production, super-lightweight competition car, not meant for road use.) All were magnificent, all had that noble vee-profiled radiator, and all are worth a king's ransom today—if you can find one, that is.

The name of Hispano-Suiza was appropriate to the origins of its founder, and its location. Marc Birkigt was Swiss-born, and although the first factory was set up in Spain, there was also a famous French assembly plant too. Hispano-Suiza built a series of splendid aeroplane engines, but they also produced three outstanding ranges of cars.

The Alphonso was a short-chassis 3.6-litre side-valve engined car, probably one of the world's first true production sports models, which featured the then advanced feature of an engine mounted in unit with the transmission. The Alphonso was only built for three years, for in 1919 the magnificent, expensive, French-built H6B came along to set new standards for every other European sports car manufacturer. Not only did the H6B have a 6.6-litre overhead-camshaft six-cylinder engine, developing about 135 bhp, but it had mechanical servo assistance for its drum braking system (which Rolls-Royce liked so much that they arranged to build it themselves, under licence).

The H6C of 1924 (made in 'Sport' and 'Boulogne' form) was even better than this, having an 8-litre engine which could produce up to 200 bhp for sports car racing. Without much doubt, Hispano-Suiza built the best cars in the world, both in design and in workmanship, in the 1920s.

About the Austro-Daimler cars of Austria, which were very rarely seen in the UK, I need only say that the Prince Henry model of 1910-14 (with a four-cylinder 5.7-litre engine) and the ADM of 1923-8 (with 2.5-litre six-cylinder engine) were both fine sporting machines in the rugged Germanic tradition, designed by Dr Ferdinand Porsche before he left to join Daimler (later Daimler-Benz). In many ways these cars were obvious predecessors of the sporting Mercedes-Benz cars which I have already mentioned.

Finally, I must also mention two marques of French sports car, Amilcar and Salmson, which were as popular in their day as MG was to become in the 1930s.

United States

Almost *anything* built in North America before 1914 is looked upon as a collectable machine by the Americans themselves but very few of these cars ever came to Europe, and are little known here.

In modern terms the most famous American 'vintage' car by far was the Ford Model T, of which more than 15 million were built between 1908 and 1927, for which a complete parts remanufacturing industry has grown up in the USA in modern times, and for which there is a great deal of affection. The Model T rode on solid axles and transverse leaf springs (something which was to be a Ford design 'trade mark' for many more years to follow). It was a car which needed to be loved for its idiosyncracies, for it had a lazy side-valve engine, a weird epicyclic transmission, a floppy, bouncy ride, and very basic standards of equipment and weather protection. Remember the song 'Get out and get under'? Many Model T owners learned to live with that!

Almost every other old, collectable American car—the vee-12 engined Packards, the Mercers, the vee-8 Cadillacs of the 1920s, and even ancients like the curved-dash Oldsmobiles—is extremely rare and extremely expensive these days in European terms, and for those reasons alone I must recommend them to collectors rather than to motoring enthusiasts.

There was even more fascinating variety to come in the 1930s and 1940s, and the cars which survive from that period tend to be more affordable than the ones I've just described. So, on to the next chapter.

Chapter 7

1930s and 1940s—fascinating variety from British manufacturers

According to the founders of Vintage Sports Car Club, and to most readers of at least one British monthly motoring magazine, few cars worth buying have been built since the end of 1930. Even if this opinion was not meant to be taken seriously, it was a meaningless statement when first made in 1934, and has come to look progressively more risible as time has passed. As far as fans of classic car motoring are concerned, the really interesting period of car design actually *began* in the 1930s, just as the die-hards were turning their backs on progress.

Between 1930 and 1950, the period covered by this chapter, the world's motor industry went through several upheavals, none more traumatic and eventful than the one in Britain. In 1929-30 the bottom dropped out of the world's economy following the 'Wall Street Crash' in America, and by 1931 European car sales had dropped considerably. Several famous marques slipped away into bankruptcy and obscurity. After that, for the next six years the recovery was steady, and impressive, but production then began to fall back at the end of the 1930s as rearmament took its toll of manpower and resources.

After the Second World War broke out in September 1939, private car production ground rapidly to a halt by the end of the year. Except in the United States, where the building of cars went ahead full blast until the end of 1941, the world's motor industry concentrated on building weapons of war between 1939 and 1945, with no real new-model development being done.

After 1945, an enormous pent-up demand for new cars was unleashed, in Britain and all over the world, and for the next few years almost everything which could be built could also be sold. Here at home, several all-new marques came into existence, but there were few brand-new models from the large companies at first, and the modern generation of cars did not truly begin to appear until 1948.

At the end of the 1940s, and into the early 1950s, there was the most fascinating variety of cars on sale, and the multi-national rationalization which has since taken place was then still many years away. Britain's motor industry, in fact, was beginning to enjoy its 'Indian Summer'.

In recent years many of the British cars built in the 1930s and 1940s have been accepted as modern classics, and I have tried to list the most significant models in the next few pages.

Small family cars

In the 1930s, this was the type of British car which tended to produce apoplexy in members of the VSCC—and in most cases, rightly so. True vintage cars, they thought, were hand-built, or at least designed and assembled by craftsmen and engineers, but the cars of the early 1930s were nasty, tinny, thrown-together devices which had been approved by cost-cutting accountants rather than lovers of motoring.

According to the VSCC, there had been a certain dignity, and something rather fitting, about the design and the behaviour of 1920s cars like the Austin Seven or the 'Bullnose' Morris Cowley, but they could see no merit in buzz-boxes like the Morris Minor, the Standard Nine, or the cheap, Detroit-designed, Ford 8 hp Model Y. Cars like the Wolseley Hornet or the Triumph Scorpion, which followed the craze of the 'small six', were despised with a venom which had to be seen to be believed.

It was all very glib, and all very persuasive, but it was not entirely true. As that authoritative motoring historian Michael Sedgwick once wrote, in his study of the period:

> How often do we hear the phrase 'the nasty 30s'? Authors have skimmed off the thoroughbreds made between 1931 and 1942 and have lumped the vast majority of the cars of the era into a symbol of degeneracy. . . . Yet the cars of the period had a character which reflected the restless era which gave them birth. . . unquestionably the cars which the man in the street could buy after 1930 were easier to drive and better suited to the tyro than some of their vintage forebears. . . .

Even so, I admit that a great many family cars made in the 1930s and 1940s have not only been neglected and rusted away, but deserve to be forgotten as well. No matter what the limited number of enthusiastic owners of such cars may say, I can see no merit, no intrinsic value and no justified collector's status for cars like the Hillman Minxes, the Austin Eights, the Morris 10s, the Flying Standards, the Vauxhall Twelves and the Ford V8s of the period.

A few cars, though, had genuine character which was obvious at the time they were on sale and is still recognized today. Character was not something that could be specified by the managing director or the sales force when the car was being conceived; it evolved during the design, and particularly during the development, of the new model—and, somehow, it began to appear as the public reacted to it.

Sometimes there is no rhyme or reason to this process—and sometimes, I have to say, there has been a well-orchestrated effort on the part of

The Morris Minor was introduced in 1928, but most cars, including this tourer, were sold in the 1930s.

owners to build up a 'character' around a car which didn't deserve to have a memorable one! A classic case of the latter (sorry about the pun. . .) is the Ford 8 hp Model Y family and its successors, for apart from the very low price of these cars, and their undoubted reliability, they had no long-term merits. The members of the post-war Austin A40/A70 'Counties' series are other cars which deserve no more than to be remembered as cars which brought profit to the Austin company in the late 1940s.

Some cars, on the other hand, will always have a following. Let's start with the Austin Seven, a car which I have already covered in the previous chapter (for it was a car announced in the 1920s, and was already reaching full maturity before the 1930s dawned). It was Austin's best-selling car between 1930 and 1932, but thereafter played second fiddle to the mundane 10 hp model, even though more than 20,000 were sold in every year until 1937. It was finally dropped in 1939. In that period it put on a bit of weight, gained extra engine and transmission refinement, and was slghtly restyled from time to time, but the cheeky, hard-riding character remained to the end. The Big Seven of 1937-39 was not the same sort of car at all, and no other memorable Austin was put on sale until the 1950s.

The Austin Seven's major competition always came from Ford and Morris. I have already dismissed the Ford 8 hp, and I am tempted to do the same to the Morris Minor of 1928-34, except that it was graced by a technically interesting but not always reliable overhead-camshaft engine. Because we should always recall that MG's M-Type Midget was little more than a rebodied Minor of the period, this car needs remembering, even if no-one could ever call it fast, or pretty.

The Issigonis-designed Morris Minor was launched in 1948, and sold well for more than twenty years. It wasn't very fast, but it had a great deal of character.

The Morris 8 hp of 1934-8 was the successor to the Minor. Since its side-valve engine was later admitted to have been a copy of the Ford 8 hp unit, and since it tried to match that car's appeal, no-one should be surprised that I do not think it worth collecting today. The post-war Morris Minor Series MM, on the other hand, was an entirely different proposition, and fully deserves its classic status today. The fact that it was jointly conceived, during the Second World War, by those two charismatic Nuffield characters, vice-chairman Sir Miles Thomas and designer Alec Issigonis, might tell us something. No doubt they should really have been engaged in war work of vital importance at the time, but let's not be beastly about this. . . .

The Minor was Britain's first post-war design of a small car, so it had little up-to-date competition until Austin's A30 appeared in 1951. The miracle of the Minor was that it had so much character in spite of having to make do with the ancient side-valve Morris 8 engine and transmission, and that it was arbitrarily widened at a late stage to suit Alec Issigonis's artistic instincts.

The original MM had a lot going for it: rigid monocoque structure, torsion bar independent front suspension, rack and pinion steering and a choice of body styles, though it always seemed to need a more powerful engine. Some 1950s derivatives were slower, and it didn't get a proper engine until 1956. Before 1971, though, more than 1.6 million Minors of all types would be built.

Middle class family cars

This is a category which is difficult to define, for there has always been an argument over 'classes'. However, I doubt if there will be much argument about the cars I choose to include:

In the 1930s, Riley of Coventry was a respected independent marque, with a reputation bolstered up by motor racing, but with most sales from family cars. Every model used one or other of the famous twin high-camshaft engines, and had pleasant and unmistakable styling; the smoothest were the six-cylinder engined cars, the fastest were the late-1930s models with the 2½-litre 'Big Four' engines, but the 9 hp models sold best of all.

There was a great deal of sporting mystique behind the Riley's reputation, which helped hide the fact that most of the cars were under-powered and too expensive. Never mind—today there is a thriving Riley restoration industry and a band of fanatical followers.

Lord Nuffield took over in 1938, but the sleek post-war RM-Series cars were still a totally Riley design. It was amazing that the cars should be shown, and put on sale, so soon after the war, and they made a great impact. They inherited the pre-war cars' greatest fault—they were really under-powered—but they had fine styling and impeccable roadholding. The longer wheelbase 2½-litre model was most people's favourite; most were saloons, but a few drop-head coupés and roadsters were also built—these are the true collectors' items today.

Triumph, also of Coventry, would have liked Riley's sporting reputation, for they also began to run out of customers towards the end of the decade. Nevertheless this self-styled 'Queen of Cars' sometimes had very graceful styling. The Vitesse was the best of the bunch, and the waterfall-grille styled Dolomite also had a following.

Bankruptcy came in 1939 and Standard bought up the remains in 1944. The post-war result was the *soi-disant* 1800 saloon, which had a tubular frame, Standard Flying 14 running gear and suspension and razor-edge styling by Mulliners of Birmingham. It was all done in a great hurry, yet it was a much nicer car than ever it deserved to be. The styling theme, though not unique, was distinctive, and gave the car a dignity which many enthusiasts like today.

In the 1930s financial problems sank two distinguished STD companies, Sunbeam and Talbot, but the two marques were bought up, stripped of all their character and components and made into a 'new' marque by the Rootes group. Both names survived, in one form or another, into the 1980s, though by that time their heritage had been lost along the way.

Sunbeam's great days had been in the 1920s, but Georges Roesch's Talbots got better and better with every succeeding year. These cars were made in London's West Kensington and were expensive but beautifully built. Any surviving example of the 75, 90, 95, 105 and 110 models is worth keeping, and restoring, for they all share that splendid and

efficient six-cylinder engine and all other facets of the same type of chassis and running gear. The most powerful 110s had more than 120 bhp and could exceed 90 mph (144 km/h), while race-modified versions went much faster than that.

After buying up the company in 1935 Rootes cynically degraded the reputation, performance and behaviour of the Talbot marque in the next three years, then compounded this vandalism by introducing the Sunbeam-Talbot in 1938, where the 'new' cars were really no more than rebodied Hillmans and Humbers.

The post-war policy did not change, but in 1948 a post-war range of Sunbeam-Talbots, dubbed 80 and 90, was introduced. The 80 used the Hillman Minx engine and was far too slow, but the 2.2-litre (Humber) engined Sunbeam-Talbot 90 was a promising car with fine four-door saloon styling which was to improve even more in the 1950s. Late-1940s 90s had a curiously old-fashioned chassis with beam front axle suspension and bodies which tended to rust away at an alarming speed, but they are still definitely classics of the period.

Alvis was another resourceful Coventry concern which produced several interesting classic cars in the 1930s and 1940s, though the post-war company (and its product) was very different from that of the 1930s. All 1930s Alvis cars had coachbuilt bodies (like Rolls-Royce, they did not build their own shells), while the best had overhead-valve six-cylinder engines, independent front suspension and synchromesh gearboxes. As engines got larger, so the performance increased, and a few models could

Left *Most RM-Series Rileys were four-door saloons, but a few Roadsters were also produced.*

Right *Post-war Triumphs were really Standards, but the 1800 Roadster's distinctive body style makes it attractive to modern collectors.*

certainly beat 100 mph (160 km/h). From a very attractive bunch I would recommend the later 3½-litre, Speed 25 and 4.3-litre models, preferably with rakish Vanden Plas coachwork, but don't expect to find a cheap one, as the word got around many years ago!

Before and during the Second World War Alvis developed a range of powerful aero engines, and car development turned into a side-line after that. The only post-war chassis design to be put on sale was the TA21 3-litre, which was launched in 1949, at which time the new six-cylinder engine produced a mere 90 bhp. However, there was a very smart four-door saloon body style (by Mulliners of Birmingham) and a top speed of nearly 90 mph (144 km/h), all of which ensured elegant progress in some style. There would be a convertible derivative in the early 1950s.

MG started the 1930s with a growing reputation for building sports cars, but ended it by producing more and more saloon cars. The purists wrongly insisted that these were tarted-up Morris or Wolseley models, even though the beam-axled chassis frame *and* body styling designs were unique to the MGs and, in fairness, they had a good deal of their own character.

Unfortunately, I rate the VA (1½-litre) too slow to qualify as an enduring classic, but well-kept SA ('2-litre') and WA models are much more satisfying machines. I particularly like the long, rakish, four-door styling of the saloons, for by comparison I found the tourers and drop-head coupés rather lacking in individual appeal. It was a pity that Nuffield's chassis design policy was so staid.

Late-1930s Wolseleys were really modified Morris models, but were nevertheless well-built and interesting cars. This is a 25 hp drop-head coupé.

Although the Wolseleys of the 1930s, to which these MGs were related, were themselves no more than better-equipped Morris models, managing director Miles Thomas saw that the late 1930s types had some extra character and a bit more style. However, in my opinion, the only Wolseleys worth considering are the 18-80 (pre-war) and 18-85 (post-war) models, which were the fastest cars in the range. Wolseley's big sales point at this time was the value for money which was offered. The same applies today.

The post-war Wolseleys included the 6/80 model, which at least had an overhead-camshaft engine to make it sound nice and go a bit better than the related Morris Six, and police use also helped its reputation. Nevertheless, I can't see why we should be forced to call it a classic car today.

You will only consider a Rover if you are looking for middle-class dignity, grace and a certain style to the equipment, rather than performance, for there were very few sporty Rovers, either in the 1930s or 1940s. Under chairman Spencer Wilks there was a progressive evolution in styling around a new family of engines.

For lovers of fine Rovers I recommend the six-cylinder, rather than the four-cylinder, cars, which means that the 16 hp, the 20 hp and the post-war P3 75 models are the most satisfying. It wasn't only the styling and the quality of construction which made these cars so nice, but the use of the free-wheel in the transmission which made it so easy to be smooth and silent.

Land-Rover? Yes, I know there is a small but persistent following for

The SS-Jaguar of 1935-37 was a sleek, fast sports saloon, styled by William Lyons who was still involved in the shaping of Jaguars produced forty years later.

the original type of Solihull-built 4×4, but I cannot bring myself to join in and recommend what is after all a very basically equipped working tool.

The fact is that almost every one of Britain's middle-class cars of this period was overshadowed by the rise, the inexorable rise, of William Lyons' SS, SS-Jaguar and Jaguar marques. With the exception of the original 1932 model SS1, every one of his cars had sleek and sensual styling which outclassed its opposition, and all were sold at very reasonable prices.

There was a lot of bitching against this company's 1930s and 1940s models—some called them 'cads' cars' and others called them 'Standard specials'—but the public didn't mind, and sales increased almost every year. Of the saloons, I would ignore the four-cylinder cars and go for the restyled SS1 of 1933-5, the 2½-litre and 3½ litre SS-Jaguar models of 1935-48, and of course the independently sprung Mk V introduced in 1948. With a 3½-litre engine a top speed of more than 90 mph (144 km/h) is assured, there is comfortable four-seater accommodation, and in every case there is the more exclusive option of a drop-head coupé body style.

An interesting post-war newcomer to this category was the Bristol. Not only was this car built by the Bristol Aeroplane Co., but it was assembled on the outskirts of that city, so there should have been no mistaking its origins. The chassis was massively strong and featured independent front suspension, whereas the six-cylinder engine, and the streamlined body style of the original 400 sports saloon, had both been cribbed from BMW of Germany by way of unofficial 'war reparations'. Right from the start, these were fine open-road cars, let down only by a lack of room inside the cabin, but by the standards of the day they were very advanced indeed.

Lastly in this section I ought to mention Jowett. The 1930s model mostly used flat-twin engines, and were remarkably successful because they combined reliability and 'slogging power' with very low selling prices, but they are not, in my opinion, classics. During the war, however, Jowett hired Gerald Palmer from Nuffield to design a new car. This was the technically advanced Jowett Javelin, which combined extremely smart fastback styling with good aerodynamic performance and good road manners. While they were in production, Javelins were plagued with engine unreliability problems and rust-prone bodies, but these have certainly been solved on the surviving cars, which have a well-deserved following.

Sporting cars

In the 1930s and 1940s Britain's designers produced a range of smart, if not technically advanced, sporting cars, and it was from this base that the hugely successful models of the 1950s and 1960s were developed. On the one hand there were popular-priced models like the MGs and the Singers, while on the other, if one had more money, there was the chance to buy an AC or an Aston Martin. In those days, of course, sports cars were not produced in large numbers, but a good proportion of those built have survived to this day, and all are well worth restoring to top-class condition.

In terms of numbers built, MG was much the most successful sports car manufacturer of the period. By 1932 fifty cars were being built at Abingdon every week, and although this figure dropped away in the next few years, the company recovered well before 1939 and positively boomed after the Second World War.

The typical MG sports car of the period had a ladder-style frame, beam axles front and rear, with hard leaf spring suspension and a wood-framed body shell incorporating sweeping wings and free-standing headlamps. Those built up to 1936 had overhead-cam engines, those after had overhead-valve engines. The majority had four cylinders and were called Midgets, but the Magna/Magnette series were 'sixes'.

To the investor, *any* MG sports car is collectable, but to the practical enthusiast some were certainly better than others. M-Types were sweet, but too slow, while the TA suffered from its old-fashioned long-stroke engine. The best, and most successful, Midgets were the J2, the PA/PB models, the short-lived TB and the post-war TC. The most numerous of all these cars was the TC, but since it was also the only MG sports car to be exported in large numbers, it is in short supply in the UK.

Although they were sometimes condemned as too expensive when they were on the market as new cars, I have always had a soft spot for the six-cylinder cars, which had a gorgeous engine noise and character

The MG PB of 1935-36, so typical of the chunky two-seater MG sports cars of the period, is much prized today.

that few other machines could approach. The problem today is that, by comparison with the straight-line performance of modern and mundane little hatchback Euroboxes, *any* classic MG sports car is outpaced. You have to get an MG out into the lanes, and drive it in the proper manner, to realize what between-wars motoring was all about.

At MG's prices, competition came from the Singer and Morgan marques. By the 1930s Singer, as manufacturers, had fallen a long way from their 1920s eminence, but they still found the time to produce a series of Le Mans sports cars which all had overhead-cam engines and which, some say, were all as fast and as nimble as their MG rivals. Yet they did not sell as well. Why? Perhaps it was something to do with the 'sell the sizzle' campaign which MG's Cecil Kimber waged in motor sport.

Even though the Nine of 1939, and the SM Roadster which followed a decade later, had the same type of overhead-cam engines, they were much more 'touring' than 'sporting', and were really no competition for the T-Series MGs. They are not at all collectable today.

Morgan, on the other hand, came into the sports car business with a fine reputation for building fast three-wheelers. With the new 4/4 of 1935 Morgan established a chassis design which they have now kept for more than fifty years: ladder-style, with Z-section side members, sliding-pillar independent front suspension, and a rock-hard ride. The styling was up-to-date by 1935 standards, but has been altered only in detail since then.

Original 4/4s had Coventry-Climax engines, but all the post-war 4/4s were fitted with overhead-valve versions of the Standard 10 unit. Per-

Above *The Riley MPH of the 1930s had all the rakish appeal of an Italian-style sports car allied to British design and workmanship.*

Left *The rear view of the smaller-engined sister car, the Imp, was attractive too.*

formance was brisk rather than startling, but all had nimble roadholding and were excellent competition cars. *Of course* they are classic cars!

HRG also produced a sports car in the same style as the Morgan (and, if that was possible, with an even harder ride!). Pay your money and take your choice—an HRG is more rare, and faster, but somehow not supported by as many fanatical followers.

Although most Rileys of the 1930s were saloons or tourers, there was also a sprinkling of fine sports cars. None was ever built in large numbers, but most seem to have survived. The Brooklands Nine was too much of a detuned racing sports car for my liking, so I would always recommend a choice between the next generation of cars, the Imp, the MPH and the Sprite models.

All were based on the same chassis layout (itself a race-proved design) and with similar styling, but with their own mechanical features. Imps had 1.1-litre four-cylinder 'Nine' engines, and really needed more power to do a proper job, while the MPH had the race-proved six-cylinder engine but was at once too expensive, and not fast enough, to be a success. The best all-round model was the Sprite, which had the new-generation 1½-litre four-cylinder engine; it was as fast as the MPH but considerably cheaper, and with slightly more modern styling. Most of these cars were fitted with Wilson-type preselector transmission. There were no true Riley sports cars in the post-war period.

In spite of having that famous personality Donald Healey at the head of their design team in the late 1930s, Triumph never produced a sports car, and one of Riley's more important competitors was AC of Thames Ditton. Like the Sprites and MPHs, the 16/80 and Supercharged 16/90 sports cars were rare, but beautifully styled. Such cars were lovely to look at and lively to drive, though expensive to buy; the cost made it certain that they would be exclusive, and this means that very few are around today.

As with the middle-class saloons, so it was with the middle-price sports cars. SS, and later SS-Jaguar, eventually got in on the act, with strikingly styled sports cars hiding conventional running gear, but at a price which made them very attractive indeed. Even though they were based on modified SS1 chassis frames and had very cramped driving positions, the SS90s of 1935 (only twenty-four were built) and the SS100s of 1936-39 (314 altogether) soon built up a formidable reputation. They were fast and accelerative and they *looked* the part. No wonder the survivors are very highly valued indeed today.

Post-war, of course, Jaguar simply stunned all their opposition with the launch of the sensational XK120 sports car. Here, at a stroke, was a car which set new standards. Not only did it have luscious styling, but it also had a beautifully engineered six-cylinder twin-cam engine. Production did not properly get underway until 1949, and most early deliveries went for export. All the original cars had aluminium bodies, and these are even more desirable collectors' items than the steel-bodied cars which followed in the 1950s.

There were two new post-war marques in the 'middle' category whose backgrounds could not have been more different. Both types are well-liked today, for different reasons. The post-war Allard was a productionized development of Sydney Allard's 'Specials' of the late 1930s, and was based on a very cheaply developed chassis frame with modified Ford vee-8 suspensions, and a choice of engines which started with the 3½-litre side-valve Ford vee-8; some had overhead-valve conversions, some were of larger capacity, and some even had Cadillac units instead. Many Allards were touring cars, but the starkly trimmed two-seaters had a rugged charm all of their own.

Jowett's Jupiter, which was announced right at the end of our period, was a much more carefully developed proposition, as its chassis was designed by Robert Eberan von Eberhorst at ERA and the running gear was all taken from the advanced Javelin saloon. Jowett aimed it between the MGs and the Jaguars of the period; the styling was very attractive, but the performance was not outstanding.

Two types of hand-built sports cars—Aston Martin and Frazer Nash— were desirable in the 1930s and 1940s, both in entirely different guises in post-war form. Both the 1930s-style cars were steadily developed on the same basic designs, and both were sold at a high price.

The Aston Martin had a simple chassis with hard suspension and an efficient overhead-camshaft engine. There was a choice of wheelbases and of body styles, all of them desirable, with models like the International being particularly sought after.

David Brown bought up the company after the war and financed the building of a few under-powered DBI models (which had 2-litre engines) and the start-up of DB2 assembly, where power was by courtesy of W.O. Bentley's design team at Lagonda (which David Brown had also bought up in 1947). DB1s and DB2s had multi-tube frames and independent front suspension, with light-alloy bodies. The best of all the 1940s cars were the early DB2s; classic car values reflect this today.

The 1930s-style Frazer Nash was the final flowering of the 'vintage' design (so the VSCC could not, and did not, complain), which is to say that the chassis had rock-hard suspension, a variety of engines (some supercharged) and a chain-drive transmission. Production at Isleworth, measured in tens a year rather than hundreds, died off in the late 1930s; as far as the die-hard 'Nash enthusiast' is concerned, they were all great cars. They had, however, very idiosyncratic driving habits, so in this case a really comprehensive test run should be taken before you consider buying.

The post-war Frazer-Nash, on the other hand, had a more conventional drive train, even if it was still a hand-built, starkly trimmed machine. This time the engine was that lofty but sweetly-revving Bristol 2-litre six-cylinder unit, which was itself a straight copy of the 1930s-style BMW 328 unit, where the power output was at least 100 bhp, but more if the customer wanted to pay for it. There was a stiff new tubular chassis with independent front and rear suspension. You could either have a narrow, cigar-shaped competition two-seater shell with cycle-type wings, or a more conventional full-width style—the open wheeler was, and still is, considered the most desirable today.

One important new post-war marque was Healey, if only because Austin-Healey evolved from it in the 1950s. All Healeys had the same solid chassis, with trailing arm independent front suspension, and most had Riley or (American) Nash engines. The most famous (and most collectable) types were the stark two-seater Silverstone and the more plushy

One of the most attractive 'new' post-war marques was the Healey, which was sold in a variety of body styles. This was the Tickford saloon.

Nash-Healey, but all types had elegant, lightweight bodies, and all could beat 100 mph (160 km/h). Don't buy one, though, and expect restoration to be easy—the last one was built in the mid 1950s, and parts are no longer available.

The carriage trade

In the 1930s, as in the 1920s, the best of the best came from Rolls-Royce, Bentley, Armstrong-Siddeley and Daimler, but there was also one new recruit: Lagonda. The Riley family made an attempt to break into this exclusive bracket with the vee-8 engined Autovia, but this was a failure. Neither Armstrong-Siddeley nor Lagonda built the same sort of cars after the war as they had done before it.

Even though they built more and more aircraft engines and progressively fewer cars, Rolls-Royce was still the standard setter for the rich man's custom. Until 1949 every rolling chassis was built at Derby, and every body was by an approved coachbuilder.

Until the mid-1930s the old-fashioned types of six-cylinder car—20/25, 25/30 and Phantom II—were continued, though improvements such as synchromesh were added to the specification; one particularly pleasing type of Phantom II was the rakish Continental of the early 1930s. Then, in the late 1930s came two innovations—a brand new (and, frankly, troublesome) 7.3-litre vee-12 engine for the Phantom III, and coil spring independent front suspension for this car and for the 4¼-litre Wraith. Rolls-Royce worked hard to make the vee-12 reliable, and surviving examples of both these types give elegant, magic-carpet motoring today.

Bodies, of course, were all elegantly produced by specialist coachbuilders like Hooper, H.J. Mulliner, Park Ward and James Young. Because most were based on wooden skeletons they tended to rot away over the years, but most have been thoroughly restored by now.

After the war, Rolls-Royce moved their car assembly facilities to Crewe (where they remain to this day) and introduced a brand new chassis design, and much modified 4¼-litre six-cylinder engine, for use in the Silver Wraith. This car was to be built until 1959, but in 1949 it was joined by the first-ever Rolls-Royce to have a standard pressed-steel saloon body; this was the shorter wheelbase Silver Dawn, a car which was only sold in export markets for the first four years of its life.

In 1931 Bentley had gone bankrupt and had been bought up by Rolls-Royce. There are a few 'W.O.' models to consider in this section: the much-loved 100 mph (160 km/h) 8-litre, and the less-liked 4-litre, which are very rare indeed, the 8-litre in particular being fought over when one of the few surviving cars comes onto the market. These, however, are vintage 'left-overs', for all other 1930s and 1940s Bentleys are really Rolls-Royces under another badge.

Three 'Rolls-Bentleys', all fine classic cars, cover this period. In the 1930s these were always advertised as the 'Silent Sports Car', and used much-modified Rolls-Royce 25/30, or Wraith, running gear in new chassis. Like the Rolls-Royce cars of the period, every 1930s Bentley had a special coachbuilt body shell, and many of them were very dashing indeed.

From 1933 to 1936 there was the original 3½-litre, which was then re-placed by the 4¼-litre model, both on the same chassis. The one engine, in fact, was an enlarged version of the other, and the change was really made to provide more power to lug around the extra weight then built into the sumptuously trimmed bodies of the period. Every Bentley of this period had a top speed of around 95 mph (150 km/h). Some of the most striking bodies were tourer or drop-head coupés, but many Bentleys were sports saloons.

From 1946, following the corporate move from Derby to Crewe, there was a brand new model, the Mk VI, with new chassis incorporating independent front suspension and with much-improved 4¼-litre engine, but also with a standard steel saloon body. This car dominated the Crewe production lines for years and was the model from which the Silver Dawn was developed a few years later. The bodies showed a distressing tendency to rust away during the 1950s, but most have now had at least one major restoration and are well worth buying today.

The third top-drawer company of the 1930s was Daimler, which built a whole range of cars (some of which carried Lanchester, and even BSA,

The Bentley of the 1930s was designed and constructed by Rolls-Royce. This is a late-1930s 4¼-litre model.

badges). Few 1930s Daimlers had independent front suspension, but almost all of them had that famous combination of a fluid flywheel and pre-selector gearbox transmission. Daimler did not build their own bodies; many came from Mulliners and Carbodies, whose premises were in the Midlands.

The most collectable were also the largest, which means that today's desirable Daimlers include the sleeve-valve Double-Six types (take care— these engines can be *very* expensive to maintain and rebuild) and the poppet-valved 25 hp Straight Eight and Light Straight Eight types. All had the same dignified approach to motoring, all shared the same fluted radiator style, and most had the sort of lofty, formal coachwork so beloved of the gentry.

During the Second World War Daimler built military vehicles, including Scout Cars and Armoured Cars (these are collectors' items in themselves. . .) and the post-war private cars were very different from the 1930s variety. Although the DB18 was an improved version of the late 1930s 15s and Dolphins, the massive six-cylinder Twenty Seven and eight-cylinder Straight Eight models had sturdy new independent front suspension chassis frames (the Straight Eight's wheelbase was an enormous 12 ft 3 in (3.7 m)), with engines evolved from the military machine exprience. Bodies, as usual, were coachbuilt, and magnificently trimmed, while the usual fluid flywheel type of transmission was standard.

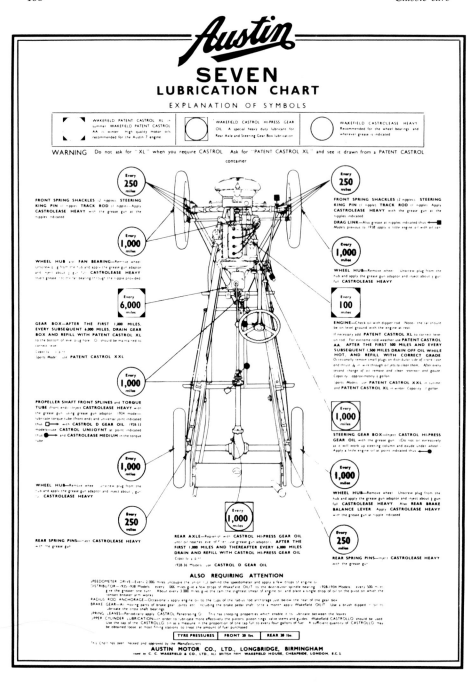

Here were cars of equal magnificence to anything being produced at Rolls-Royce, but somehow without the same charisma. Not even the most costly limousine bodies, from companies like Freestone & Webb, and Hooper, were quite as graceful or quite as nicely built as those supplied to Rolls-Royce, and few have survived into the 1980s in as good a condition.

Armstrong-Siddeley entered the 1930s with a growing reputation for building sensible, well finished, dignified cars, which meant that most were heavy cars with conventional styling and no outstanding features. One car, the Special, had an excellent engine and was not only the largest but the fastest Armstrong-Siddeley of the period. But how many remain out there today?

After the war, Armstrong-Siddeley introduced a new range of 16 hp cars which had independent front suspension, a pre-selector transmission and a 2-litre pushrod engine. The bodies of all these types—Hurricane, Typhoon, Whitley among them—tended to rot away quite badly, but they were considered to have sensational styling for the day. Today? Curiosity value only, perhaps?

Lagonda was a new arrival at this price level, for in the 1920s its products had had smaller engines and had been altogether more sporting. In the 1930s they produced two classic series of cars, each having its own type of sturdy separate chassis frame. The 4½-litre range, introduced in 1933, was powered by a Meadows six-cylinder engine, and the sporty-bodied versions were as fast as any Bentley of the period, but at first they felt a bit rough and ready. They were better by 1936, and in later Rapide or independently-suspended LG6 form they were quite outstanding.

W.O. Bentley moved from Rolls-Royce to Lagonda in 1935, and his masterpiece, which went on sale two years later, was the vee-12 model. This had a sturdy type of chassis with independent front suspension, but was powered by a magnificent new 4½-litre vee-12 engine, and was usually clothed in magnificent bodies constructed by Lagonda themselves. All vee-12s could beat 100 mph (160 km/h), which was better than anything Rolls-Royce or Bentley could offer, and by 1939 even the build quality was reaching for the same standards.

For Lagonda, the war spoilt everything, and neither of the 1939 models was put back into production afterwards. The post-war Lagonda design was the all-independent 2½-litre model, whose engine (taken up by the Aston Martin DB2) was more important than the rest of the design. Even so, it was a thoughtfully detailed car which deserves its classic reputation today.

Left *The trouble with everyday maintenance of cars of the 1930s and 1940s was that they needed frequent greasing and lubrication. This is a typical Castrol chart, for the Austin Seven.*

Chapter 8

1950s and 1960s—the true 'classic' period for British cars?

Look around any British gathering of classic cars today and I guarantee that you will see that most of them were originally built in the 1950s and 1960s. Although no-one tries to limit the definition of a classic car to the year in which it was built, this is the archetypal period on which everyone—friend or foe—is agreed. Since the 1919-30 period has already been defined as 'vintage' by one group of enthusiasts, then the best and most characterful cars of the 1950s and 1960s can certainly be dubbed 'classic' by others.

Some of the cars I will be listing in this chapter were certainly designed, and introduced, in the late 1940s, but all of them were famous in the years which followed. In those twenty years, Britain's motor industry was at the height of its prosperity; in view of the decline which followed, we can certainly call this a motoring 'Indian summer'.

It wasn't only the styling and engineering of British cars which changed completely between the 1930s and the 1950s; the *type* of cars which were so popular and became so famous was also very different. Several long-established marques disappeared, but new marques came into existence. There were mergers, and then more mergers yet to come in the future!

Having fought and won the Second World War, Great Britain Ltd was financially shattered, mortgaged up to the hilt, reliant on the USA for so many things, and needed to send most of its products abroad to try to pay off the debts. Rigidly applied government systems for material supply made sure that this happened.

Britain's long-established export market was her Empire, but now the huge American market beckoned as well. The Americans wanted style, performance and dash above all—so that is what we sent them. In the 1950s and 1960s, therefore, Britain built fewer and fewer middle-class cars of the traditional type, but produced more and more sports cars instead. Our small cars and our bread-and-butter family saloons sold well, and were exported in large numbers too, but it was the Triumphs, the Jaguars, the Austin-Healeys and the MGs which laid down a reputation for the future.

For today's classic car enthusiast, however, there is a paradox to be solved. British sports cars were built in much larger numbers than ever before—101,000 MG MGAs, compared with 10,000 MG TCs, is a perfect example—but not all that many appear to be still in the UK. Why not? The reason is simple: to take the MG example, more than 91,500 of those MGAs were sold overseas (81,000 of them in the USA alone. . .), and that is where the survivors are to be found.

It was a fascinating era during which the best of our sporting cars changed in character. In the 1950s, many were still based on 1930s design practice—which is to say that they had separate chassis frames, beam axle rear suspension, drum brakes and two seats—but by the 1960s more and more featured monocoque structures, 2+2 (if not four-seater) accommodation, disc brakes and all-independent suspension. Although British car production did not peak until the 1970s, the character of its cars was at its height in the 1960s.

Incidentally, far too many cars built in this period which were neither distinguished nor all that successful have since had their reputations artificially boosted. In some cases the only obvious justification for this was that (a) they were built at the right time and (b) they were built in limited numbers. They find no place in this book.

My problem, in fact, has been to find space for every car which deserves a mention. Here, then, is a very compressed list of the models which I believe deserve their place in classic car line-ups of the future.

Small family cars
Britain was on the winning side in the Second World War, and its car-producing factories were little damaged by enemy bombing, but in the years which followed, its family design standards were rapidly left behind by the French and the Italians. Although many and various low-priced cars were built in Britain at this time, very few of them deserve to be remembered as classics.

For a small car to be listed as a classic, it needs to have a well-proven character and, preferably, advanced or idiosyncratic technical features. To sell in large numbers is not enough. Right away, therefore, I propose to eliminate several small cars from my list on the grounds that they were, frankly, ordinary or are overrated today.

First of all, that list must include all the non-sporting Fords—Anglias, Prefects and Escorts of all types. Until 1953 these were 1930s designs in any case, and thereafter they had front engines, conventional pressed-steel monocoque structures and no character.

Next on my hit list is BMC's Austin A30/A35 series, which has come in for a degree of hyping in recent years. This car's small overhead-valve A-Series engine *was* important, as it powered so many classic BMC/BL cars of the next generation, but the rest of the cramped little Austin's design was very conventional indeed. The A40 Farina which followed it was at least smart and practical, but no more. And as for the frightful

Above *The Morris Minor matured as the Minor 1000 in 1956, and was given a 1.1-litre engine in late 1962 (this model). The Olde Englishe estate car derivative has great period charm today.*

Below *The BMC Mini Cooper S was launched in 1963, and became Mk II from late 1967. It was a nimble little 100 mph sports saloon.*

Nash Metropolitan which also built at BMC's Longbridge factory. . . !
Vauxhall built nothing worth remembering throughout the 1950s and
1960s (and any attempt to convince me of the charm of a Vauxhall Victor
will be met with a horse-laugh), while Rootes simply didn't attempt to
produce a small car before the Hillman Imp appeared in 1963; just one
type of Imp family car had merit—I discuss this below.

For many years, Standard-Triumph's small cars were all lumpy and
undistinguished, and an attempt to produce something different with the
oddly-styled Triumph Mayflower (who was it who saw one and
commented: 'Queen Anne front, and Mary Anne sides'?) was also a
failure. The Herald of 1959, however, was a different proposition.

Both the famous small British cars of the period came from BMC—the
Morris Minor and the Mini. I have already mentioned the Morris Minor
in Chapter 7, for it was launched in 1948, but it was at its best, and most
prolific, in the 1950s. Even when it was new, the Minor had something—
and in old age that 'something' has also acquired period charm.
Performance was never up to much but the handling, the choice of body
styles (a wood-framed Olde Englishe estate car was added in the 1950s)
and the unmistakable styling all helped. There were Minor 1000s from
late 1956, and the engine became 1.1-litre for 1963.

By that time, though, the Minor had been overshadowed by the
astonishing Mini, which was launched in 1959. Here was Alec Issigonis'
masterpiece, a tiny but roomy 10 ft (3 m) package which had everything,
including a transverse engine, front-wheel drive, all-independent
suspension, amazing roadholding and an irrepressible character. It didn't
matter that there were big quality problems at first, for everyone loved the
Mini—and everyone still does. They had rather floaty Hydrolastic
suspension from 1965, but this was dropped again at the end of the
decade.

From 1961 there was the faster Mini-Cooper, and from 1963 a growing
family of even faster Mini Cooper S models. The last of all was built in
1971. 100 mph (160 km/h) from a 1.3-litre saloon seemed indecent in those
days, and there were hundreds of racing and rally victories to add to the
charisma. These days, interest continues to grow, and you can still get
most of the parts.

Rootes' Imps suffered quality problems, particularly in the engine
department, but a properly sorted twin-carb model (an Imp Sport) was
a nimble, good-handling little roller skate. A few cars became 1-litre
Rallye Imp saloons which could, at least, keep up with the Mini-Coopers
and are now very rare. The best of the bunch, though, was the Sunbeam
Stiletto of 1967-72, which combined the 55 bhp engine with a smart coupé
body style and an up-market interior. It didn't sell very well at the time,
which was a pity—a well restored one is at least as satisfying as any
Mini-Cooper.

I am including the Herald (four-cylinder) and Vitesse (six-cylinder) family as classics for one very good reason—here was a genuinely fresh solution to producing modern-looking cars at minimum investment. At a time when everyone was turning to monocoque construction, these cars had separate chassis, but they also had all-independent suspension, modular body construction, and a wide choice of styles. The handling and the build quality of early types was very dodgy indeed, but it improved dramatically after Leyland took control in 1961. The 12/50 and 13/60 types were the best Heralds, while the best Vitesse was undoubtedly the 2-litre Mk 2 (introduced in 1968), which had a completely different rear suspension layout.

Middle-class family cars

Compared with the 1930s and 1940s, the choice was falling, but there was still a great deal of variety. Coventry's independent manufacturers (like Alvis and Armstrong-Siddeley) gradually faded away, but Jaguar's reputation continued to rise, and the Rootes Sunbeam-Talbots also continued to sell well.

From this period more than a dozen marques can now claim to be classics, and all have their own distinctive character. Helped along by the reputation of its sports cars, the most famous of them all was Jaguar, with every model powered by a version of the legendary twin-cam XK engine.

To replace the 1940s-style Mk V saloon, Jaguar produced the Mark VII, which had the Mk V's chassis, the new engine and a smart, if somewhat bulbous, body style. It was a big, heavy and rather ponderous car, but even the original 160 bhp model could achieve 100 mph (160 km/h), and the later Mark VIIM, Mark VIII and disc-braked Mark IX derivatives were even faster.

From 1955, however, Sir William Lyons produced a new type of Jaguar, the 2.4, which had a much more compact, and plainly styled, monocoque body structure. This car was crab tracked, only had drum brakes, and wasn't very fast by expected Jaguar standards, but when it was up-

Jaguar's Mk II saloon of the 1960s, one of the most obviously 'classic' cars of all time.

Alvis's post-war chassis was given a Graber-styled body from the mid-1950s which was built by Park Ward from 1958. This is the TE21 derivative.

engined and given disc brakes, to become 3.4, it was a much more formidable 120 mph (192 km/h) proposition.

For 1960 the car was restyled, given a wider rear and a wider choice of engines. This, the MK II range, was most popular of all, the 3.8- litre version in particular being excellent value, and in later years it also gave rise to the long-tail S-Type and the squared-nose 420 models, the latter being the fastest of the bunch.

In 1962 came the massive Mark X (which was renamed 42OG in 1966), which had the same engine tune and similar all-independent suspension to the famous E-Type sports car. It hasn't got the same high reputation as other Jaguars, mainly because of its size, styling and bulk. Will it even fit your garage?

At the end of the 1960s, of course, there was the sensational new XJ6, but as that car was to be built into the late 1980s, it really qualifies as a 'sleeper' (see the next chapter).

Faced with such competition from Browns Lane, all the other Coventry-based middle-class marques had a hard time. Riley had already left Coventry at the end of the 1940s, and there were really no BMC-Riley designs which could be called classic. Lea-Francis gave up the struggle in the early 1950s and was never revived.

Armstrong-Siddeley tried very hard when they introduced the separate chassis Sapphire, which had a splendid cross-pushrod type of six-cylinder engine and graceful styling; when it was new, though, it always lost sales to the cheaper Jaguar Mk VII family, and when it was older it

The famous 'Auntie' Rover was built from 1949 to 1965, with many different engines. Each and every car had great dignity and refinement.

was seen to have a very rot-prone body. It didn't help that the 234/236 saloons of 1955 were so abysmally styled. Armstrong-Siddeley gave up car manufacture in 1960, and concentrated on the aerospace industry instead.

The 1949 Alvis 3-litre soldiered on into the mid 1950s (the final, 100 mph (160 km/h) Grey Lady was a very smart, but essentially old-looking, sports saloon), but its replacement, the 'Graber'-styled car, was more popular and better looking. It used the same basic chassis as the 3-litre, and in final TF21 form its engine produced 150 bhp. Park Ward (which was owned by Rolls-Royce) produced saloon or drop-head coupé bodies, the last of which was delivered in 1967.

Daimler produced many different models in the 1950s before being absorbed by Jaguar in the 1960s. All had separate chassis frames and rather staidly styled bodies, with lots of wood and leather. Nearly all of them had the familiar fluid flywheel, plus pre-selector gearbox, transmission system. The best of a varied up-market bunch were the Regency and One-O-Four models. The smaller type, called Conquest or Conquest Century (75 bhp or 100 bhp respectively, from 2.4 litres), was surprisingly nimble; their bodies were from Pressed Steel, they rotted readily, and few good ones have survived. Values are still very low, even today.

Triumph's 1940s-style 1800 became the Renown of the 1950s, still with that quaint styling but now with the Vanguard-type chassis, engine and running gear. These cars look better than they go, and low values reflect this. They were, alas, the last of the larger 'classic' Triumphs, as I am afraid the 2000/2.5PI family do not seem to qualify for inclusion.

Rover moved out of Coventry at the end of World War Two, after the Luftwaffe had redistributed their factory walls during the blitz. From Solihull, however, they produced a succession of fine saloons which are certainly seen as classics today. More than 230,000 of the separate-chassis P4 types—always numbered 75, 90, 105, and so on—were built from 1949 to 1965, and because of their sedate image and impeccable manners they came to be known as the 'Auntie' Rovers; except that the bodies rotted badly, these were sturdy cars but not sporty cars—buy for quality rather than for performance. The best P4s have six-cylinder engines; four-cylinder versions like the 60 and the 80 are best forgotten.

Next up was the altogether larger monocoque 3-litre model announced in 1958 (which, naturally enough, came to be known as 'Great Auntie'), which had a six-cylinder 3-litre engine until 1967 and (as the 3½-litre) the new light-alloy GM-licenced 3½-litre vee-8 thereafter. It was just as ponderous, and just as well built as, but considerably faster than, the old P4 types. However, it was also a car much used as 'official' transport by Government ministers, and it was also the car used by Rover to mark an entry in big-time rallying in 1962. The V8-engined cars in particular were surprisingly fast.

The 2000 family, which was born in 1963, had an advanced 'base-unit' structure, De Dion rear suspension and other arresting technical features, but as it was so numerous and so prone to mechanical degradation in old age, I cannot in all honesty call the four-cylinder versions classic. However, from 1968 there was the vee-8 engined 3500 (sometimes known as the Three Thousand Five), which was a much more intriguing proposition.

Two other firms—Bristol and Lagonda—were quite unperturbed by the rise of Jaguar because both were priced considerably above that level. Bristol have never changed their chassis design in forty years (but it was a distinguished chassis design in the first place. . .), so you need only choose between styles and engines.

The best of the Bristol-engined Bristols was probably the two-seater coupé, the 404, but as this is virtually unobtainable today, perhaps you should settle for one of the 403, 405 or 406 types. These could all be described as expensive indulgences, for values are beginning to break £7,000 at the time of writing, and it is costly and time-consuming to rebuild the obsolete engine and the hand-finished bodies.

From the early 1960s and the 407, Bristol adopted Chrysler vee-8 engine power allied to automatic transmission, which helped to produce a lot more performance, the chassis being quite capable of handling it. 408, 409 and later models in this family are all excellent classic cars which need lots of good money spending on their upkeep.

David Brown's Lagonda always took a back seat to the Aston Martin marque, in which he was much more interested. The 1940s-style 2½-litre was up-engined into the 3-litre from 1953 but was dropped in 1958 when sales had died to a trickle. However, on the basis that 'everyone' buys Aston Martins, the elegant Lagonda is an intriguing alternative. The 1960s-style Rapide was a commercial failure—and as a long wheelbase four-door, heavier version of the Aston Marin DB4, perhaps it deserved that fate.

The Bradford-built Jowett Javelin ran on to 1953 before it ran out of customers, while MG's sweet little YA and YB saloons also sold slowly until the same year. The MG Magnette ZA and ZB, Gerald Palmer style, of 1953-8, were elegant, though under-powered, sports saloons, which had fine handling but deserved a lot more than the BMC B-Series engine to power them. However, when you see what styling horrors BMC inflicted on the name on the following version, you may understand why the Magnette is so popular today. On no account buy a Mk III or a Mk IV. . . .

Rootes' Sunbeam-Talbot 90 carried on into the 1950s and was eventually renamed Sunbeam Mk III, but not even a Monte Carlo rally win in 1955 could hide the fact that it was a lot heavier, and slower, than it

The Bristol 407 of the early 1960s was the first Bristol to use Chrysler vee-8 engine power. Many subsequent derivatives have followed it.

The Y-Series MG saloon, of pre-war design but post-war manufacture, was built until 1953.

looked. By comparison with other Rootesmobiles, though, it was a stylish creation, the drop-head coupé in particular being a nice, old-fashioned classic car today.

The long-running series of Sunbeam Rapiers followed the Mk III. Although these cars were really dressed-up two-door Hillman Minxes at first, they were relentlessly improved during the 1960s. In spite of a successful rally record, however, I cannot bring myself to call a Rapier a classic car.

Even though they had humble beginnings, two families of Vanden Plas models deserve a mention. Out of the Farina-styled Austin A99 BMC produced the Princess 3-litre saloon; it neither went, nor handled, better than the Austin, but there was real class in the trim and furnishing, which makes it a 'different' proposition today. Funnily enough its replacement, the 4-litre Princess R of 1964-8, which had a Rolls-Royce six-cylinder engine, was not really any better, though classic values are significantly higher.

Similarly, the Hydrolastically-suspended front-drive BMC 1100/1300 family do not qualify as classics, but the retrimmed and refurnished Princess 1100/1300 cars probably do. This is one of the few cars I know where a contrived facelift, and a contrived image, has actually improved the product. A Princess with a proper paint job and well-preserved leather furnishing and woodwork is a very silent and pleasing little car.

Sports and sporting cars

In the 1950s and 1960s, the most famous British classics of all were the sports cars. To make my point I need do no more than list models like the Jaguar E-Type, the Triumph TR3A, the Austin-Healey 3000, the MG MGB and the Morgan. There were a dozen more like that. There were so many fine sports cars that there is no need to start searching for favourites; however, it is worth recalling that the MGB sold most of all (more than 500,000 were built before it was finally dropped in 1980) and that the E-Type was one of the world's fastest cars, and one of the most charismatic, for a long time.

As with the saloons, so the sports car story must begin with Jaguar. Not only was Jaguar running a very successful team of racing sports cars in the 1950s (C-Types to 1953, D-Types from 1954), but it was selling fast, twin-cam engined XK sports cars to overseas markets at absurdly low prices: when the XK140 was launched in 1954, its British price was £1,598, while the (slower) Aston Martin DB2/4 sold for a whopping £2,782; nothing else came close in performance or value. And, if that wasn't enough, the 1950s-style XKs were displaced by the sleek and sexy E-Types of the 1960s, which were even more amazing pieces of machinery.

Although the XK120 was a 1940s design, it got better and better throughout the 1950s in XK140 and XK150 form, and every single example is a worthy classic car. All were very fast, but to summarize, the

Three famous classic MGs of the late 1960s/early 1970s period — the MGB Roadster, the MGB GT hatchback, and the Midget sports car.

XK140 had more cockpit space, better steering and roadholding than the XK120, while the XK150 was even faster and had disc brakes but a much restyled, less sleek, body style. The XK150S, especially in 3.8-litre form, was fastest of all; it could beat 135 mph (216 km/h). I think the two-seater open Roadsters were—and are—the most desirable XKs, but these days a fixed-head coupé seems to be the most practical, while a drop-head coupé somehow has the most style of all.

Then, of course, there was the E-Type, one of the best-known sports cars of all time. All the 1960s types were six-cylinder cars, and all could exceed 140 mph (224 km/h) (but *not* 150 mph (240 km/h)—except specially prepared road test cars. . .). Up to 1964 they had 3.8-litre engines, and 4.2-litre units plus all-synchromesh gearboxes after that. They became 'Series 2' from late 1968, no faster but better equipped than ever. The longer wheelbase 2+2 model came along in 1966, not quite as beautiful but an excellent compromise package. E-Type prices had gone through the roof by 1986—you simply couldn't buy one for less than £10,000.

The most numerous, then as now, were the British 'Big Three' marques—MG, Triumph and Austin-Healey. These are the cars which you see most of in classic car circles today.

MG started the 1950s with the new (but old-looking) TD, the first MG sports car to have independent front suspension, then replaced it with the slightly sleeker TF; even in TF1500 form in 1954 and 1955, none of these cars could exceed 85 mph (136 km/h). I call that disappointing, but traditionalists love them.

The MGA of 1955-62 was a much better car, with a rigid chassis and pretty styling plus 100 mph (160 km/h) top speed. I loved the bubble-top coupé option which arrived in 1956. MGAs got better over the years (1600 from 1959, 1600 Mk II from 1961), though the short-lived Twin-Cam of 1958-60 was an unreliable disappointment at the time. Surviving Twin-Cams, with modified and rebuilt engines, are delightful to own.

The monocoque MGB took over in 1962 and became MGB Mk II in 1967, with all-synchro. gears and a (rare) automatic transmission option. The Roadster was neat, while the fastback GT was very attractive indeed. They all had the 1.8-litre BMC engine, and they could all beat 100 mph (160 km/h). These days MGB ownership is backed by the largest one-make car club in the business—the MG Owners' Club.

From 1967 to 1969, too, there was the 3-litre engined MGC which, when new, was faster but suffered from a sluggish engine, heavy steering and worse handling than the MGB. Only 10,000 were built before it was dropped. Modern conversions can make an MGC handle much better than before.

Then, of course, there was the MG Midget, launched in 1961 as a rebadged Austin-Healey Sprite and identical in all important respects. More details below. . . .

The Austin-Healey marque came into existence in 1952, and in the next

There were two types of Austin-Healey over the years — the 'Big' Healey coming first, seen here in 3000 Mk II form. The Sprite followed at the end of the 1950s, this being a Mk II model.

two decades just two basically different models were produced. The 'Big Healey' began as the four-cylinder Austin-Healey 100 of 1953-6, with sturdy 'he-man' handling and character. Everything you have heard about minimal ground clearance and roasting cockpits is correct, but you can't ignore the styling or the performance.

The 100 Six models of 1956-7 were disappointingly slow, but later versions, and especially the 3000 types, were much better. The civilized wind-up windows/convertible hood version came along in 1962, and the 3000 Mk III of 1964-7 was the last, and the best developed. The 'Big Healey' died ahead of the MG MGC, which was no sort of replacement for an appealing car.

The little A-Series engine Sprite was built in various forms from 1958 to 1971 (only badged as an 'Austin' in the final year). For the first three years it was sold as the frog-eye variety which, these days, seems to have most charisma (and higher classic values than any other type), yet it was neither as fast, as civilized nor as practical as later types.

The restyled, and altogether more conventional, Mk II came along in 1961 (of which the new MG Midget was a clone), and it progressed through Mk III and Mk IV types before the end of the 1960s; the 'Healey' part of the title was dropped for 1971 when Donald Healey's royalty deal expired. There were worthwhile improvements along the way, including wind-up door windows for the Mk III and the 1,275 cc engine for the Mk IV. The Mk IV was the best car, in spite of what frog-eye values say.

The best-selling Triumph of the 1950s was the TR family, which started with TR2 in 1953 and culminated in TR3B (USA only) in 1962. All such TRs had a hard ride and a bump-steering chassis, but all beat 100 mph (160 km/h) with ease and had unburstable wet-liner engines; they looked good, too, without being pretty-pretty. There were disc front brakes for 1957 and the wide-grille TR3A for 1958; TR3As were best, and most numerous.

In the 1960s there was a succession of new TRs—the Michelotti-styled TR4 in 1961, a new all-independent chassis'd TR4A in 1965, the 2½-litre fuel-injected TR5 in 1967, and a face-lifted (by Karmann) TR6 in 1969; one model always developed from the last, and all had the same hairy-chested character. American-spec TR5s were TR250s with carburettors, the same

The cheekiest character of all Austin-Healeys was contained in the original 'frog-eye' built from 1958 to 1961.

The Sunbeam Tiger of 1964-67 was the vee-8 engined version of the pretty Alpine.

engine also being used in USA-spec. TR6s. MG fanatics mock the TRs, while TR owners snarl back at the MGs—which means, surely, that each was formidable opposition for the other?

What made MG enthusiasts even more angry in the 1960s was the success of Triumph's pretty Spitfire. Michelotti styling, more roomy and more practical than that of the Midget/Sprite, topped a short wheelbase backbone version of the Herald's chassis. Until 1970 and the arrival of the Mk IV, the roadholding was poor (too much sudden swing-axle oversteer), but performance was also on a par with the BMC opposition. It outsold the Sprite/Midget combination at the time, and is easier to restore today; values, surprisingly, are still lower.

Rootes tried hard with the Sunbeam name on two occasions. The separate-chassis Alpine of 1953-5 is best forgotten, a heavy, not-very-fast two-seat tourer version of the Sunbeam-Talbot 90, but the monocoque Alpine of 1959-68 (which was Rapier-based) was a good MGA/MGB competitor. It wasn't quite as quick but it handled well, and was a very pretty and practical car.

The 'Q-Car' version, of course, was the Tiger of 1964-7, where a Ford-Detroit vee-8 engine was mated to the Alpine's structure; performance was better than roadholding or braking, even on the rare 1967 model Tiger IIs—and these days a Tiger is rather a sought-after rarity, twice as valuable as any Alpine.

There were lots of specialist-manufactured sports cars which deserve a mention. Until 1968 a Morgan looked, felt *and* drove much as before, with a choice of Triumph TR (Plus 4), and four-cylinder Ford (4/4) engines from 1955. The fibreglass-bodied Plus 4 Plus car of the early 1960s was an unsuccessful aberration, which explains why its classic value is high today. Then, for 1969, came the fearsome Rover vee-8 engined Plus 8 model, an instant classic if ever I saw one, and of course it's still made today.

Reliant wished they could have achieved Morgan's reputation, but their GRP-bodied coupés never quite made it. Their first generation Sabre model was too much of a kit car, though the Scimitar two-seater of 1964-70 was much better, especially with Ford vee-6 power from 1966. Then, from 1968, there was the Scimitar GTE hatchback, which set a precedent followed by many larger companies, ran to the earlier 1980s and is still something of a 'sleeper'. Many people were surprised when a GTE was pronounced British concours champion in 1986.

Surprisingly, I can now mention Daimler in the sports car section. If only because it was a rare and ungainly two/three-seater version of the Conquest family car, I ought to mention the Conquest Roadster of the mid 1950s, but it was the GRP-bodied SP250 which was a much more serious project. Here was a car with a chassis copied from Triumph's TR3A, and with rather nasty styling, but with a magnificent home-brewed 2½-litre vee-8 engine. If only it had been built properly—and promoted properly—then more than 2,600 would have been sold. The third and last series was best, but all have a certain period charm.

I have already mentioned the Frazer Nash, the Healey, the HRG and the Jowett Jupiter marques in earlier chapters. All these cars were built

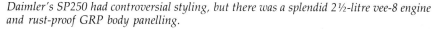

Daimler's SP250 had controversial styling, but there was a splendid 2½-litre vee-8 engine and rust-proof GRP body panelling.

until the mid 1950s, but none was replaced by a new model. New and interesting models came along from AC, Gilbern, Lotus, Marcos and TVR to take their place; surprisingly, four out of these five survived (if tenuously at times) into the 1980s.

The 1946-53 AC 2-litre models were boring and old-fashioned in the extreme, but the Ace (Roadster) and Aceca (coupé) family were altogether different. The basic tubular chassis design, with all-independent suspension, was by Tojeiro, and the styling was typically mid 1950s Ferrari; the result, even with the ancient AC engine, was a *real* sports car with superb handling and character. Later cars had Bristol, then modified six-cylinder Ford engines. Popular opinion is that the 120 mph (192 km/h) disc-braked Ace-Bristol is best of the bunch.

Then, even more charismatic, was the Cobra of the 1960s, which evolved from it, with larger and ever larger Ford vee-8 engines, and even more performance. One self-styled motoring sage described it as an 'obscene' car, but hundreds of happy owners don't agree with him. Like Jaguar's E-Type, the Cobra is a definitive car of the 1960s.

Gilbern started building multi-tube framed, GRP bodied GTs at the end of the 1950s which used BMC four-cylinder engines, and followed it in 1966 with the similarly engineered, Ford vee-6 engined Genie. Gilbern's problem was that the cars were undeveloped—but these days the simple chassis and rot-proof body is thought to be a classic advantage.

Marcos also evolved from being a special to being a respectable manufacturer, and for years used a marine ply *wood* chassis (which was replaced by a steel tubular frame in the late 1960s) to support GRP bodies, and a variety of proprietary engines. The GT of the mid and late 1960s was an attractive and ultra-low coupé. It dropped out of production in the early 1970s but has been revived, as the Mantula, in the mid 1980s.

TVR, too, evolved along the multi-tube frame/GRP body route, with all-independent suspension, many different engines, and almost as many different managements! The Grantura Mk III of 1962 was a much better car than the original TVR, especially when the Tuscan derivatives came on the scene with larger and more powerful Ford engines.

The outstanding newcomer, though, was Lotus, which made its name with multi-tube framed racing cars but went on to produce some light, excellent-handling, independently-suspended, GRP-bodied but oh-so-fragile road cars. *All* the road cars are classics, these being the two-seater Elite coupé of 1959-63, the Elan two-seater introduced in 1962, the Europa of 1966 and the Elan Plus 2 of 1967. In every case they got better as development proceeded, so if you are shopping around, look for a late model, if possible; in all cases develop a sense of humour to deal with the failings which are sure to occur.

By the 1950s, Aston Martin had stopped building sports cars and were producing GT cars instead, while Jensen steadily raised their reputation in an attempt to join them. There were three generations of Aston Martins

The Elite (with Coventry Climax engine) was the first practical road car from Lotus.

The Aston Martin DB6 was a close-coupled four-seater, and the last of a family which started with the DB4 of 1958.

which are definite, timeless classic cars today. The DB2 of the late 1940s turned into the DB2/4 of 1953, and eventually into the DB Mk 3 of 1957, getting a 3-litre engine (1954) and front-wheel disc brakes (1957) along the way. All were nicely developed, fine-handling cars; the latter types could exceed 120 mph (192 km/h).

Then came the DB4, DB5, DB6 family of cars, launched in 1958 and built to the beginning of the 1970s. These had a new platform frame and massively powerful new six-cylinder engines. For rarity choose the short wheelbase DB4GT (which will be expensive), or for *extreme* rarity (and an incredibly high price) try to find a DB4GT Zagato. For ordinary mortals, though, the best choice is probably a well-preserved DB5 complete with Vantage engine and five-speed ZF transmission—though the slightly more roomy DB6, often with automatic transmission, is an even more practical alternative.

Finally, in the 'Supercar' category, there are the DBS and DBS-V8 series of cars, which made their debut in 1967 and 1969 respectively. Originally there was the DBS, with DB6-type six-cylinder engines, but the vee-8 version then took over, and is still made today. Bigger, wider and heavier than the DB6, and equipped with De Dion rear suspension, the DBS is still an amazingly easy-to-handle four-seater—and these days it still changes hands for less money than, say, an E-Type.

Jensens improved steadily throughout this period. I would not recommend the early generation Interceptors (of the early/mid 1950s), but the 541 family of the next dozen years or so have considerable charm. A solid platform chassis was clothed in a fastback GRP 2 + 2-seater body, with six-cylinder engine power by BMC, giving high top speeds and creditable economy. The 541R was best: the final 1960s type, 541S, had lost its edge in performance and looks. To take over, then, there was the CV-8 range, based on the same structure but, like the Bristols, having Chrysler vee-8 engines. To some eyes these were ugly cars, though significantly faster than before; surprisingly, their classic values are significantly higher than those of the six-cylinder Jensens.

Finally in this period there were the beautifully styled but steel-bodied (and therefore rust-prone) Interceptor and FF coupés, which had new body styles on the well-proven chassis and Chrysler vee-8 engines. The FF was the first production car (but only about 300 examples were built) to have four-wheel drive and anti-lock braking, which made it a trend-setter, even if there were all sorts of teething troubles which have not all been eliminated on surviving models. For the average classic car buyer, a late-model Interceptor (which was built until 1976) is probably a better bet. You would probably pay one-third E-Type price, these days, and get just as much enjoyment, especially if the 2 + 2 seating appeals.

Although Ford's 1950s offerings were distinctly mundane, in the 1960s the company produced a series of fine sports saloons, all being much-modified versions of bread-and-butter machinery. If you can face the

Two of Britain's best 1930s-style sports cars were the MG TA (right) and the Singer 9 Le Mans (left).

One of the most instantly recognizable shapes of the 1940s and 1950s is Jaguar's XK range — this is an XK140 drop-head coupé.

Below left Concours standards in the UK are very high — and improving! Left to right are Roger Rowley's Reliant Scimitar GTE, Paul Garland's Morris Minor 1000 Traveller and Dave Horton's Jensen CV-8.

There's no doubt about the potential of Ford's RS200 as a 'sleeper' — only 120 road cars were sold in 1986 and 1987.

Jensen's Interceptor was introduced in 1966 and built for nearly ten years. There was also a four-wheel-drive version, the FF.

(eventual) aggravation of rebuilding a Lotus-Ford twin-cam engine, then consider buying a Lotus-Cortina (the Mk 1 of 1963-6 is still worth a lot more money than the more civilized Mk 2 of 1967-70—which makes no sense, but is a fact), or even an Escort Twin-Cam (which was introduced in 1968).

Otherwise go down-market, spend a lot less money, and look for a Cortina 1600E (more plush, less engine, but something of the character of a dolled-up Lotus-Cortina) or a Cortina GT instead. This was only the beginning for new types of 'Fast Fords'—as the next chapter makes clear.

The carriage trade

At this level of the market it is amazing how rarely the contenders change. In the previous thirty years Rolls-Royce had set the standards and others had followed. So it was, again, in the 1950s and 1960s.

Until the mid 1950s the eminently collectable Rolls-Royce cars were the Silver Dawn and the Silver Wraith models, both of which have been detailed in the previous chapter; the Silver Wraith, in fact, was built until 1959.

From 1955 Rolls-Royce introduced the Silver Cloud model, which was really the last of the old-style separate-chassis Rolls-Royce cars with a six-cylinder engine and drum brakes. Automatic transmission was standard by this time. Beautifully built but ponderous, it became the much better (115 mph (184 km/h)) Silver Cloud II with the new light-alloy vee-8 engine in 1959, and the slightly more powerful four-headlamp Silver Cloud III in 1962, and was built until 1965-6. A small proportion had splendidly lavish coachbuilt body shells, but most were 'standard steel' by Pressed Steel (and just as liable to rust away as the more mundane Daimlers and Jaguars of the period).

A mere sixteen straight-eight Phantom IV limousines were produced in the 1950s, which means that they are as rare as unicorn's eggs today, but the Phantom V, introduced in 1959, was a more serious proposition. This gargantuan machine had a long wheelbase version (144 in (3.66 m)) of Silver Cloud II's chassis and the new vee-8 engine, and always had huge coachbuilt bodies, mostly from Mulliner, Park Ward or James Young. Phantom V became Phantom VI in 1968 with relatively minor changes, and a few such cars are still being built in the late 1980s. Hundreds have been built, and dozens change hands every year, so if you have a *lot* of money to spare on purchase and upkeep, why not join the nobility?

The new generation Rolls-Royce of 1965 was the Silver Shadow, of which more than 30,000 would be made by the time the Silver Spirit took over in 1980. These cars were everything the Silver Clouds had not been—they had monocoque structures with rather plain styling, all-independent suspension, disc brakes, ultra-complex high-pressure hydraulics—yet the 1960s examples now change hands for no more than the price of a good E-Type. Which is the bargain? I'm afraid it isn't the Rolls-Royce which, like all cars of this marque, can cost a respectable fortune to maintain and cherish.

On that basis, you simply can't afford one of the coachbuilt variety which came along towards the end of the decade. . . .

For every Rolls-Royce of the 1950s and 1960s there was also a Bentley, the differences getting fewer and fewer as the years progressed. The R-Type already mentioned, was significantly faster than the Silver Dawn, but from 1955 (with the S-Series) and from 1965 (with the monocoque T-Series) only the badges and the radiator distinguished one standard-steel saloon from another.

Collectors therefore tend to home in on the coachbuilt cars, particularly the R-Type Continental of 1952-5 and the S-Type Continental of 1955-65. S-Types have the same running gear as the standard cars, but graceful coachbuilt bodies, some with two doors and (from 1957) an increasing number with four doors. That special coachwork does a lot to values—expect to have to pay 300% to 400% *more* than for the same car with a

The Rolls-Royce Silver Cloud III was the last of the 'separate chassis' designs from Crewe. Although it had a fine vee-8 engine, it was still afflicted with drum brakes and a beam axle rear suspension.

standard saloon body. Is it worth it? Every year hundreds of people seem to think so. . . .

There are only two other marques in the 'top drawer', as far as this era of classic cars is concerned. One, clearly and obviously, is Daimler; the other, though with a less obvious pedigree, is Vanden Plas.

Before it was taken over by Jaguar at the beginning of the 1950s, Daimler produced more and more middle-class cars, fewer and fewer for the carriage trade. The 1940s-style DE27s and Straight-Eights disappeared in the early 1950s, after which the only truly large, series-production Daimlers were the 4½-litre models of the 1950s (especially the massive DK400 limousines), the 3.8-litre Majestic, introduced in 1958 (a better, faster One-O-Four), and especially the 4½-litre vee-8 engined Majestic Major and DR450 Limousine models of the 1960s.

Each of these cars had a solid separate chassis frame and beam axle rear suspension, but big and graceful coachwork, often by first-grade companies like Hooper. The Majestic Major, in particular, handles almost indecently well for a 120 mph (192 km/h), two-ton car. Compared with a Rolls-Royce, a Daimler of this type costs about one-tenth as much (yes, that's right, one tenth), but paradoxically, such cars are much more difficult to restore as parts supply is patchy.

Just falling into this period is the Jaguar Mk 10-based Daimler Limousine, which combines Vanden Plas furnishing with Jaguar chassis engineering. Perhaps it really qualifies as a 'sleeper', as these cars are still made, in limited numbers, to this day.

Lastly, there is the Vanden Plas marque, which gradually evolved from the big 4-litre Austin models of the 1940s. In my opinion, a 1940s/1950s style Austin Sheerline is a clumsily styled car which is best ignored, but the same six-cylinder chassis clothed by Vanden Plas was a different proposition. All were well built, but some were beter than others. I liked the Princess II and Princess III models (but not the Princess IV which followed), and was especially impressed by the Princess 4-litre Limousine, which was built in almost exactly the same style between 1952 and 1968. With this sort of car, however, you have to look hard, and compare with an expensive coachbuilt Rolls-Royce, before deciding if you want to pay ten times as much money for that famous badge from Crewe. Think about it.

Chapter 9

Modern times—collecting your 'sleeper' for later!

'Sleeper'—a slang word often used in espionage circles for an agent recruited but then ignored for many years by his masters. Only activated when the time is ripe.

Also applied to objects whose values are not appreciated when new, which are neglected for years, and gain popularity in later life.

Was there ever a time in the 1970s when you thought the 'classic car' breed was already dying out? Was this the time when you thought that a 'classic', like a 'vintage' machine, would eventually end up in a time warp of its own? And weren't you delighted to be proved wrong?

I don't blame you, for looking around today's Motor Show displays can be a very depressing business. Most of the unique character which helps to create a classic car seems to have been squeezed out of the latest new models. It's true that most of the famous marque badges are still in evidence, but many cars are quite obviously cloned from others with different badges, and there has certainly been a great deal of amalgamation, integration and collaboration world-wide in recent years. Many new cars have clearly been designed to satisfy the legislators and the cost accountants, and don't seem to have any soul any more. As I have already made clear, this was one of the major reasons for the growth of the classic car movement in the 1970s in the first place.

In the case of middle-size, middle-price saloons, here's just one perfect example. In the mid 1970s the Alfa Romeo Alfettas, Fiat 131s, Lancia Betas and Saab 99s were all so obviously different; now, in the late 1980s, their successors are all very obviously based on the same 'Type 4' layout.

It is also quite clear that, in recent years, many of the smaller, energetic car makers have either disappeared altogether, have been absorbed into larger combines, or have lost their own design independence following policy changes. You want examples? Consider MG, Triumph, Alpine-Renault or Matra. No thrusting new marque has established itself in the last decade or so; the De Lorean project looked promising for a time, before it collapsed into bankruptcy amid accusations of financial chicanery.

The miracle, therefore, is that exciting and technically 'different' new

Ferrari Testarossa of the mid-1980s — there's no doubt about its classic status in years to come.

cars have continued to appear, year after year, and from almost every car manufacturing country. There have been new cars like the mid-engined Ferrari Testarossa, the amazing Porsche 911 Turbo, and the original Audi Quattro, all with character which shouted 'instant classic' from the day they first appeared.

In some cases, however, it took time for a modern car's character to become apparent—the Range Rover and the Saab Turbo were two such models—and sometimes such cars looked too expensive when new. Then, over a period of time, they began to attract a following and build a status of their own. These were the 'sleepers'—the cars we will surely be calling 'classic' any day now, while wondering how we could have missed their significance when they were new.

In some ways, and with experience, you can pick a 'sleeper' from the day it is announced, but the logic is not always apparent. It was obvious that 'homologation specials' like the Lancia Stratos or the BMW M1 *should* be stunning road cars, but one had to wait to try them out before making the decision. On the other hand, it was not at all clear from the data sheets that the Ford Capri 2.8i was going to feel so much better than the 3-litre version which it replaced, and in the case of 'hot hatches' like the VW Golf GTi and the Peugeot 205 GTI, a test drive was essential before the enthusiast could even begin to get excited.

The importance of this discussion, of course, is not only to emphasize that great cars, with great character, continue to appear even in the late

1980s, but that they can often be bought at surprisingly reasonable prices. However, anyone looking to buy a 'sleeper' which will turn into an acknowledged classic one day has to find the right time to do that.

Clearly, if you buy an 'instant classic' when it is new, you have to pay full price and watch the car's value plummet due to normal depreciation for a number of years. If you hang around and wait for too long, until the word has got around and demand has built up, the value will have shot up through the roof once again.

A perfect example is the Aston Martin DB6. In the UK in 1970, when it was near the end of its current-model fame, a DB6 sold for £5,500, but by 1975 or 1976 you could pick up a scruffy example for around £1,600/£1,700. Now, in the late 1980s, any DB6 in good condition commands at leat £10,000, and some go for a great deal more than that.

As a general rule, the best time to buy (and not to sell!) a car you consider to be a 'sleeper' is when it is about five years old. At that point its first (or maybe second) owner will have found that his car has begun to suffer corrosion, the big reconditioning bills will all have rolled in at least once, and the owner will probably have become attracted to something newer, glossier, and one needing less care and attention. Take a deep breath, weigh up the problems facing you over *long-term* ownership, and pounce. . . .

Here, then, is a personal view of the cars of the 1970s and early 1980s

Lancia's mid-Ferrari-engined Stratos was a cramped two-seater rally car, with ferocious performance and excellent road-holding.

which surely qualify as 'sleepers', some nascent classics already, and all set for secure classic status in the future:

UK

Let me start at the top, among the 'carriage trade'. Even though there seem to be so many of them around at the moment, there's no doubt that *any* unit-construction Rolls-Royce/Bentley is a car to keep. In spite of the myths which surround any car built at Crewe, don't forget that these cars can go expensively rusty, and don't expect them to handle and perform as well as they are built and equipped. Forget the current criticism about styling, and similarity to some American designs—it *will* all be forgotten in the end.

All of them—Rolls-Royce Silver Shadows and Bentley T-Series—are good, but some are more desirable than others. On the 'rarest is most valuable' basis, look at the Bentley badge before the Rolls-Royce, the Corniche (especially the convertible) before the four-door saloons, and the Camargue coupé before all of them. The problem, quite simply is, that they are *all* expensive.

If, on the other hand, you want as much space as a Rolls-Royce limousine at a fraction of the price, consider the charms of the vast Daimler Limousine, which was introduced in 1968. The running gear was pure Jaguar, with a 4.2-litre XK engine and modified versions of the Mk 10 suspension, while the body was by Motor Panels/Vanden Plas. This car is surprisingly fast, if somewhat ponderous, and unquestionably a

Rolls-Royce Camargue — horrendously expensive today, but in ten years, who knows?

All the Jaguar XJs were fine cars, but the two-doors coupés (this is an XJ6C with the 4.2-litre engine) were more rare, and more desirable.

very impressive eight-seater indeed. It is, however, a large car, and the styling might not appeal to everyone.

Space, of course, is also no problem with a car like the Range Rover, a remarkable machine which is not only a nearly unstoppable 4×4 (arguably the best in the world) in the most appalling conditions, but is a very well-equipped five-seater estate car with a great deal of style, and a lasting reputation with the Green Wellies set. It's not all good news, of course, for against the traction, the supple ride and the 100 mph (160 km/h) top speed, you have to set the 12-16 mpg of most examples. Even so, there can't be many classics which are equally at home, and recognized, in the Mall as in the heather, on the M1 or on a 1 in 2 hillside—and no other 4×4 comes close.

Another spacious 'sleeper' which is already becoming more fashionable is the Jaguar XJ range of saloons, which had a long-running career from 1968 to 1986. These cars admittedly had a wobbly reputation in their early and middle years, over quality, reliability and protection against corrosion, but no-one ever argued about their styling, their refinement, their handling or their performance.

From a very wide range, which included two different wheelbases as well as six-cylinder and vee-12 engines, I would pick the Series 3 cars (1979-86) as the most desirable in terms of product quality, the vee-12s as the most exciting in uncannily silent performance terms, and the two-door XJCs for their rarity or their styling.

Most people agree that the 2.8-litre and 3.4-litre models had a slightly disappointing performance, and that the vee-12s were really too thirsty to be practical for classic car enthusiasts looking for value for money.

Aston Martin's mighty Vantage saloon, with 170 mph potential. Historically, Aston Martins have always become very cheap by their tenth birthday, then seem to pick up in value again.

Unfortunately, far too many XJ6s (and their Daimler-badged equivalent) have been handed down, and sold on, to owners who did not appreciate them, and there are some *very* scruffy examples indeed.

The other spacious 'sleeper' which already has its rather quirky following in some quarters is the famous Carbodies taxicab, the famous 'London cab' style. Yes, I know, this only has its obvious character (and its well-known rugged reliability) as advantages, but we can't all own Lamborghinis and Ferraris, can we?

Consider, next, a clutch of stylish coupés or Grand Tourers. An obvious range of 'sleepers' is the modern Bristol range, with models as diverse as the 411s, Brigands and Britannias. All are based on the same rugged chassis, with Chrysler vee-8 engines and automatic transmissions. With production at the rate of little more than fifty cars a year, all sales handled from the company's headquarters in London and a great deal of hand-work in every model, these are not cars to be bought casually. Not only are they expensive to buy when new, they are costly to keep up in later years. They are, on the other hand, beautifully built, fast, well-balanced machines.

Bristols are perhaps even too rare to be completely practical classic cars in the 1990s, but the modern Aston Martins and Lagondas are much more numerous, better understood by restoration specialists, and considerably cheaper to buy at any time. Perhaps it is already too late to describe a vee-8 as a 'sleeper', as it has been around since 1969 under one name or another and has already been enjoyed, at length, by all the 'classic' magazines. However, the long wheelbase, four-door derivative of this design, the Lagonda, of which the Newport Pagnell factory has been building four or five examples every week since it went on sale in 1978, is still a fast-depreciating car at the moment, and early examples must now be near the bottom of the value trough.

The Jaguar XJ-S, too, is a well-known and readily-available model today, for it has been in production since 1975. The vast majority of these cas have vee-12 engines and fixed-head body styles, but don't forget that the new 3.6-litre AJ6-engined six-cylinder version has since been available since the autumn of 1983 in coupé *or* cabriolet guise, and that the vee-12 cabriolet was also launched in 1985.

The XJ-S's advantages and disadvantages are now known to all enthusiasts—the doubtful build quality of those cars built in the first five years or so (and their eagerness to rust!), the hefty thirst of the vee-12 engined cars and their rather large size—but the car is nevertheless an amazingly refined, fast, good-handling package. The best vee-12 engined cars were built after mid 1981 when they were given redesigned, more fuel-efficient 'HE' engines. Accordingly, my XJ-S 'Best Buy' of the moment would be a 1982-ish HE coupé, though *any* cabriolet is likely to become collectable in years to come.

Still on the theme of coupés, you might consider the Triumph Stag of 1970-77, which was built in considerable numbers and was a very smart and practical car available with a removable hardtop, or with T-Bar protection and a folding hood. The cars which survive today have all had their early vee-8 engine problems sorted out, and there are specialists in restoration and maintenance to make classic ownership worthwhile. The MG MGB GT V8 of 1973-6 was a different type of car from the Stag, this time with the light-alloy Rover 3½-litre vee-8 engine, but with a two- (or, if we are being charitable, 2 + ½!) seater fastback/hatchback style. In many ways the MG could have been a great car, but as its styling was identical to that of the four-cylinder MGB GT, it was not 'different' enough to be successful in its day.

Three other coupés, if not already classic, will certainly qualify in the 1990s. The Ford Capri 2.8i, introduced in 1981, was considerably better than any other Capri, thanks to its relatively low price, its 160 bhp fuel-injected engine, its 7.0 in (18 cm) rim alloy wheels, its firmed-up suspension and a hairy-chested character. For 1983 there was a five-speed gearbox, and for 1985 a limited-slip differential and RS-style wheels, and all these cars had a near-130 mph (208 km/h) top speed. In West Germany (but theoretically not sold in the UK) there was a short-lived, factory-produced carburettor/turbocharged version of the car, with no less than 188 bhp and even more performance.

Above *The mid-engined Lotus Esprit, especially in turbocharged form, will always be desirable, if you can keep it running...*

Below *TVR's first ever open-top car was the Convertible of the late 1970s. Under that skin is a backbone chassis frame with all-independent suspension and four-wheel disc brakes.*

Bottom *Vauxhall's best-known 'homologation special' was the Chevette HS which went on sale in 1978. Only 400 of these 120 mph machines were ever built.*

Naturally, the Lotus Esprit and Lotus Elite/Eclat/Excel families, introduced progressively from 1974 (Excel, actually, was the Eclat's replacement in 1982), have to be considered. In some ways their backbone chassis/glass-fibre body construction promises so much as far as long life is concerned, though in practice the slant-4 16-valve twin-cam engines can cost a fortune to maintain and rebuild, and there always seems to be a lot of work to be done on the suspension, steering and chassis components. But they look so good, have so much performance, and such good road-holding. . . .

Lastly in the 'coupé' category there is the TVR family of the 1970s and 1980s, all of which have multi-tubular chassis with all-independent suspension and glass-fibre bodies. Most of the UK market M-Series models of 1972-9 had 3-litre Ford vee-6 engines, but a good proportion had hatchback, or even full convertible, styles. The most fearsome of all were the Turbos—just sixty-three of them—which had a 140 mph (224 km/h) top speed and real tyre-stripping acceleration. the Tasmin, which took over in 1980, had entirely new chassis and body engineering with Ford-Germany vee-6 power, and was a better car all round then before. Later examples (called 350i) had the big 3½-litre Rover vee-8 engine in 190 bhp Vitesse tune. In both cases, it's best to avoid the rather slow four-cylinder Ford-engined models (1600M and Tasmin 200 respectively).

Time now to turn to the 'homologation specials', usually produced for a short time only, in the lowest possible number to satisy the sporting authorities, so that they could be used in rallying. In many cases these cars are not nearly as refined as one might hope, but all, without exception, have a great deal of character and rarity value. As 'sleepers', they qualify easily.

To summarize, therefore, you might start by considering any of the Ford Escort RS models—Twin-Cam, Mexico, RS1600, RS1800, RS2000 and RS Mexico—which were really ordinary Escort Mk I or Mk II cars with engine transplants and some attention to handling and braking. Road cars are surprisingly docile, and you can still get parts for most of them, for cars like the RS2000s were built in their thousands; there is a thriving one-make club, the Ford RS Owners' Club.

Two interesting Vauxhalls were the Firenza 'droop snoot' of 1973-5, of which only about 200 were made, a hopped-up and restyled version of the Firenza, and the Chevette HS of 1978-80, which combined the familiar Chevette hatchback body style with a 135 bhp 2.3-litre twin-cam engine and Getrag gearbox; there were 400 of these, and most seem to have survived.

The Talbot Sunbeam-Lotus of 1979-81 was an amalgam of the Talbot Sunbeam's hatchback style with the 150 bhp version of the 2.2-litre Lotus 16-valve engine and a ZF gearbox. Compared with the Vauxhall, this was a much more genuine road car, for over 2,300 were built, of which a number were 'customized' by Avon Coachworks after production had

Just 5,000 Ford Sierra RS Cosworths were built, all with 204 bhp turbocharged engines and a 150 mph top speed — plus that large rear aerofoil section.

ceased. All in all, though, this was a very similar type of car to the Chevette HS.

The Ford Sierra RS Cosworth of 1986 is still too new for everyone to afford (its price, as new, was £15,950), but as only 5,000 were built, and as the car combines startling styling (it has a huge rear aerofoil) with a turbocharged 204 bhp 2-litre Cosworth engine and a 150 mph (240 km/h) top speed, it is not likely to be ignored by posterity.

The RS200 of 1986, on the other hand, was probably too fierce for nearly everyone. With a high-tech body shell including liberal amounts of Kevlar, a mid-mounted 250 bhp turbocharged 1.8-litre engine, four-wheel drive and distinctive Ghia styling, it was the ultimate in Group B 'specials', and was making no money for its makers at £50,000 a time! Nor was it all that refined, either. Only 200 were built, and I doubt if more than 100-120 cars will ever be used on the road. This was the car being used for *everday* motoring by the author in 1987. Impractical and too expensive? Remember what happened to the other Ford homologation special of the 1960s, the GT40: cars changed hands for derisory prices five years after production had ceased, but now at least £100,000 is needed to finance the purchase of any one of the survivors.

The rest of my British-made selection of 'sleepers' are all sports cars, pure and simple. Perhaps you didn't like the Triumph TR7, first announced in 1975 and put on UK sale in 1976? Maybe you didn't like the rather odd wedge-nose style and hump-backed rear? I wouldn't argue with any of that, but I would commend the later (1979 onwards) TR7 Convertible as a car which will certainly take on classic status in the 1990s, especially as most such cars were sold in five-speed transmission form. Similarly, you should certainly consider any *genuine* (as opposed to privately constructed) Triumph TR8 which has ended up in this country complete with 3½-litre Rover vee-8 engine, matching gearbox and light-alloy road wheels. But beware! A number of TR7s have been converted to vee-8 power by resourceful private owners, and that's not the same thing at all.

On the other hand, no-one is ever going to argue against the inclusion of a Morgan, which carried on into the 1980s in much the same way that it had ended the 1960s. Every Morgan has a wooden body structure which rots and a body shell which eventually goes rusty, but that never stopped anyone buying an older example in the past. . . .

Do you agree that the De Lorean DMC12 was a sports car? I hope so, and I also hope you agree that it *must* become a classic one day, if only because of its unique reputation and finish. Because John De Lorean's whole concept was engineered for production by Lotus, its relation to a modern Lotus was obvious—backbone chassis, glass-fibre body structure, all-independent suspension and all. The twin problems were that it had a rear (not mid) Renault vee-6 engine, which made the handling very spooky at high speeds, and every car had unpainted stainless steel skin panels, which are the very devil to keep clean. However, several thousands of these stunningly styled cars with gull-wing doors were built in 1981 and 1982, and they already have a cult following in the USA.

Personally, I am quite happy to include the Jensen-Healey/Jensen GT in this list, though I know of several people who suggest that the cars lack character. On the other hand, they are certainly very pretty (if slightly bland-looking), with power by courtesy of the ubiquitous Lotus 16-valve unit and simple, rugged Vauxhall front and rear suspension systems. The GT version is an estate-like conversion on the same base, with an interesting layout but not much extra carrying capacity. Both types, having pressed-steel shells, have an unfortunate reputation for rusting away, but this problem can be dealt with during a thorough restoration. Nearly 11,000 of all types were built from 1972 to 1976.

Even though the car is rare, and not nearly as fast as its looks suggest it ought to be, I feel that the AC 3000ME is a classic car already, and will certainly confirm that rating in future. The name 'AC' is good enough to ensure that, surely, and the transverse/mid-engined design (the engine is a Ford vee-6 of 3 litres) is unique enough to make it interesting to enthusiasts. How many are on the roads? No more than 100, I'd say.

Lastly, of course, I must include the Lotus Esprit/Esprit Turbo models, which combine the established advantages of Lotus ownership (steel backbone frame, glass-fibre bodywork, all-independent suspension and striking styling) with mid-mounting of the 16-valve twin-cam engine, splendid roadholding and sparkling performance. Any normally aspirated Esprit which can't achieve 130 mph (208 km/h), or a turbo-charged example which can't nudge 150 mph (240 km/h), is not in a good state of preservation. The bad news, however, is that (as with the Elites and Eclats) the cars seem to get scruffy and worn out alarmingly rapidly. You need a real sence of adventure to own a modern Lotus—and a big bank balance. . . .

Europe
There is, of course, a goodly supply of 'sleepers' from Europe as well as from Britain, many with even better reputations for long life, quality of construction and great character.

Starting, as I did with British products, at the 'space' end of the scale, I must naturally include many of the petrol-engined Mercedes-Benz saloons and coupés of the 1970s and 1980s. Once you have understood that every such car had a massively strong steel body/chassis unit, all-independent suspension, disc brakes all round, power-assisted every-thing, and a build quality of which even Rolls-Royce would be proud, there is no need to draw back again. Naturally, a Mercedes goes rusty after a time (but so, too, does a Rolls-Royce), and of course they all cost a lot of money to keep in the proper manner, but it is usually worth it. At between five and ten years old such cars are usually bargain purchases, and I don't think anyone would regret this.

The best of all are those with vee-8 engines—350SEs and 450SELs, for example, to say nothing of the even more modern 380SEC and 500SEC coupés—the most fuel-efficient being the most modern light-alloy variety which came in with the 1980s. The only drawback is that vee-8 engined cas from Stuttgart all have automatic transmissions, which may take the edge off enjoyment for some enthusiastic drivers.

Incidentally, I hope I do not demean the name of Ferrari by listing one of its most desirable models as a saloon? The car I have in mind was intro-duced as the 365GT4 2+2 in 1972, grew up into the 400GT in 1976, then became the 400i in 1979 and eventually matured as the 412 in 1985. All are based on the same elegant, Pininfarina-styled two-door four-seater shell, with front-mounted vee-12 engine of between 4.4 litres (original) and 4.9 litres (final). Need I say more?

There is a very healthy list of coupés, some of which are already recog-nized as classic cars and some of which are still 'sleepers'. The most obvious of these, of course, are the various Ferraris and Lamborghinis.

Because of the well-known nature and quality of all these Ferrari types, I need do no more than mention the 365GTC/4 (a rather Daytona-like 2+2 seater), *all* the mid vee-8-engined 308 and 328 coupés and Spiders (the most desirable of all, it is generally agreed, are the Spiders), the charismatic mid vee-12-engined Boxers, and of course the sensational 1980s-style Testarossa. Very few people indeed can afford to run a Boxer, even fewer a Testarossa, as a 'toy'—what a pity!

The modern Lamborghinis encompass the front-engined and rather angular Jarama, the mid/transverse vee-8 engined Urraco/Silhouette/Jalpa family, and the simply stunning Countach supercars. Lamborghinis, some people say, are not as well built or as well developed as Ferraris—and there certainly isn't the same preservation cult at the moment. One day, though (and that is what choosing a 'sleeper' is all about), their high performance, their looks and their magnificent power plant engineering will become fashionable again.

For some reason, Maserati models have never attracted as much adoration as that lavished on their Italian rivals, yet some of their cars looked as good, and certainly went just as fast. Of the more recent models, the mid-engined Bora and Merak coupés are certain 'classic material', as are the front-engined Indy (1969-75) and Khamsin (introduced 1972) coupés. Except for the Merak, which had a 90-degree vee-6 engine, all had one or other version of the famous four-cam vee-8 engine, which was powerful, yet at the same time relatively simple.

The Audi Quattro, introduced in 1980, was the first of the modern-generation four-wheel-drive cars, and had a 140 mph top speed. It was also a great rally car.

I'm not yet sure that the Kyalami (which was really a re-engined and rebadged De Tomaso Longchamps), or its longer wheelbase, four-door version, the Quattroporte III, deserve classic recognition, though on scarcity grounds they are sure to achieve it one day. Somehow, too, the modern BiTurbo may be too common, and too bland, to attract attention for a while—but keep an eye on it for the time when other Italian prices have rocketed out of reach.

There are, of course, many other splendid coupés well worthy of recognition. First and foremost I must mention the Audi Quattro, which caused a sensation when it was launched in 1980 because of its modern interpretation of the four-wheel drive theme, and because of the colossal performance produced by a front-mounted five-cylinder 200 bhp 2.1-litre engine. It soon became an established rally winner, which confirmed its reputation as a go anywhere, do anything machine, and it has been built at the rate of ten cars a day almost ever since. Forget the fact that the Quattro's technology has now been overtaken by a host of more modern four-wheel drive machines—it was *first*, and important because of that. Most people could probably afford to buy an early 1980s Quattro today (there were no right-hand drive examples, incidentally, before late 1982), but very few indeed could raise the money to buy one of the 300 bhp Sport Quattro models, of which only 200 were built as rallying 'homologation specials' in 1984 and 1985, had short wheelbase versions of the 'normal' Quattro style, and were as fast and specialized as any Ferrari or Lamborghini. Like the Ford RS200, less than 100 will certainly be left by the time prices fall far enough, and they will be *very* expensive indeed to preserve.

Incidentally, if you are not only a car enthusiast but a masochist as well, you might consider the Citroen SM of 1970-75. The specification (Maserati vee-6 engine, front-wheel drive, typically Citroen powered-everything in the suspension, steering and braking departments, and a very cramped 2+2 seating layout) was exciting enough, and a top speed of 140 mph (224 km/h) was possible, but the complications, and the cost of restoration, can be enormous. Nearly 13,000 cars were produced, all officially with left-hand drive. They're cheap today, probably because *everyone* is frightened to tackle a maintenance job of such complexity. Worth a gamble?

No gambling is needed with the decision to choose one of the Mercedes-Benz SL coupés. This second-generation 'pagoda-roof' style, which took over from the original type in 1971, was so successful that it was built into the late 1980s, and was seen in a myriad different forms— long wheelbase, short wheelbase, two-seater, 2+2-seater, open or hardtop six-cylinder or vee-8 cylinder. *All* of them wil be classic one day, but the 'Best Buys' at the moment are certainly the vee-8 engined convertibles with the highest performance—which means choosing a 4.5-litre or a 5.0-litre example. None of them is cheap, nor ever likely to be. At

Top *There were many desirable Mercedes-Benz coupés in the 1960s and 1970s. This was the original two-seater 350SL, as launched in 1971.*

Above *Porsche's model range for 1979, with the front-engined, water-cooled 928 in the foreground. The 924 (left background), really no more than a Porsche-designed Audi coupé, sold well for ten years.*

least the Mercedes-Benz reputation for build quality was intact on these cars.

One day, too, the Cosworth-engined 190E 2.3-16 saloon will be accorded classic status, but while in production it was far too expensive for most people to consider.

Next there is Porsche, whose 911 family carried on into the late 1970s and 1980s (and now looks likely to make it into the 1990s as well!). Their

1970s offerings were based on two different families—the 924/944 breed and the 928 types—both having water-cooled engines mounted up front, driving the rear wheels, and 2+2 coupé seating.

The 928s, of course, have massively powerful vee-8 engines (the smallest is a 240 bhp/4.5-litre type. . .) and are all beautifully built, but you have to match the sleek looks, the colossal performance and the impeccable road manners against the high cost of ownership and the extremely sparse dealer network in the UK.

Some people call the 924 (which was introduced at the end of 1975) a poor man's Porsche, and some would like to deny its Porsche heritage altogether (much of the drive line is Audi-based, and its original concept was for use as an Audi-badged model), but the fact is that it is a relatively simple, conventional car which has been treated to the usual meticulous Porsche detail development over the years. Buy the ordinary 924 if you want 130 mph (208 km/h) Porsche motoring without needing a resident mechanic to keep you sane, but by all means buy the fastest 924 Turbo (170 bhp, and more than 140 mph (224 km/h)) if this attracts you instead. The mid 1980s 924S is still a new car on the Porsche scene, and will certainly become classic material one day.

The 944 of 1981 was effectively a 924 with a 2½-litre Porsche four-cylinder engine transplant, a more robust transmission, and flared wheelarches to signal the differences. Everyone loved the combination of performance (the same as the 924 Turbo), handling, quality and looks which were offered, and it is always in demand. The 944 Turbo of the mid 1980s was an even better car, but it would cost you a great deal more to keep it in shape for its old age.

Next I come to four pretty coupés, all with similar reputations—attractive to look at, with powerful and advanced engines but otherwise conventional front-engine/rear-drive layouts, and well-earned reputations for rusting away if neglected!

From Alfa Romeo of Italy there is a choice between the Montreal and the Alfetta Coupé/GTV models. The Montreal was announced in 1971 and was really a combination of a 2.5-litre 200 bhp vee-8 engine, new Bertone styling and an established (Giulia-style) floorpan and chassis. It was a fast car—the top speed was about 140 mph (224 km/h)—but it never really caught on, and only 3,925 were built in four years. A poor Montreal can be dreadfully scruffy, but these days they are cheap to buy, if not to run.

The Alfetta Coupé/GTV was Ital Design's smart transformation of the very ordinary-looking Alfetta saloon, with crisp lines and almost-four-seater accommodation. All had rear-mounted gearboxes, in unit with the final drive, and most had one or other of the famous twin-cam four-cylinder engines, but there was also the GTV6 from 1981, with the complex new vee-6 engine. They all look attractive, and there is a lot of performance and character, but it is going to take years to eliminate Alfa's

Introduced more than ten years ago, the 6-Series BMW Coupé still sells well. This is the fiercest type of all, the 286 bhp 24-valve M635CSi.

rust-bucket stigma. For the Alfa fanatic, however, the consolation is that asking prices are still very low.

The same sort of reputation has always dogged the BMW coupés. The six-cylinder cars of the late 1960s which culminated in the 3.0CSL were certainly very prone to rust, but the 6-Series models which took over in 1976 are really much better in every way. The joy of such a BMW is in the singing character of the overhead-cam engine, but the problem for BMW is that the classic car enthusiasts have still not taken them to their hearts. As with the Alfas, BMW prices are still low, and likely to remain so. To my mind, the largest-engined examples, particularly those with factory-approved M-Power fitting, are undervalued.

The same can certainly be said of the beautiful Fiat 130 Coupé of 1971-7, which used to be undervalued by the critics, and is now by posterity. The underpan, chassis and running gear were pure Fiat 130 saloon (and included a magnificent 165 bhp 3.2-litre vee-6 engine), but the four-seater body style was Pininfarina at its best. Except for the use of rectangular headlamps (four circular units would have been nicer. . .), I thought the styling was flawless. The problem at the time was that it had little charisma, and only 4,491 cars were sold in six years. *Definitely* a sleeper for the future. . . . I have an idea, too, that people will come to appreciate the rear-engined Alpine-Renault A310 models more as time passes. The basic specification first seen in 1971, featuring a backbone frame, a glass-fibre body and tail-heavy handling, is not outstanding, but this was a pretty car (the second, new-generation, machine is even prettier), and at least it can't easily rot away with the passage of time. The best A310s were

The Fiat X1/9 was launched in 1972, and was still selling steadily in the mid-1980s. Under that skin is a transversely-mounted mid-four-cylinder engine, and a very effective little chassis.

those fitted with the PRV-type vee-6 engine; these were phased in from the end of 1976.

Two other mid-engined Italian coupés will certainly be fully-fledged classic cars one day. Both were designed at the same time in the Fiat-Lancia stable and had similar layouts, though one was a commercial success and one was a partial failure.

The success, without a doubt, was the Fiat X1/9 range, first seen in 1972, of which nearly 200,000 cars have now been produced, which is one good reason why classic status will inevitably be delayed for a time; the

1.5-litre engined cars, introduced from autumn 1978, are the best bet, but all of them look quite a bit faster than, in fact, they are. X1/9s do most things very well indeed, for the good looks (styling by Bertone) are matched by the handling *and* the practical details—there are two luggage containers, for instance, which is remarkable for such a small car. Their only let-down is that their original reputation for being technically advanced was soon submerged under a rather namby-pamby or 'feminine' image. Don't worry—the car will make it, one day.

So, too, will the Lancia Monte Carlo, in spite of the fact that it was a miserable commercial failure in North America and was once withdrawn from production in 1978, three years after its introduction, so that Lancia could sort out the indifferent handling and braking performance. It came back, refreshed, in 1980, and was then built steadily until 1984. In all that time just 7,595 of these Pininfarina-styled machines were produced, all of which had attractive mid-engined styling, but all of which suffered quite badly from the dreaded Italian tin-worm disease. A Monte Carlo had a very similar transverse mid-engined layout to the Fiat X1/9, but every component was larger, and different, for the car was based on the 2-litre twin-cam engine/transmission power pack. It was a 120 mph (192 km/h) car when in good health, and I always marked it down as an unlucky car.

North America
This is a very short list, I'm afraid, which tells you a lot about the sort of cars which have been introduced in North America since the beginning of the 1970s, and about the taste, in general, of classic car collectors. In fact, I would choose a mere handful of the hundreds of models put on the market in that time.

First of all, there are the two later generations of Chevrolet Camaro/Pontiac Firebird coupés, which were mechanically no more exciting than the original 1960s types. The 1970s breed were most famous for their rugged, he-man styling, while those introduced as recently as 1981 had such startlingly sleek styling that they must qualify as 'sleepers' right away. They all had rather rust-prone steel body structures. For the enthusiast who likes a degree of exclusivity in his cars, however, there seem to have been so many of them. . . . At least that ought to mean that you would never have a spares problem!

Then there was the latest type of Chevrolet Corvette, which arrived on the scene in 1983, and which seemed to have everything. Not only was it the sexiest shape to come out of Detroit for many years (once of a day, I'm sure, Ferrari and Pininfarina would have been proud to own it), but this style hid a very advanced backbone chassis, all-independent suspension, power-assisted everything and a great deal of performance. Like all previous Corvettes it had a GRP body, which was corrosion-proof. In terms of refinement and breeding, several European coupés leave it standing, but in terms of pizzazz the Corvette reigns supreme.

Above *The 1980s-generation Chevrolet Corvette combines an advanced chassis with sleek styling and a rust-proof GRP body shell; it's an attractive 'classic' prospect for future years.*

Below *It was a miracle that this neat little two-seater coupé, the Pontiac Fiero, ever got through all the committees at GM, but it was launched in 1983 and has been a great-handling and pretty-looking success ever since.*

Once again, though, although it is rare in Europe, it is very well-known at home.

Except that I ought to make mention of the Cadillac Seville introduced in 1980 (the combination of Cadillac nose, Bentley Mk VI razor-edge tail and front-wheel drive will be irresistible one day), the only other American car in this list is the Pontiac Fiero. Here is a car which looks so good, and does so many things very well indeed, that I have to ask how on earth it ever slipped through the corporate net at General Motors without being rendered ordinary.

The Fiero was really an Americanized Fiat X1/9 in its layout. The early four-cylinder examples were much slower than the Italian car, but the later vee-6 engined versions not only performed better, but looked even more sensational. The other advance was the use of GRP composite panels over a steel structure, which should help its 'sleeper' status in years to come.

Postscript: the homologation specials

As I have already mentioned the British 'homologation specials', which were built in small numbers with competitions in mind, it is now time to line up the various European examples of the genre. Some have already achieved classic status (the Stratos and the M1, for instance), and by their very nature, all will eventually qualify. In each case, I will give the *official* count of numbers built:

Any such group of collectables must start with the Lancia Stratos (which was sometimes affectionately known as the 'plastic pig' because of its stubby, short-nosed looks). Some 492 of these cars styled and built by Bertone, were produced between 1973 and 1975, with mid-mounted 190 bhp Ferrari Dino 246GT engine/transmission packs in a rugged chassis and with GRP panels. Tiny, cramped, noisy and 'nervous' to handle on the road, they have a great deal of character and a growing preservation interest.

After the Stratos came the Lancia Rally 037 of 1982 (200 built), another mid-engined car with beautiful Pininfarina styling whose mid-section was from the Monte Carlo, but whose front and rear tubular chassis sub-frames were special. The 200 bhp engine was an in-line supercharged (not turbocharged) 2-litre twin-cam linked to a ZF transmission, but the road cars were very comfortable and acceptable machines, lacking only in luggage space.

The third such Lancia was the Delta S4, which superficially resembled the ordinary Delta hatchback but was entirely different underneath. Here was a multi-tube framed, four-wheel drive, mid-engined two-seater rally special, of which just 200 were made, which came complete with a 1.8-litre engine which was turbocharged *and* supercharged to produce 250 bhp in 'road car' trim. If you could put up with the busy noise of all those transmission gears, the S4 was a surprisingly good little road car, as fast

Above *The Lancia Rally 037 was designed as a 200-off Group B 'homologation special', but road cars are fast, pleasant to drive sports cars too.*

Below *Peugeot's 205 Turbo 16 was a 200-off 'homologation special' with a mid-mounted engine and only two seats. It was a very successful rally car and a very practical road car too.*

as any Ferrari on twisty sections though let down by bluff aerodynamics in a straight line.

BMW produced only one such machine, the M1, which was first seen in 1978 and of which just 450 were produced. Originally this was to have been produced by Lamborghini, which explains the typically Italian mid-engined tubular-chassis'd layout, but final assembly was eventually carried out at Baur, in West Germany. The 24-valve, twin-cam, 3.5-litre engine has since been used in other BMWs (the M5 and M6 models), but it was ideally suited to the Ital Design-styled M1, which was a real Super-car, could exceed 160 mph (256 km/h), and was as civilized as a Ferrari Boxer or Lamborghini Countach.

I must dismiss the two four-wheel drive Citroens (the Visa Mille Pistes and the BX4TC) in a sentence, as neither was competitive in motorsport and neither was attractive to look at. Both also offered very crude solutions to the question of a four-wheel drive installation.

On the other hand, I have no reservations about the Opel Ascona 400 and Opel Manta 400 models, both of which used the same front engine/rear-drive installation in lightly modified standard bodies. There were 448 and 236 cars manufactured respectively of these types. Having driven the Ascona 400 for long distances, I can confirm its habitability, and the torquey abilities of its 140 bhp 2.4-litre Cosworth-developed engine. At the moment these cars are surprisingly cheap, though very rare.

Lastly, there was the very appealing little Peugeot 205 Turbo 16, a car which (like the Lancia Delta S4) looked like a mundane little hatchback but was a real firebreather under the sleek skin; Peugeot built just 200 road cars during 1984. To enjoy driving a 205T16 you needed to wear ear-defenders and carry very little luggage, but otherwise this 200 bhp turbocharged 1.8-litre mid-engined machine was a real pleasure to use, in traffic or on the open road. I can vouch for this from personal, pleasurable, experience. Classic status must be assured because of the way the 'works' cars dominated World Championship rallying for more than two busy seasons.

Chapter 10

The European scene—a wide choice

In this section I would like to make a choice of sensible (if not always affordable!) cars which were built in Europe during the 'classic' era. This, let's not forget, covers a very long period, say from the 1920s to the mid 1970s. It isn't going to be easy.

I have to take a pragmatic British attitude. On the one hand this means that I refuse to include some strange family cars which somehow got themselves a reputation on the British market because of their idio-syncratic design, and on the other I see no point in talking about the rarest Bugattis, Ferraris and Pegasos, which never seem to change hands these days at understandable prices.

The problem with nominating European classic cars from a British view-point is that we sometimes feel differently about a model which is not 'native' to us. The Mercedes-Benz range of cars is a perfect example—we tend to revere the engineering of *all* of them, while in some parts of Europe a small Mercedes-Benz is treated as nothing more than a worka-day taxi. This works both ways, of course—for I am sure the British veneration of the Morris Minor is not at all understood by the Italians or the West Germans.

Compared with the British suggestions already made, my list of recognized European classic cars has an entirely different balance. In my opinion, there are fewer small family cars or quality middle-class machines worthy of preservation, and a very sparse selection of 'carriage trade' models, but there is a fascinating collection of sporting cars and a mouth-watering selection of Supercars.

After pausing to remind everyone that it is more difficult, and usually more costly, to run a European classic car than one originally built in the UK, here are my comments on the scene:

Small family cars

Far too many European cars have been overpraised in the past. I do not mean that they were all technically inferior, or worse built, than British products of the day, for this was definitely untrue in many cases. It is just that I see no merit in nominating a small car as a classic merely because it *was* small, recognizable or idiosyncratic.

Examples? Just because the Citroen 2CV takes such a unique approach to motor design, it does not mean it is worth preserving. Just because there were so many VW Beetles, this does not mean that it will ever be a classic car—personally, I have always thought Beetles to be noisy, badly packaged and hard to handle; longevity does not necessarily make *anything* a classic car. Just because the Renault 4CV, or the Renault Dauphine, was so successful, it doesn't deserve to be remembered by posterity.

I have only two nominations for a *British* classic car enthusiast to consider: the original 1930s-style Fiat 500 Topolino, and the original two-stroke engined Saabs.

The Fiat Topolino was introduced in 1936, ran on until 1955 (with a restyled body from 1949) and has been hailed by other shrewd historians as 'the first entirely new "baby" car since the Austin Seven'. In spite of what Fiat's own Fiftieth Anniversary publicity would have you believe, it was built around a separate chassis frame and had a tiny, 569 cc side-valve engine. Independent front suspension and a price of only £121 when launched here were great attractions, though the Topolino was really only a two-seater with extra space for willing children. Until an overhead-valve engine was adopted in 1948 it struggled to reach 50 mph (80 km/h), but it had enormous character.

The Saab 92 of 1950-55 was more distinctive than any of its descendants because of the original thinking which had gone into it. Before it started building cars, Saab was an aircraft manufacturer, and this influenced the style and structure of the 92. It looked strange, but was aerodynamically efficient, and had a transversely-mounted engine and front-wheel drive, yet that engine was a smoky twin-cylinder two-stroke unit of 764 cc. Top speed was about 60-65 mph (96-104 km/h), and handling was excellent.

If you want more performance, go for the three-cylinder 93 of 1956-9 or, especially, the 45 bhp Saab 750GT of 1958-9. After that came the 96, also three-cylinder engined, which was heavier, and suddenly more familiar to motorists world-wide.

Sports and sporting cars

Although Britain's budget-priced sports car sold in great numbers and made many headlines during this period, many fine cars were also produced in Europe and have attracted justified 'classic' reputations in recent years. An astonishing variety has to be considered, as complex as the best Mercedes-Benz models and as flashy as the VW Karmann-Ghia, as out-and-out sporting as the Alfa Romeos or as technically efficient as the German Porsche.

Since a lengthy period has to be covered, I think it best to survey marque by marque rather than decade by decade, and hope the model-by-model development of important cars becomes clear.

Among the affordable cars, the Alfa Romeo marque has one of the

Above *The Alfa Romeo Giulia GT style, produced for many years with several different engines, was beautiful and practical, though rust prone.*

Below *The 1950s-style Lancia Aurelia GT combined Pininfarina styling with a powerful vee-6 engine.*

longest continuous histories, and there are many fine cars to be collected today. Although I would like to have included the hand-built sports cars of the 1920s and 1930s, these cars now sell for ferociously high prices (the time to buy an 8C 2300 was twenty years ago. . .), and my story really begins after the Second World War with the twin-cam engined models, which were produced in quantity. In almost every case, a collectable Alfa has a unit-construction body/chassis unit, and the recurring bad news is that these all tend to be very rusty and cost a fortune to restore.

The 1900 four-door saloon, introduced in 1950, looked somewhat like an early Jaguar 2.4, and was a surprisingly effective sports saloon; the fastest type was the 115 bhp 1900 TI Super of 1953-5, but few remain in good condition.

In the next ten years, though, there were tens of thousands of Giulietta models, of various shapes and degrees of performance. All had the sensational new 1.3-litre twin-cam engine, and the most special, near-competition types had a five-speed transmission as well. A Giulietta has great *joie de vivre* (though you might find it lacking in sheer steam by 1980 standards. . .) and enormous Latin character.

It's best, I feel, to ignore the saloons, and go for the Bertone-styled Sprint/Sprint Veloce coupés or for the Spider/Spider Veloce cars by Pininfarina. 'Veloce' means 90 bhp and 100 mph (160 km/h) performance. Limited-production off-shoots which are even more collectable are the Giulietta SS (by Bertone) and the Giulietta SZ (by Zagato), both with 100 bhp engines and five-speed gearboxes; the SS looks more sexy but the SZ is lighter, more nimble and had an excellent competition record.

Ignore the 2000 and 2600 saloon/coupé/spider range (most people did, even when they were new. . .), and turn next to the Giulia range instead, which was introduced in 1962 and ran through to the 1970s. As with the Giuliettas, my advice is to look for coupés or spiders, not the very angular (some say ugly) saloons. The Giulia Sprint GT/Veloce and Giulia Spider/Spider Veloce models were by Bertone and Pininfarina respectively, and were sold in 1.3, 1.6, 1.8 and 2.0-litre engine form; coupés stopped in the mid 1970s, but the Spider is still with us. The Zagato-styled GT Junior is an intriguing alternative to the better-known models.

Just down the road in Turin are Lancia and Fiat. From pre-war days you really ought to consider the angular, but technically interesting, Lambda series, but the quantity-production Lancia possibilities really begin with the vee-6 engined Aurelia coupés and spiders of the 1950s, and should then go on to the 1960s-type front-wheel drive, flat-four engined Flavia Coupés by Pininfarina. There is no doubt in my mind, however, that the most collectable Lancias are the sporting, narrow vee-4 engined Fulvia Coupé and Fulvia Zagato models of the 1960s and early 1970s. The Coupé looks gorgeous, while the Zagato's appearance is, how shall I say, 'individual'; they share the same nicely-developed front-wheel drive chassis and nimble handling characteristics, and have vast reserves of Italian charm.

Prettiest of all the early 1970s Lancias were these 1.6-litre front-wheel-drive Fulvia HF Lusso coupés.

The best of a nice bunch are the HF and HF Lusso types, with 1.6-litre engines and five-speed transmissions, but even the less powerful 1.3-litre models can still beat 100 mph (160 km/h), and make you feel like an Italian racing driver in the process. Pity about the rust, the cost of spares and the general complexity of this period of Lancia, for these are very attractive little cars in every other way.

Although Fiat makes its profits by churning out millions of family cars (*small* family cars, at that. . .), over the years it has produced some pretty sports car as well. In the 1930s there was the sweet little Balilla Sport, which was head-on competition for the P-Type MG Midgets, and in the 1950s 114 vee-8 engined 8V sports cars were produced (now worth a lot of money, if only because of their rarity), but my choice of collectable Fiats begins in the 1960s.

I liked the neat Pininfarina-styled 1500/1600S Cabriolet range of 1959-66, but the only version fast enough is that powered by the OSCA-designed twin overhead-camshaft engine. The 1600S version had disc brakes from 1963, and a new five-speed transmission from 1965. In the words of one motoring cynic, it was 'almost a good car. . .'—rather let down by handling not as pin-accurate as that, say, of a Midget or an MGB.

850 Coupés and 2300S Coupés were much too standard, under the skin, to impress me very much, but on the other hand I was always a great fan of the 124 Sport Coupé and 124 Spider models of the late 1960s and early 1970s. They were built with 1.4, 1.6 and 1.8-litre twin-cam engines and (nearly always) five-speed transmissions for the first ten years. The first and second generations of Coupé were prettiest, for from late 1972 the facelift job didn't really work; the last was built in 1975. Spiders (from Pininfarina) got better looking as grilles, wheels and decoration

It might look like a vintage racing car, but this Type 51 Bugatti could also be used on the road.

If you aspire to owning a truly patrician car, the Rolls-Royce Enthusiasts Club will be delighted to hear from you...

Right To add to the competition at a concours, there is sometimes a 'suitable dress' event as well. This is Derek Green, his lady and his Lagonda M45 Tourer at the 1986 'Benson & Hedges' final.

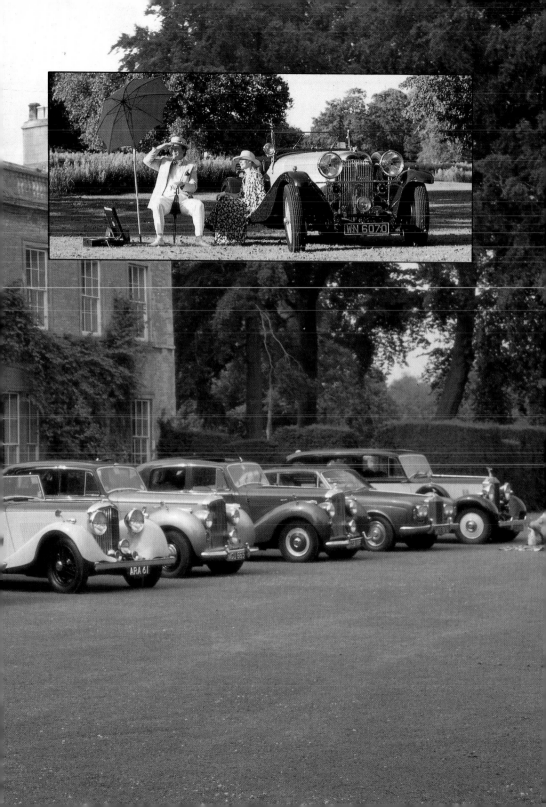

*Post-Second World War British rivals — the
Lea Francis and Triumph 1800 Roadsters.*

Styling by Pininfarina, engine by Ferrari, structural design by Fiat — the Dino Spider of 1966-73 (this is a 2.4-litre version) was an intriguing design.

improved, and a 2-litre engine was adopted from 1978. Pininfarina carried on making this body until the mid 1980s.

The most famous Fiat sports car, however, was the Dino family of 1966-73. This combined coachbuilders' styling (two-seater Spider by Pininfarina, four-seater Coupé by Bertone), a simple but rugged chassis by Fiat—and a four-cam vee-6 engine by Ferrari! Up to 1969 all Dinos had 160 bhp/2-litre engines and a solid back axle beam, and thereafter they had 2.4 litres, 180 bhp, ZF transmission and a new independent rear suspension layout. Unlike Ferrari's race-bred Dino of the period, which shared the same engine, this Fiat model family was thoroughly practical in all respects; more than 7,500 of all types were built.

Moving over the border into West Germany, the most important marque, of course, is Porsche. The easy way to summarize this company is to emphasize that *all* air-cooled Porsches are classics, but some are more classic than others. However, don't let the 'German-built' label convince you that these cars last for ever; on the contrary they are cars which rot away persistently, and can cost a lot to restore.

The first generation of Porsches was the Type 356 range, which ran from 1949 to 1965. All cars were based on the VW Beetle's underpan, suspension and running gear, but more and more Porsche parts were fitted as the years passed by. From 1955, Type 356A models were better developed than the original types, and I would always recommend you to buy a 1.6-litre model if possible. Steer clear of cars fitted with four-cam 'Carrera' engines unless you have a bottomless pocket and a personal engine builder. Coupés are most common, but the Speedster and Cabriolet derivatives are probably more desirable these days.

No-one, surely, needs to be introduced to the 911 family, which has now been on sale for more than twenty years? If you accept the facts—that

Left *All Porsche 911s are pretty, but when you add the massive rear spoiler and flared wheel arches of the Turbo, the attraction is even more obvious.*

Right *The mid-engined VW-Porsche of 1969 was also joined by this faster derivative, the 2-litre Porsche-engined 914-6. The styling was always controversial.*

early 911s could exhibit vicious oversteering handling if provoked, that their body shells cost a great deal of money to renovate from a rusty condition, and that your insurance company will hate you for buying one—then a 911 is everyone's typical classic car.

911s got better as more and more development took place, so my recommendation is that you choose the newest, largest-engined version that you can afford. Targa-styled cars are most desirable of all, but nobody seems to like cars fitted with the optional semi-automatic Sportomatic transmission.

The last Porsche built in the recognized 'classic' period was the mid-engined 914 series, of which there were VW four-cylinder (914) and Porsche six-cylinder (914/6) types. This was, and remains, a controversial machine, if only because they carried 'VW-Porsche' badges and because the styling was not to everyone's tastes. Functionally, it was a fine car, though the performance of the four-cylinder cars was disappointing. There were 115,600 of them but only 3,300 914/6 models, which explains the difference in so-called 'investment' values. If you find one of the very rare 916 types, buy it at once. . . .

There are several BMW models worthy of note, though surprisingly enough, the classic value of some is surprisingly low. BMW did not actually start making cars of their own design until 1932, but in 1936 they produced the splendidly modern 328, which had a tubular chassis, a powerful six-cylinder engine and independent front suspension. Bristol liked it all so much that they stole the engine design for their post-war cars. There were only 461 of these cars, so today's values are very high indeed.

After the war, BMW produced the vee-8 engined 503 (a 2+2 coupé), the

507 (a fast and sexily-styled two-seater tourer—only 253 were made) and then the Bertone-styled 3200CS, which spanned 1956 to 1965. All were big, ponderous, heavy, but extremely attractive propositions.

Then in the 1960s (and into the 1970s) came the monocoque-shelled coupés, first the four-cylinder 2000CS of 1965, then the 2800CS of 1968, and finally the limited-production bewinged 3.0 CSL of 1972-5. All had four-wheel independent suspension and 2+2 seating, with power gradually creeping up from 100 bhp to 206 bhp over the years. They *all* rusted very badly, which might explain why the classic values are still limited today.

There are no *affordable* Mercedes-Benz classic cars from the 1920s and 1930s, so we must jump ahead to the post-war period. Having rebuilt its shattered factories and introduced a new range of saloon cars, the company turned to sporty cars in the 1950s, and there were three distinctly different types in the next twenty years; one of them, the 300SL, belongs to the Supercars section of this chapter.

From 1955 to 1963 there was the 190SL, a smart rather than sexily-styled '2+0' convertible based on a shortened version of the 180 'Ponton' saloon car's underframe. Like other Mercs of the period, it had high-pivot independent rear suspension and drum brakes, and with a 150 bhp four-cylinder engine it could reach 105 mph (168 km/h). Nearly 26,000 were built. The 190SL's biggest problem was that it was made at the same time as the 300SL and missed a lot of the limelight. Quite unjustly, it got something of a 'call girl's transport' reputation at one time.

Next, there was the 230SL family of cars, which had six-cylinder overhead-cam engines and were built from 1963 to 1971. All types looked the same, but there were three different engines and model names—

The Opel GT is the only two-seater car to have been made by the West German company since the Second World War, and is all the more collectable because of that.

2.3-litre 230SL, 2.5-litre 250SL and 2.8-litre 280SL. There was no overlap, for the 250SL was only built in 1967 and the 280SL thereafter. All had that distinctive styling, with the 'pagoda roof' hallmark if the optional hardtop was fitted, and because times were changing, many were fitted with automatic transmission. Compared with the old 190SL there was a lot more performance, and because rear suspension was now by low-pivot swing axles the handling was much better too.

Somehow, the 230SL family got rather a 'lady's car' reputation, which hid the fact tht it was hugely strong and good enough to win the roughest and longest of rallies. Even today it is not considered as 'macho' as, say, an E-Type or a Big Healey.

Two other West German cars also qualify as classics in their own way. One was the 1950s Karmann-Ghia version of the VW Beetle (which in fact was all flash, and had very little performance but a certain amount of charm), and the other was the Opel GT of the late 1960s, which had a sweetly curved coupé body style hiding mundane Kadett and Rekord running gear. Opel didn't have the resolve to build the bodies of that car themselves—instead they were imported from a French coachbuilder.

The French themselves recognize rather more of their sporting cars as classics, but I must ignore notable machines such as the early Bonnets and Matras, and some pre-war sports cars, merely because they are virtually unknown in the UK.

The best-known French sports car of the inter-war period was of course Bugatti, and every one qualifies as classic, vintage (if pre-1931) or thoroughbred (if built after 1930). I really don't have to make any recommendations here, for popular opinion has it that every Bugatti is collectable. In the end, your choice will be limited by the price you have to pay—and that will always be *very* high. The best-known, and the most numerous, road cars of the period were the Type 57 family, some of which had stunningly attractive sports and touring bodies.

Incidentally, if you do set out to buy a Bugatti, don't expect to own a car which is easy to maintain (who was it who said that when you want to adjust the valve clearances, you begin by removing a rear wheel. . .?), and don't be surprised by the hard ride.

It is an interesting challenge for a competent mechanic to consider running any large Citroen, but the ultra-complex Citroen SM coupé (which was announced in 1969) was the most demanding of all. Not only was this car extravagantly long for the cramped four-seater accommodation offered, but it had a four-cam Maserati-built vee-6 engine to add to the aura. Add in all the expected hydraulic complexities of a 1950s/1970s Citroen, including self-levelling suspension and the wire linkages necessary to make *four* of the six headlamps swivel as the steered (and driven!) front wheels were turned, and you have a real conversation stopper. . . . Almost all of them were left-hand drive, but a handful have been converted to right-hand drive by a British engineer.

The Alpine-Renault sports cars, on the other hand, were in complete contrast—simple where the Citroen was complex, crude where it was sophisticated, and with rear engine/rear drive instead of front engine/front-wheel drive. A Citroen SM understeered at all times, whereas the Alpine-Renault, if shown a corner, would fling out its tail with gay aban-

The fabulous, and complex, front-wheel-drive Citroen SM of the early 1970s, complete with four-cam Maserati vee-6 engine.

don. An Alpine-Renault restoration is not at all difficult for the resource-ful enthusiast, as the backbone chassis is simple, the body shell is glass-fibre, and almost all the running gear is modified from standard Renault material.

There are three generations of classic Alpine-Renaults—A106, A108 and A110—of which the A108 and A110 types (built in Dieppe from 1957 to 1963, and 1963 to 1977) were always the most popular. A few were cab-riolets or rather stubby 2+2s, but the streamlined, cramped two-seater fastback coupés were the most desirable. The best of all were the late 1960s/early 1970s examples with 1.6-litre engines and five-speed trans-missions, for anything up to 125 mph (200 km/h) was available.

One day, maybe, we will look upon the mid-engined Matra Simcas of the 1970s and 1980s as classics, but for the moment they are too new. A 'sleeper' for the future, perhaps?

I now want to mention two sporty cars from Scandinavia, one a Saab and one a Volvo, the two being as different from each other as only a Saab and a Volvo could be!

To cater for the American market Saab produced the two-seater Sonett family between 1966 and 1974, a front-wheel drive machine using the Sport and V4's underpan and running gear, but with fastback coupé body styles in glass-fibre. There were three distinct types. Sonett II (1966-7), with a 60 bhp, 841 cc two-stroke engine, Sonett V4 (1967-70), with a 1½-litre Ford vee-4 engine of 65 bhp, followed by a completely restyled

One of the few genuine three-abreast sports coupés ever made — the mid-engined Matra Simca Bagheera of the 1970s. Left-hand-drive only, but a smart and 'different' little sporting car.

Volvo's P1800 sports coupé was built in several different guises starting in 1961, but for the last two years the car was produced as this smart 'high-performance estate' derivative.

Sonett III (1970-74), with 75 bhp/1.7-litre vee-4 engine. As with other earlier-generation Saabs, these Sonetts had a great deal of character, though they are virtually unknown in the UK.

Volvo's P1800/1800S family of coupés were much more conventional, much heavier, and much more like small saloons than sports cars. Production began in 1961 and ended in 1973. Styled in Italy (with a high waistline and a low seating position) and always using the four-cylinder engine and running gear of the 120/140 Series, these cars were carefully developed and equipped two-seaters with front engines and rear drive. Original cars were assembled by Jensen in the UK, but Swedish assembly (as the 1800S) began in 1963. They had two-litre engines from 1968, 130 bhp injected engines from 1969-70, and a Scimitar GTE-like sporting estate car restyle (as the 1800ES in 1971. All in all, 39,500 coupés and 8,100 'ES' models were built.

Middle-class saloons
The list of what I call classic 'middle-class' European saloon cars is considerably shorter than that of the sporting cars. Indeed, I propose to list only six different marques.

In spite of its famous name, I do not think that any Alfa Romeo saloon

The NSU Ro80 was the world's first series-production Wankel-engined saloon car. It had a twin-rotor unit which helped to give the car a 115 mph top speed, but there were big engine reliability problems to be solved at first.

(except the 1950s-type 1900TI, already mentioned) deserves to be called a classic, even though these were the products which kept the state-owned company out of the bankruptcy courts for so long. In almost every case the saloons had serious corrosion problems, and in every case there were coupé and Spider derivatives which were more appealing.

From West Germany there was one car which deserved every accolade except that of a reliability award—the Wankel rotary-engined NSU Ro80. The pity was that the twin-rotor engine tended to wear itself out very rapidly in the early years, which ruined the car's reputation later on even though the entire design had by then been considerably improved; the semi-automatic transmission was 'right' for the engine but not liked by everyone. The rest of the car—aerodynamic styling, front-wheel drive chassis and general innovation—was remarkable, and deserves to be remembered. Even today, though, values are very low—well down on that of a Morris Minor, for instance.

West Germany's other middle-class car makers, BMW and Mercedes-Benz, are remembered much more fondly for more conventional machinery.

As far as BMW is concerned, the classic touring cars include the 326 and 327 models of the late 1930s (which had much in common with the 328 which has already been recommended), the big and bulbous vee-8 engine 501, 502 and 3.2 models of the 1950s (which were related to the 503/507/3200CS types), and to a lesser degree the less common, overhead-camshaft monocoque saloons such as the 2002 Ti and 2002 Tii models of the 1960s and early 1970s. One late-developing derivative of this car which set many modern trends was the 2002 Turbo of 1973-4, which was Europe's first turbocharged saloon car to go into production.

Since all post-war Mercedes-Benz saloons have been well built and long-lived, many of them now qualify as classics. I hope you'll excuse me, though, if I ignore all the diesel-engined cars and all the four-cylinder engined machines. There were many highlights among many good cars. The 300/300S of the 1952-62 period, a car which combined a backbone chassis, all-independent suspension and a six-cylinder overhead-cam engine, was also distinguished by some splendid body options, including the most desirable coupés and cabriolets; this was the car which gave all its running gear to the legendary 300SL sports car.

The most distinguished of the 1960s crop were the 220SE and 300SE families of coupés and convertibles, which used the standard monocoque underbodies and running gear of the appropriate saloons but had much more flamboyant two-door coachwork. Don't expect me to list all the different six-cylinder engines *and* the early vee-8 engines used in these cars—it would be a brave author who tried to do that!

There was one quite stupendously fast saloon which deserves its place in the hall of fame—the 300SEL 6.3 of 1967-72, of which a mere 6,526 examples were made. This combined the luxurious early S-Class structure with the gargantuan 250 bhp vee-8 engine of the 600 limousine. It could do 134 mph (214 km/h) but only 15 mpg, and weighed 4,300 lb (1,950 kg)—what a car! Mercedes-Benz have been building splendid cars ever since, with several models already queuing up to become classics in years to come.

From Italy I cannot, in all honesty, include any Fiat saloons, and it is difficult even to include any Lancias. However, because they were so closely related to the famous sporting coupés and Spiders, I would like to make mention of the vee-6 Aurelia and the vee-6 Flaminia saloons of the 1950s and 1960s respectively.

In France, above all other machines I must nominate the Citroen traction-avant (1933-57) and the Citroen DS (1955-75) families of cars, both of which had front-wheel drive, and both of which were technically ahead of all their rivals when announced. Both types, of course, also rust badly and need ingenuity to restore and maintain, but their worth is recognized in many countries.

The 'traction' style was low and wide-tracked, but otherwise similar to other 1930s cars, and there were several different engines over the years. The most powerful, if not the best balanced, were the six-cylinder cars, and there was hydropneumatic suspension for the last two years. In the UK the *Maigret* TV series made it famous, years after its reputation was assured.

The DS19 of 1955, which went on to become DS21 and DS23 in later years, was quite simply the most advanced car in the world at the time, with front-wheel drive, disc brakes, all-independent hydropneumatic self-levelling suspension, high-pressure hydraulics, power-assisted steering, aerodynamically efficient styling, and quirky controls and instruments. Saloons and, eventually, enormously roomy estate car styles were offered. In France, there was also a two-door cabriolet by Chapron.

From 1965 there was the DS21, complete with new four-cylinder engine. Later cars had swivelling headlamps linked to the steering gear, and even later there was a fuel-injected version of the DS23's 2.3-litre engine. Do you still want to buy one?

In Sweden the Saab marque has many friends, but it is Volvo who provide the classic middle-class machinery. Pre-war models were all worthy but dull (except for the hideous, and thankfully rare, Carioca saloons), and the only interesting post-war cars were the PV444/PV544 and 120/Amazon series models. But not all of them, not by any means—the only collectable versions are the sporty two-door types, the sort which won Swedish, Acropolis and RAC rallies in the 1950s and 1960s. Leave all the rest to the environmentalists, the lentil eaters and the Friends of the Earth.

The carriage trade
Over the years, Rolls-Royce has had more competition from the United States than from European car makers, for at this level the only makes really to give the British company sleepless nights have been Hispano-Suiza and Mercedes-Benz.

Hispano-Suiza was a worthy and direct rival for Rolls-Royce in the 1920s and the 1930s, but did not make any cars after the Second World War. The vintage H6B actually carried on in production until 1938, although its great days were over after the depression. On the other hand, every rich collector should try to have at least one Type 68 Vee-12 model in his collection; the problem is that they are so valuable that few people can ever afford to indulge themselves.

The original Type 68 of 1931 had a 190 or 220 bhp, 9.4-litre over-head valve vee-12, a choice of wheelbases going up to an enormous 13 ft 2 in (4 m), and any number of magnificent body styles from the best coachbuilders in the world. The Type 68 Bis which followed had a 250 bhp/11.3-litre engine—it was no wonder that every such Hispano could beat 100 mph (160 km/h), and that it left the opposition gasping. The last such car was built in France in 1938.

At this level of the market there were three Mercedes-Benz models which are obvious classics, two being 1930s creations and one being a Rolls-Royce competitor of the 1960s and 1970s. All of them, officially or unofficially, were called Grosser ('Large'!), though some were more gross than others.

From 1930 to 1937 there was the Type 770 Grosser, which had a vintage-type chassis, beam front and rear axles and a 7.7-litre overhead-valve

The most complex Mercedes-Benz car built up to the 1980s was the gargantuan 600 model. Even in 'basic' form it was a very large car, but with long-wheelbase it was almost a boardroom on wheels. These days, though, they are much cheaper than the equivalent Rolls-Royce.

straight-eight engine which could produce up to 200 bhp when the 'optional' supercharging was brought into play. Most of the 114 cars built had seven- or even eight-seater tourer, cabriolet or limousine body styles, and all were heavy, thirsty, difficult cars to drive.

The second-generation Grosser of 1938-9 was a car bound up so completely in the story of the Nazi party that every surviving car seems to be advertized as being 'ex-Hitler' or 'ex-Goering'. Only eighty-eight were produced, for high party officials or for potentates, and many weighed up to 8,000 lb (3,629 kg) and could do 110 mph (176 km/h) but only about 5 mpg! The old-type engine had been boosted to 230 bhp, but a new tubular chassis had independent front and De Dion rear suspension. Many were at least 20 ft (6 m) long, some were armour plated, and most looked vulgar and vainglorious.

The 600 of 1963-81, of which 2,677 were built, was a much more practical machine whose design pre-dated the Rolls-Royce Silver Shadow in so many ways. It had a monocoque shell, all-independent suspension, a 6.3-litre vee-8 engine and complex hydraulics. Most examples had four passenger doors, but nearly 500 had much longer wheelbases, four passenger windows at each side, sometimes six passenger doors, and occasionally a landaulette top into the bargain! Compared with the Silver

Shadow the styling was more angular and, somehow, not quite so dignified. Strangely, in spite of the reputation of Mercedes-Benz it didn't sell at all well, and classic values are much lower than those of the equivalent Rolls-Royce. A bargain today?

Supercars

I have left coverage of these mouth-watering machines till last so that I might get a bit of vicarious enjoyment out of describing exotic cars which I am never likely to be able to afford. The marques to be mentioned almost choose themselves; only two of them, both 'USA-European mongrels', need any real justification.

Let's start with those two marques, which are Facel Vega and Iso, one French and one Italian. The Facel Vega evolved from a company which had been building bodies for other companies for some years. There were Supercars and others, but the others (Facellia and Facel III) had smaller engines, and are not really worthy of preservation today.

Three generations of the same basic chassis design—Facel Vega, HK500 and Facel II—were produced from 1954 to 1964, each with large-capacity Chrysler vee-8 engines. All had the same characteristic slab-sided styling, four seats (but two passenger doors) and top speeds of up to 140 mph (224 km/h). They were splendid *grand routiers* for autoroutes and motorways, but not nearly as manageable on minor roads. Even though the company was a body building specialist, the bodies rotted out badly and they have limited value today.

Facel Vegas were the most glamorous French Supercars of the 1950s and 1960s, complete with Chrysler vee-8 engines and very high performance. This was the Facel II model of 1964.

Neither is the Iso marque of 1962-74 all that well thought of today, even though the Grifo model in particular had startlingly sleek styling. All types shared the same type of pressed steel platform frame, with De Dion rear suspension and stable roadholding, and all had large-capacity Chevrolet vee-8 engines.

In my opinion, cars like the Rivolta, the Lele and the Fida all had disappointing styling, but there was never any doubt about the Grifo A3L two-seater coupé of 1965-74, which was graced by a beautiful Bertone style. Most had 5.3-litre engines and could exceed 160 mph (256 km/h); a few even had 7-litre power and top speeds of more than 170 mph (272 km/h). By comparison with the engine complexities of a Ferrari or a Lamborghini, this is an attractive thought for latter-day preservers. It's a pity that the steel bodies rot so badly, and so persistently.

The other 'USA-European mongrel' of the period was the Swiss-built Monteverdi, whose power came from Chrysler and whose body shells were supplied by Fissore of Italy. As you might expect, chassis frames were tubular and there was always De Dion rear suspension. Such Supercars were built only from 1967-77 and could be coupés, convertibles or even four-door saloons.

The sleekest coupé was the front-engined 375C (which was actually the original style), and the most exclusive of all was the mid-engined Hai 450SS (1970-76), which was a very rare machine trying (but failing) to outdo the Ferrari Boxer and Lamborghini Miura approach to building ultimte road cars. There isn't the same cachet as in owning a Ferrari, but then you don't have to pay as much for one either.

Before going on to review the Italian 'Big Three' there are two other, widely different 'Supercar Classics' to be listed, one being West German and one Italian. The Italian contender was the Alfa Romeo Montreal, which was actually sold in the early 1970s and was an unlikely-*sounding* combination of Giulia Sprint GTV chassis platform and suspension, detuned Type 33 vee-8 racing engine, and a rot-prone, two-seater body style by Bertone. It was a 200 bhp car which could beat 135 mph (216 km/h). Perhaps not E-Type performance, and certainly there were not many right-hand drive examples, but at about half E-Type prices it is surely some sort of bargain.

No-one has to make any excuses for the fabulous Mercedes-Benz 300SL of the 1954-63 period which, when announced, was probably the fastest production car in the world. Ferraris overtook it in later years, but nothing else ever had the attraction of the Gullwing model of the mid 1950s. Not only did it have those distinctive lift-up doors (which De Lorean was to copy so many years later) and a complex multi-tube chassis space frame of small-diameter tubes, but it combined huge performance (and over 150 mph (240 km/h) with the highest gearing options) with truly perilous over-steery roadholding in the wet. From 1957 the 300SL Roadster took over, without the unique doors but with low-pivot swing

The gull-wing Mercedes-Benz model of 1954-57 built, and still holds, the most phenomenal reputation. The more modest 'sister car' is the 500SL Roadster of 1981.

axle suspension and better roadholding; it was more efficient and more practical, yet people still pay over the odds for a 'gullwing' today. There were 1,400 'gullwings' and 1,858 Roadsters made, many of which survive to this day. You need a resident mechanic, or a deep pocket, to keep one in the right manner today.

The Italian 'Big Three' manufacturers were, and of course are, Maserati, Lamborghini and Ferrari—and I have listed them in my own opinion of rising importance. In general, all these marques exhibit the same characteristics as far as the classic restorer is concerned. They all have splendid chassis and excellent engines, but they are nevertheless expensive to renovate and maintain. They all have beautiful styling, but the bodies were usually panelled in steel and tended to deteriorate at an alarming rate.

Since such firms tend to generate new classics with every year that passes, I have quite arbitrarily had to draw my line in the early 1970s. By leaving Ferrari to the end, I am also ensuring that the First shall be Last. . . .

Maserati came into existence in the 1920s but built no road cars until 1946. The early A6G and A6G/2000 cars were fast, but very rare indeed, and I have not seen one for a long time. In addition the 5000GT of 1959-64 was a hand-built rarity (only thirty-two cars were made) which has almost disappeared today.

Since the mid 1950s, all the best classic Maseratis have used one of three engines—a straight-six twin-cam, a four-cam vee-8 or a four-cam vee-6—but there have been several different chassis. Compared with Lamborghini and Ferrari, the later chassis were of simpler design, which makes them a bit more practical for restoration purposes.

The first series-production Maserati was the straight-six engined 3500 model of 1958-66, which was produced with a fuel-injected engine from the early 1960s to become first the 3500GTI, then the Vignale-styled Sebring in the final years. To follow up this model there was the Mistral of 1963-9 (with 3.7-litre or 4.0-litre engine), the total production of this entire series being well over 3,000 cars.

The front vee-8 engined family of Maseratis began with the big four-door Quattroporte saloon of 1963-70 (which has very low classic values compared with the more sexy styling of the two-seaters), and on the same shortened chassis led to the rather conventional-looking Mexico and to the simply beautiful Ghia-styled Ghibli two-seater of 1966-73. The rich loved the Ghibli when it was on the market (1,273 examples, some with 4.7 litres and a 155 mph (248 km/h) top speed, were sold in seven years), and so do today's collectors. The Indy of 1969-75 looked somewhat like the Ghibli, but it was a 2 + 2 coupé styled *and* engineered by Vignale, with a unit-construction shell (which makes restoration that much more complex, and expensive); there were 1,136 of those cars. The Khamsin, Kyalami and Quattroporte II/III models are all too recent for inclusion here.

There was, of course, one splendid range of mid-engined cars with the same brutish Giugiaro style—the vee-8 engined Bora and the vee-6 engined Merak models. These had unit-construction body/chassis and all-independent suspension. In theory the Merak had 2 + 2 seating, but both were really two-seaters. Sales began in 1972, and the Bora's top speed was more than 160 mph (256 km/h).

The history of Lamborghini is much shorter, and financially more turbulent, than that of Maserati, for the first cars were not sold until 1964, and there were several changes of management (and backing) in the 1970s. Two types of engine are involved, the original four-cam vee-12 and the later two-cam *or* four-cam vee-8, and these remain in production, in modified form, in the late 1980s.

The first classic Lamborghinis were the 350GT, 400GT and Islero models, all based on the same ruggedly simple front vee-12 engined tubular chassis. The first cars were styled by Touring, while the Islero of 1968 was by Marazzi of Milan. The engines are fabulous (top speeds of up to 160 mph (256 km/h) have been recorded by the media), and the all-independently suspended chassis are good, but the bodies usually need lots of restoration work. Choose between the curvey, sensuous styling of the Touring models and the angular Marazzi-styled Islero—there were 393 and 225 cars respectively, and most people now favour the originals.

Lamborghini's only true four-seater was the Espada of 1968-78, which

Lamborghini's Miura was unique when introduced in 1965, and still turns every head today. Under that smooth exterior is a transversely-mounted vee-12 engine, mounted behind the driver.

had quite unmistakable Bertone styling, a platform chassis, and could beat 150 mph (240 km/h). Because it was never fully developed (the more exotic Miura (see below) always took precedence at Sant'Agata), and because it had a rather cramped, messily detailed interior, it isn't much liked today, but it still offers 150 mph (240 km/h) performance with a great deal of style; more than 1,200 were made. The Jarama of 1970-78 was a short wheelbase version of the same chassis, with 2+2 seating and *very* angular styling, and was even faster, but it made few friends, then as later.

The classic Lamborghini of all time was the remarkable mid-engined 4-litre Miura of 1966-73. Not only did it look so amazing, it was also the world's first transverse vee-12 engined road car which went, handled and stopped just like a racing car. It also made *every* Ferrari look out of date from the day it was released, and that is reason enough for buying one today! Chassis rot, bodies rot, and engine/transmission units cost a fortune to restore these days (but it *can* be done. . .), yet the 170 mph (272 km/h) Miura's appeal is unmistakable. There were three versions, the best of all being the final 385 bhp 400SV types of 1971-3.

(The later Countach is likely to be even more charismatic than the Miura, but as it is still a production car in the late 1980s its 'classic' status must wait a while. . . .)

Even though the mid vee-8 engined Urraco family had Bertone styling, it is not at all as popular as the larger Lamborghinis, probably because it was always overshadowed by the Miuras and, later, the Countachs. Even so it had '2+0' seating, and it was certainly fast enough (143 mph (229 km/h) for the P250, 158 mph (253 km/h) for the later P300 models). But there are some reputations which can never be rebuilt. . . .

The Ferrari marque is probably the best-documented in the motoring world, so very little explanation of the varous types is needed here. For the collector, however, it is always worth remembering that Ferrari, like Maserati and (mostly) Lamborghini, did not build its own bodies. These were produced by specialists like Scaglietti or Pininfarina, and even though these are illustrious names I have to say that in general they were all prone to go very rusty very quickly. Restoring a Ferrari engine usually costs a lot of money, but rusting a Ferrari body can be equally costly.

For many years all Ferrari production of road cars was concentrated on tubular chassis with front-mounted vee-12 engines. Sales built up very slowly from 1947, and although the 166/195/212 Inter family of 1947-53 is old, rare and desirable, it was the 250/250GT/250GT 2+2 cars of 1954-64 which sold in higher numbers and are now established classics.

In the same period there was a *very* limited series of America/Superamerica/Superfast two-seaters, some with engines of up to 5 litres and more than 300 bhp. Technically these were much like the 250GTs, but larger-engined and more powerful. Their scarcity makes them even more valuable today.

Any two-seater 250GT is a high-value classic, but some are even more sought-after than others. Expect to pay a great deal of money for short wheelbase Berlinettas and Lussos, and naturally expect to have to pay extra for a convertible style. Any or all of them should be good for 150 mph (240 km/h), if you can find the right piece of road.

To succeed these cars Ferrari produced a new chassis, with front engine, rear-mounted gearbox and all-independent suspension. This was used for the two-seater 275GTB/275GTB4/Daytona coupé family of 1964-74, the first two models sharing one style, and the Daytona having its unique shape. All had sleek, curvy styling and colossal performance, the Daytona being so powerful (362 bhp!) that it could reach nearly 175 mph (280 km/h) when flat out.

During the 1960s there was a confusing choice of vee-12 engined 2+2 and full four-seaters. The 250GT 2+2, (4-litre) 330GT and (4.4-litre) 365GT 2+2 models were all based on the original type of tubular frame, though the 365GT 2+2 had independent rear suspension too. The 330GTC/365GTC cars used the later '275GTB' type of frame with rear-mounted gearbox, whereas the short-lived 365GTC/4 was a unique hybrid. All of

The Ferrari Daytona, announced in 1968, is probably the fastest front-engined car ever put on general sale — it could reach well over 170 mph.

which goes to show that there is no lack of choice, or difference in specification, in the Ferrari range.

More affordable for those of us who do not have numbered bank accounts in Switzerland was the compact (Porsche-sized) Dino 206GT/Dino 246GT series of two-seater mid-engined coupés and spiders built from 1968 to 1974. Strictly speaking, according to the factory these were not 'Ferraris' but 'Dinos'—it was a fiction which the customers always ignored, and many surviving cars have had Ferrari badges substituted for the originals. All had the same robust tubular frames, all-independent suspension, transverse mid-mounted vee-6 engines and stunning Pininfarina-styled bodies. The 206GT had a 2-litre engine, the 246GT a 2.4-litre version of the same design, and all performed beautifully. They are much loved today, and probably worth up to three times as much as the equivalent Porsche 911.

Is that all, then, from the world of exotic cars? Certainly not—the 'sleepers' are building themselves a reputation at this very moment, and will certainly have to be added to this list in future years.

Chapter 11

North America and Japan— choose carefully

North America

Who was it who originally said that the British and the Americans were two great nations, separated by a common language? It might have been a flippant remark, intended to show up the way the English language has been modified in its passage across the Atlantic, but the result certainly has an effect on the cars we are considering in this book. My definition of a classic car built in North America is by no means the same sort of machine as some Americans would choose.

As I have already pointed out in an earlier chapter, according to the Classic Car Club of America a 'Classic Car' is one which that club chooses to recognize, and which was built between the years 1925 and 1948. This is a very restricting definition which the club might now have cause to regret, although in the 1950s when it was made, there was good reasoning behind it.

The dates chosen now seem to be quite arbitrary, for there have been several great American cars built, both before and since, and many magnificent machines world-wide both pre-date and post-date that period. I have never understood, for instance, why a 'Springfield' (US-built) Rolls-Royce should be eligible from 1925 but considered inferior before that date, why a Hispano-Suiza or a Bentley of the early 1920s should not qualify, and why one of the famed Packard Twin-Six (vee-12 engined) models should *never* qualify. The 1948 date, too, was only chosen so that the last of the original Lincoln Continentals (the 1940-48 variety) could be included. It doesn't make such sense to me, but perhaps if I lived in North America I would think differently.

Although I would be one of the first to agree that tens of millions of truly uninspired cars have been built in North America (though they fulfilled a need), I am also happy to pick out some amazingly different cars which can now be considered as classic. The miracle, these days, is that cars of character continue to appear. The concentration of USA car-making marques into four large groups, and total reliance on the 'product planning' process, has produced lots of look-alike/do-alike/be-alike models, some of which look as if they have been conceived by a computer. (Only recently, someone stated that a range of modern GM cars was 'one body style, and the clever use of a photo-copying machine'. . .).

In North America, and in Europe too, a great deal of nonsense is still talked about the cars which are designed in Detroit. In this case, therefore, more than in any other, I find it necessary to point out that there is a difference between 'classic' and 'flash': just because a car looked spectacular, or even bizarre, this does not mean that it has any worth at all. Far too often these days, at shows all round the world, an American car with fins, false wire wheels or rainbow-like colour schemes is paraded as a 'classic' of its period. It is not! Vulgar, yes, but classic—never!

Although the French and the Germans began building cars a few years before a motor industry was established in the United States, they did not enjoy dominance for long. As soon as 'can-do' American entrepreneurs got to grips with the technology of mass production and changed the motor car from a rich man's toy to a necessary adjuct to American life, production figures leapt upwards. By 1910, certainly, the USA was already making more cars every year than any other nation, and by the 1920s it was making more cars than the combined total of every other country in the world.

Over the years, an astonishing number of different cars, by marque, have been built in North America, which means, by definition, that I am going to offend *someone* by ignoring their favourite. Even eminent American historians disagree on these numbers, except that they certainly exceed 3,000! In her monumental encyclopedia, The *Standard Catalog of American Cars 1805-1942*, Beverly Rae Kimes writes:

> There are thousands of American automobiles here—steamers, electrics, gasoline cars, high-wheeled motor buggies, cycle cars, light cars, touring cars, taxis, assembled cars, grand classics, juveniles, racytype roadsters, streamlined experimentals, Doctor's specials, stanhopes, dual cowl phaetons. . . .cars that are magnificent, cars that are ungodly, cars that are, well, just cars. . . .

By the end of the 1920s and the period the CCC of A agree is 'classic' but which we Europeans call 'vintage', most of the one-offs and no-hopers had disappeared and the industry was settling down to dominate Detroit and the Michigan countryside around it. Three massive industrial corporations—General Motors, Ford and Chrysler—sold the great mass of American cars, with independent concerns like Nash, Hudson, Studebaker, Willys and Packard still significant and profitable. The most glamorous American cars of all at this time included the Auburns, the front-wheel drive Cords, Duesenbergs, Marmons, Pierce-Arrows and Stutz models.

The 'Big Three' all had several different marques to sell, spanning a wide range of selling prices. From GM, then as now the world's largest

If you ever found a genuine Tucker Torpedo (this is a 1948 model in the Henry Ford Museum), you would be envied by every other classic collector in North America.

car-making business, there was Chevrolet, Buick, Oldsmobile, Pontiac, La Salle and Cadillac. From Ford there was Ford and Lincoln, while Chrysler offered the Chrysler, Plymouth, Dodge and de Soto marques.

After the Depression, which erupted with the Wall Street Crash in 1929, the motor industry was hit hard, and during the 1930s nearly all the truly great cars disappeared. The balance of the industry shifted down-market, so instead of the Cords, Duesenbergs and Pierce-Arrows we saw the emergence of cars like the Mercury and the Lincoln Zephyr from Ford, and vee-12 and vee-16 engined models from Cadillac. Ford's indulgence of the period was the famous Lincoln Continental (now known as the 'Mark 1' because there were later 'Marks'. . .).

The industry's output expanded considerably after the war, but the number of different marques kept on decreasing. One attempt by the multi-millionaire shipping tycoon, Joe Frazer, to mount an onslaught on Detroit failed when the Kaizer-Frazer empire stopped building cars in 1955, even though he had bought up Willys in 1954; the only lasting result of that business was the famous Willys Jeep 4×4 vehicle, itself already agreed to be a classic. No other large new ventures even showed signs of succeeding.

Packard bought Studebaker before Curtiss-Wright bought the ailing group and eventually closed it down, and Nash got together with Hudson to form the American Motors group, which emerged as the fourth largest corporation in the business (with AMC, Hudson, Nash and

Rambler marque names in its line-up), though it was small even by comparison with Chrysler.

In the 1950s, 1960s and 1970s the four major corporations—General Motors, Ford, Chrysler and American Motors—all prospered, mainly by making more and more very similar cars indeed, though various marques continued to disappear. There were no De Sotos after 1961, no Hudsons or Nashes after 1957, no Packards after 1958, and no Studebakers after 1966; on the other hand, Chrysler introduced the Imperial, which was a success, and Ford introduced the Edsel, which failed ingloriously.

In those years manufacturers concentrated most of their design, development and marketing efforts on selling mass-produced family cars, usually large ones with four-door saloon or estate car bodywork, massive gas-guzzling engines, and almost always with automatic transmission, air-conditioning and soft, sick-making suspension. The only cars to exude a character of their own (which is something quite different from the non-existent character advertised for other models!) were the *very* rare sports models, and the more conventional machines which either had advanced engineering, exotic styling and equipment or extraordinary performance. However, in thirty years the only two-seater 'sports' cars to come out of Detroit were the original Ford Thunderbird and the Chevrolet Corvette, for the big bosses were convinced (and seemingly could consult figures to prove it) that a car needed at least four seats to make it saleable.

Until the astonishingly pretty two-seater mid-engined Pontiac Fiero came along in 1983, the only potential Detroic classics with advanced engineering were rear-engined machines like the Chevrolet Corvair (until, that is, Ralph Nader's book *Unsafe at Any Speed* crucified its reputation) and front-wheel drive monsters such as the Oldsmobile Toronado and its design-related derivative, the Cadillac Eldorado.

Before the new anti-exhaust pollution laws began to take effect there were many high-performance American cars on offer, but those which also provided better-than-average handling and a generous dash of charisma were the so-called 'pony cars' such as the Ford Mustang and the Chevrolet Camaro, the 'muscle cars' (of which the Pontiac GTO was a perfect example) and the limited-production NASCAR racing specials like the bewinged Plymouth Roadrunner Superbird.

For exotic styling, most enthusiasms were reserved for sporty cars like the Camaro, Firebird, Rambler Javelin/AMX and most up-market convertibles, or for the magnificent excesses of *any* Cadillac or Lincoln Continental. In addition, any convertible, even that sold as an option of a car that was never very popular when on the new-car market, would develop a following in later life.

For the European lover of classic cars, or even for the enthusiast who would like to buy a good-condition American car which does not have acknowledged classic status, there are two major problems: one is that of availability in Europe, the other is the price of such cars in North America.

As an example, let us consider the Chevrolet Corvette, which certainly qualifies as a classic car in any language except that of the CCC of A and the VSCC. Although these cars have sold in hundreds of thousands over the years (there were more than 28,000 of the original 1968 model-year Sting Rays, for instance), relatively few were ever sold in the UK or Europe. On the other hand there are ample supplies in the USA, but as the USA is so much more prosperous a country than any in Europe, and as the Corvette is an ongoing cult there, you would have to pay $10,000-$20,000 for a reasonable car to bring home—and then it would be left-hand drive and probably not road-legal over here. Then later on there is the question of acquiring spare parts and keeping such a car up to scratch. . . .

My advice for anyone smitten by the attractions of American cars is therefore to choose very carefully indeed, to make sure that the attractions of a glittering body style do not outweigh the more basic features, and to be sure that all the aggravation of ownership in later years is going to be worth it. Bear in mind, too, that the whole concept and make-up of an American car is different from that of a European machine with styling, straight-line performance and equipment generally being thought more important than elegance, handling and refinement. In other words, don't buy on the evidence of your own eyes, but be sure to take a good long drive *before* signing the cheque!

Naturally there are some amazingly desirable American-built cars, but those like the vee-16 and vee-12 Cadillacs, the Stutz DV32 and the early 1930s Duesenbergs fall into the 'expensive investment' category rather than being cars to own and enjoy today. You would buy a Corvette for driving fun, but you would buy a Duesenberg instead of a magnificent painting or a weekend cottage!

Here is my selection of the *sensible* North American classic cars which could be enjoyed on this side of the Atlantic:

General Motors
The corporation was founded in 1908, and by the mid 1920s it was not only a large and complex organization in the USA, but it had also bought control of Opel in Germany and Vauxhall in Great Britain. At this time most of the General Motors marques in the USA were dedicated to producing strictly ordinary, value-for-money motor cars. Chevrolet offered the cheapest models and fought head-to-head with Ford, while in order of ascending price and prestige there was also Pontiac, Oldsmobile, Buick, La Salle and Cadillac. Except that La Salle (a 'junior Cadillac' in all but name) was dropped in 1940, that line-up of cars, and that corporate pecking order, have continued to this day.

Until the 1950s Chevrolet had nothing exciting to offer, for all their cars had side-valve six-cylinder engines, but in 1953 they surprised everyone by introducing the Corvette. Not only was it the first sports car ever produced by Chevrolet, but it had a glass-fibre body shell and attractive styling.

Sales were alarmingly low at first (only 300 were sold in the first year, 3,640 in 1954, and 700 in 1955), but after the first restyle things looked up, and the Corvette has been a firm favourite ever since. There are five different types to consider, all with two seats and all with glass-fibre styles. The first generation (of 1953-5) was technically and visually the least exciting, but this was followed (1956-62) by a larger, more flamboyant, considerably faster machine; these cars had four headlamps from 1958 and up to 360 bhp with some vee-8 engine options.

From 1963 there was the Sting Ray type, complete with horizontal waistline styling, a choice of coupé or convertible bodies, all-independent suspension, and up to 435 bhp from 7-litre vee-8 engines. Then, for 1968, came the long-running 'Mako Shark' Stingray style, on the same all-independent chassis as before but with sleeker, lower body lines and even more performance.

This type was built until 1983, sometimes at the rate of 45,000 to 50,000 a year in the late 1970s. There were regular detail style changes, incorporating features like '5 mph' bumpers, and a fastback coupé, but throughout the 1970s performance dropped off as exhaust emission laws tightened. Then, for 1984, the stunningly styled fifth-generation Corvette was announced, and that car was immediately dubbed 'instant classic'. Not only did it have a magnificent body style incorporating a hatchback and lift-off roof panel, but there was an advanced new chassis with all-independent suspension and engines with fuel injection and other advanced features. The ride of the car built for the European market was bone-shattering, but no-one minded that. . . .

Also from Chevrolet was the Camaro, first seen in 1967. Also built to this day in the usual GM scheme of things, it had a close relative in the Pontiac Firebird (see below). The first-generation cars were GM's answer to the Ford Mustang (see below), and were fast, close-coupled four-seaters, though they looked quite ordinary. The high-spec. Z28 derivatives were best of all, for these could be turned into formidable racing saloons. The second-generation Camaros (1970-81) looked sleeker but were not as fast as before; they still retained a beam rear axle and steel coachwork, but they had no convertible option. As ever, the Z28 was the most desirable, and there were significant facelifts for 1974 and 1978. The third-generation Camaro/Firebird range was launched in 1982, with styling from the same inspired team which was also to produce the mid 1980s Corvette. These were smaller and lighter than before, with a hatchback body style, the largest engine being a 5-litre vee-8; the style will certainly outlive the 1980s.

The only other Chevrolet worth considering was the controversial rear-engined, air-cooled Corvair, and then only in its 1960-64 Monza Coupé/Spider forms (in which the handling was very spooky), or the 1965-6

Corsa Coupé (in which there was new rear suspension and *much* better handling).

There were no Pontiac models worth getting excited about until John De Lorean (yes, *that* De Lorean) rose to power in the engineering division. The first exciting car was the GTO, of which the first-generation (1964-7) and *early* second-generation (1968-72) models were fastest of all. But let's make no mistake about these 'muscle cars'. All the emphasis was on straight-line performance and hard ride as a substitute for good road-holding, for some GTOs had up to 360 bhp and tyre-stripping accelera-tion; on the other hand, you'd never accuse them of being refined, or civilized.

Then from 1970 there was the Firebird, a derivative of the Chevrolet Camaro and similar in most respects, though with its own unique engines. The first-generation cars, of which the Trans-Ams were the fastest and most collectable, lasted from 1970-81; then, for 1982, came the beautiful new cars already described under Camaro, distinguished by hidden-headlamp noses. Keep buying the Trans-Ams. . . .

All these cars look ordinary, however, by comparison with the Fiero, which was 'instant classic' from the day it was launched in the autumn of 1983. GM didn't deny that they had closely studied the Fiat X1/9 and the Lancia Monte Carlo before freezing the design of the car, for this was a neat transverse mid-engined coupé which made an immediate impact on its public. Apart from having a thoroughly well-developed chassis, the Fiero also had body skin panels of advanced composite materials. The original version was the 2M4, with an under-powered 93 bhp four-cylinder engine, but a vee-6 version with 140 bhp came along for 1985 to make the performance worthy of the looks. Having driven that car, I can assure everyone that this is the most European American car I have ever sampled.

For years and years Oldsmobiles were middle-class, middle-price GM cars, slightly more expensive and desirable than the Pontiacs, slightly less so than the Buicks—but for 1966 their engineers astonished the world with the new front-wheel drive Toronado. Not only because of its very advanced mechanical layout (which featured Morse chain drive from massive 7-litre engine to automatic transmission), but also because of its smooth four-seater coupé styling, the Toronado was a critical success right from the start; a year later there was a Cadillac equivalent, the Eldorado (see below).

There have been front-wheel drive Toronados ever since then—they got progressively larger, thirstier, more ponderous and more angular until 1977, then got smaller but remained angular thereafter—but only the rounded, first-generation coupés are truly collectable. The front-drive, incidentally, is more of a curiosity than an engineering advantage, for the suspension has always been very soft, the tyres not at all as grippy as a European would wish, and the accent more on what the Americans call 'personal motoring' than on sporting character, but for many years it was so very different from anything else being built in Detroit that it simply had to be considered as a classic. There are small, but significant, quantities of these interesting cars in Europe.

The only Buick car worth even considering was the original Riviera of 1963-5, and this was purely on the grounds of its sleek, two-door four-seater coupé body style and its slightly larger successor offered for 1966 and 1967.

On the other hand, there was usually something to enthuse about from Cadillac. Once you come to terms with the fact that a Caddy is the largest, most expensive, most flamboyant General Motors car, that it is styled and built for wealthy Americans, and that equipment and pizzazz is more important than road behaviour, its virtues become more and more clear. In spite of what its fanatical followers would have you believe, a Cadillac is *not* as well built as a Rolls-Royce or a Mercedes-Benz, but by Detroit standards it is, and always has been, the most carefully assembled car of all.

Sixteen and twelve cylinder models had surprisingly ordinary chassis and coachwork, but because their engines were so extraordinary they all sell for huge amounts of money these days. Don't even consider buying one unless you can spend as much again on maintenance in the years to come.

On the other hand, almost any of the Series 62 and Series 70 models, of whatever post-war model year, are well thought-of American cars, the most desirable of all being convertibles, coupés or those amazing long wheelbase limousines. Tail fins grew progressively larger in the 1950s, reaching their greatest height in 1959—you might like that sort of thing.

Save your dollars, however, for the front-wheel drive Eldorado models, especially the originals built from 1967 to 1970, for these combine the same basic chassis engineering of the Oldsmobile Toronado with sharp-edged Cadillac styling, and of course their own designs of vee-8 engine which peaked at 8.2 litres and 400 bhp (all driving the front wheels, don't forget!) in 1970. As with the Toronados, Eldorados with front-wheel drive are still with us, but it is the earlier cars, and the 1970s convertibles, which are the most desirable machines today.

Ford—which includes Mercury and Lincoln

As everyone surely knows, Ford's massive financial reserves and market penetration were founded on the incredible sales record of the Model T, which breathed its last in 1927. Even though more than fifteen million of these cars were built in nearly twenty years, survivors are quite rare today and are not only considered 'vintage' but 'classic' by some enthusiasts.

Ford bought up Lincoln in 1922 and allowed it to retain its individuality for many years, before inventing the Mercury (1939) and Lincoln Zephyr (1936) marques to make more of a corporate fight with General Motors.

The model on which the Ford dynasty was built — the Model T. Surprisingly, this is not at all rare these days, so it isn't a very desirable collector's car.

The fact is, however, that Ford (under Henry I before the Second World War, and Henry II afterwards) tended to stick to building lots of conventional cheap cars, aiming to sell to the mass of American buyers rather than the sportsmen or the individualists.

Apart from the original V8 models there were really no collectable pre-war Fords, and Dearborn was also a dull place to be until 1955, when the first Thunderbird was shown. The original type was a direct competitor to Chevrolet's Corvette, and outsold that car completely in its three years as a two-seater convertible model with optional removable hardtop. The separate chassis, powerful vee-8 engines and automatic transmission were all out of the company (Fairlane, particularly) parts bin, but the steel body was crisply styled and quite unmistakable.

After that the Thunderbird became the 'Squarebird' and was not at all desirable, yet many were, and still are, sold. Not even the Americans, however, would call the 1960s and 1970s variety classic; in the 1980s,

Left *The Thunderbird was introduced in 1955, and soon made its mark as a very classy little two-seater model. It was available in open or coupé form — this is a 1956 model with those well-known 'portholes' in the hardtop.*

Right *The most successful of all Ford's 1960s new cars was the Mustang, a car which invented the 'pony car' era. This fastback version, introduced in 1965, is now one of the most desirable of several well-liked Mustangs.*

though, with their rounded styling and NASCAR racing record, there are signs of a renaissance.

The most charismatic Ford car of the post-war period, without a doubt, was the Mustang, whose concept is generally credited to Lee Iacocca, although several other ex-Ford personalities are now ready to take the credit! (Read the latest 'tell-all' biographies if you want to get the background.) Whatever, this amazingly successful concept, first seen in 1964 and built in larger, more powerful and more flamboyant form until 1973, when it was dislaced by the smaller and less exciting Mustang II, captivated America's younger generation and sold in huge numbers. The first million were completed in less than three years, which was excellent even by Detroit's high standards.

All such Mustangs had conventional chassis engineering with a big choice of engines, transmissions and options. The six-cylinder base-model cars were very boring, but the broad-shouldered vee-8s were another proposition. There were notchback coupés, fastback coupés and convertibles, all with four seats, the most powerful of all having up to 7 litres and 390 bhp. There were major restyles for 1969 and 1971, with the cars getting larger all the time. To many eyes the fastback 1971 example was the most elegant of all such cars. The best of all the mainstream cars were the Boss and Mach 1 derivatives of 1969 and 1970, which hit the streets just before exhaust pollution laws began to strangle the engines.

For every Mustang of this period there was an equivalent Mercury Cougar, and though most were as fast, and all were better equipped, none seemed to have the same charisma.

One must not, however, forget the Shelby GT-350 and Shelby GT-500 derivatives of the 1965-70 Mustang models, which had 4.7/4.9-litre and 7.0-litre vee-8 engines respectively. Carroll Shelby, already famous for his work on the AC Cobra and with the GT40 race car programme, further modified high-specification Mustangs with hotter engines, sturdier trans-

missions, better brakes and suspension and special striping jobs. Measure their production in thousands a year rather than hundreds of thousands, and you can soon see why these cars attract premium prices. . . .

In the 1920s and 1930s the classic Lincoln had a vee-12 cylinder engine (the Lincoln, rather than the cheap-and-cheerful Ford/Zephyr unit which followed), but the Lincolns which everyone remembers, and considers classic, are the several series of Continental Mark models (as the Americans like to call them). Some, incidentally, did not *officially* carry 'Lincoln' badges, being called 'Continental' in their own right.

Henry Ford's son, Edsel, inspired the original Mark, which had a sportier version of the Zephyr's vee-12 engine and was made from 1940 to 1948 (with a four-year break during the war years). Only 4,988 of these four-seat coupés or cabriolets were produced, this and their undoubted elegance ensuring desirability in later years.

The Continental Mk II of 1956-57 was a debadged Lincoln with a 300 bhp vee-8 engine and unique close-coupled four-seater styling, but it didn't sell at all well, and there was then an eleven-year gap before the Continental Mk III of 1968-71 came along. According to legend, Ford's Lee Iacocca asked for a Thunderbird with a Rolls-Royce grille—the result was a long, low, extravagantly dimensioned four-seater coupé, with a huge bonnet seemingly large enough to land a helicopter on. It was all in the best over-the-top Detroit tradition, aimed squarely (and success-fully) at the Cadillac Eldorado market. The Continental Mk IV of 1972-6 was bigger, larger-engined and thirstier than the Mk III, but with less accommodation than before, while the Continental Mk V of 1977-9 was a lighter restyle of that gargantuan machine. Thereafter, the cars were down-sized, and lost their charisma.

Chrysler Corporation
Walter P. Chrysler had already made his name (and his fortune) at Buick

and Willys before setting up his own business. The first Chrysler car was launched in 1924, and by the 1930s the group had expanded to include several different marques. Without any doubt, the most famous 1930s model was the unit-construction, 'aerodynamically styled' Chrysler Airflow, but the public hated its looks, and it looks even more bizarre today; in the best badge-engineering tradition there was also a De Soto Airstream version, this being just as bizarre as the Chrysler.

My American friends assure me that some of the post-war Chrysler 'woodies' are worthy of mention (there now, I've mentioned them. . .), and that *any* of the C300 models built between 1955 and 1965 are classics, but from this side of the Atlantic I think that only the following are collectable:

Chrysler's most interesting 'muscle cars' of the late 1960s were the Dodge Charger and its related model the Plymouth Road Runner, of which the 1968-70 Charger was the most exciting of all. As used in NASCAR racing (and by the *Dukes of Hazzard* TV series), the Charger was an engine-bellowing, tail-swishing extrovert with sensational styling and immense performance if the 425 bhp 7-litre 'hemi'engine was fitted.

The most extreme example of this genre was the Dodge Charger Daytona of 1969 (505 cars built), or its look-alike sister the Plymouth Road Runner Superbird of 1970 (1,920 cars produced). These extraordinary NASCAR 'homologation specials' are certainly classic, because of their rarity and their single-minded design intentions. Not only did they have a choice of 7.2-litre/375 bhp or 7.0-litre/425 bhp 'hemi' vee-8 engines, but onto the sleek Charger style was added a long needle-nose extension and a large rear aerofoil mounted high on pylons above the rail. These cars were so successful in racing that they were banned after a couple of seasons!

By comparison with these machines, the Dodge Challengers and Plymouth Barracudas were tame, unsuccessful Mustang competitors.

American Motors
This group, the fourth largest of the Detroit car-building combines, always struggled to remain profitable and to stay alive, and for many post-war years they relied on the ubiquitous Jeep to subsidize the slow-selling cars. The Jeep, like the Land-Rover, has generated a following all of its own, though it seems that the genuine ex-military 'GPs' (which means those of Willys or Ford manufacture) have a greater following than the slightly more civilized peace-time developments of the same design.

American Motors cars have included some controversially styled (perhaps it isn't fair to call them ugly!) machines, such as the Gremlins and the Pacers, but for a short time in the late 1960s they had a family of coupés which are worth preserving today. The originator was the very smart Javelin coupé of 1968-70, which was a four-seater 'pony-car' competitor for Mustang/Camaro sales, just as conventional as its rivals, but with six-cylinder and vee-8 engine options up to 340 bhp. AMC, however, were rather unlucky in not selling as many as they should, for Mustang-mania was at its height, and GM could sell so many more Camaros through so many more dealers. The same basic body shell was retained until 1974, though larger and more bulbous on the same structure and not nearly as attractive.

Even more special (only 19,134 were built) was the AMX of 1968-70. Effectively, this was a 12-in (0.3 m) shorter wheelbase version of the Javelin (perhaps 200 lb (90.7 kg) lighter), with only two seats, the same vee-8 engine options (no sixes) and altogether tighter, more sporting handling and behaviour than the Javelin itself; it was a car I particularly enjoyed driving on a visit to Detroit in 1968.

Studebaker, later Avanti

The last car in my list of American 'collectables' is that long-running, low-production phenomenon, the Avanti. In post-war years there had been a number of strikingly styled Studebaker family cars from South Bend, Indiana (with shapes provided by the Loewy studios), but no sporty cars at all. Suddenly, when the Studebaker corporation's finances were already rocky, and when its image was as dull as ditchwater, the company produced the Loewy-styled Avanti coupé. Like most new Studebakers of the period this was cobbled up from existing resources, being based on the Lark Convertible's chassis with beefed-up suspension

The Studebaker Avanti, styled by the Loewy Studio, came too late to save the South Bend company's fortunes, but it lived on as the Avanti II until the mid-1980s.

and the existing 4.7-litre vee-8 engine (though up to 335 bhp and optional supercharging were available), but with disc brakes and a sensationally sleek four-seater coupé style, the body being constructed from glass-fibre.

In Studebaker form, only 4,643 cars were built before South Bend assembly closed down. Studebaker passenger car production was then concentrated in Canada, but the Avanti was abandoned. Two years later the design was resurrected, under private ownership, as Avanti II, looking just the same, but powered by Chevrolet Corvette engines of 300 bhp and up to 5.7 litres. In that form, little changed except in detail (it was once described as the 'Best kept secret in the American motor industry'. . .), it was produced in antediluvian surroundings at South Bend until 1986 when the business finally folded. No more than 100-200 Avanti IIs were ever made in a full year.

The two great joys of Avanti motoring are that they really are *very* rare, especially in the wide-open spaces of the USA, and of course they have corrosion-proof bodies.

Japan

Although the Japanese motor industry has risen so rapidly in the last thirty years, it has produced very few memorable cars for enthusiasts to want to keep, cosset and enjoy driving. For many years, indeed, the industry concentrated on building millions of ultra-ordinary, but ultra-reliable family cars, many of which were quite obviously copied from the European or North American competition. Even so, one has to be impressed by a nation which restarted from scratch in 1945 and worked, and worked, and worked—such that annual car production exceeded 5 million in 1976, and reached 7.6 million ten years later.

In the early and mid 1980s, more and more interesting and sporting cars were revealed (cars like the mid-engined Toyota MR2 and the latest front-wheel drive Toyota Celica are sure to be considered 'classic' in the 1990s), but this followed a long period in which there was very little indeed on offer:

Datsun

The Nissan Motor Co. Ltd was founded in 1933, building some very dreary cars indeed, and it was not until 1962 that the first true sports car, the Fairlady 1500 SP310, went on sale. This was replaced by the more angular, still mechanically conventional 1600 SP311 in 1966, and a larger-engined version (2 litres) was the SR311 in 1967; 40,000 of the '311' family were made, but they have now sunk without trace.

From 1969, however, there was the famous 240Z family, with a shape originally inspired by the West German, Albrecht Goertz—and there have been 'Z-Cars' ever since. I ought to state, right away, that for many years these cars were Datsuns in some markets and Nissans in others, some called 'Fairlady' at home but never overseas, and with different engine

The Datsun 240Z of the early 1970s was usually nicknamed the 'Z-Car' — it was a great road car, and successful in rallying too.

options available in different markets. In every respect, however, they were great sports cars with great character. It was as if Nissan had bought and studied an Austin-Healey 3000, added their own new styling, ruthlessly developed all the obvious Big Healey faults out of the result, and put it on sale. 'The Big Healey lives. . .' was a regular response to the Z-Cars—except that no such BMC car ever had independent rear suspension, such elegant shark-nose styling, or such useful accommodation. Nor did the BMC car have an overhead-camshaft engine or a five-speed gearbox.

According to all the facts and figures, the fastest and 'purest' Z-Cars were the 2.4-litre 240Zs of 1970-73, for the 2.6-litre 260Z which followed (1973-8) had a larger engine which did not rev, or breathe, as well. On the other hand there was a useful long wheelbase 2 + 2 version of the 260Z which made a lot of friends, and there is also no doubt that the later versions of this family (there was a 2.8-litre 280Z version sold only in the USA) were better developed and more refined than the originals.

As you might expect from the diligent Japanese engineers, this family of Datsuns went well, handled well and was potentially reliable; strangely, it was also rust-prone, the result being that many early Z-Cars have been scrapped.

The second-generation model was the 280ZX, sold as a two-seater or as a 2 + 2. Built on an entirely new chassis and structure, it was even less

Second-generation Datsun Z-Cars 'went American', as this study of the Targa 2 + 2 type confirms. My guess is that these will never be true collectors' cars.

sporting than before, heavier, and less fuel-efficient; one plus-point was the option of a 'Targa' version with lift-out roof panels. That car, and the 3-litre vee-6 engined 300ZX which followed in 1984, have yet to make any sort of impact on the classic car market.

Honda
In the beginning Honda made its name with motor cycles, and its original four-wheeler, a tiny two-seater sports car, was unveiled in 1962. The first production cars had 531 cc and 606 cc engines, but from 1966 the first 791 cc S800 models were delivered to Britain and other European countries. A fastback coupé version of the style was also put on sale. On the one hand, the Sprite/Midget-sized machine had neat styling, and the 70 bhp (gross) twin overhead-camshaft engine specification was exciting, but it had to be revved to 8,000 rpm to produce all its performance; neither was it very reliable, and in old age it could be expensive to maintain, so its classic reputation is still somewhat mixed. There were no more British imports after 1970.

In the years which followed, there were many successful Hondas, but none has shown any tendency to develop into a classic.

Mazda

Most people forget, but at Mazda there *was* some sporting life before the arrival of the RX-7. Mazda started building cars in 1960, and took up a development licence for the new Wankel rotary engine in the same year. Once committed to a production programme, Mazda stayed faithful to the Wankel engine, in spite of problems in getting reliability or meeting tough emissions regulations, and have had rotary-engined cars on sale for the last twenty years.

Their stabilizer was the Cosmo Sport, which was also known as the 110S, a two-seater hardtop coupé looking for all the world like a cross between Japanese and USA design thinking; it was the world's first Wankel-engined sports car. This was a technically fascinating machine, whose 110 bhp twin-rotor engine (nominally of 2-litres capacity) helped to produce a 115 mph (184 km/h) top speed (so the aerodynamics must have been reasonable), and there were front wheel disc brakes and De Dion rear suspension. As far as is known, only one car reached Great Britain, and the Cosmo was a limited-production machine by any standards. Even so, if you found one with its rotary engine intact, *of course* it is a classic.

It was a long time before Mazda tried again, but their next collectable Wankel-engined car was, of course, the very pretty RX-7, which was called the Savanna in Japan. Launched in 1978 and built in hundreds of thousands until 1985, this was an unmistakably styled two-seater coupé complete with 2.3-litre (nominal) engine and a five-speed gearbox. At first with 105 bhp, these cars had 115 bhp from 1981, they were good for up to 120 mph (192 km/h), and in some respects they were head-on competitors for cars like the Porsche 924 or (in the USA, where prices were more equal) the Triumph TR7.

You only have to look at the shape and study the specification (the rear window doubling as a hatchback, four-wheel disc brakes from 1981, and an automatic transmission option for USA-market cars) to see why the cars already have classic status. The second-generation RX-7, which appeared in 1985, was an even better car in all respects, and should also be in great demand as it grows gracefully older.

To emphasize what I recommended concerning American cars, a European should only buy a Japanese car as a classic, or potential classic, if he is convinced that he can gain access to spare parts and restoration expertise when he needs them. The Cosmo, for instance, might be an intriguing rarity, but I doubt if *any* spare body parts are now available; on the other hand, there are thriving one-make clubs looking after Datsun Z-Cars. It's better to ask around regarding support *before* you take the plunge into the exotic, oriental unknown.

Chapter 12

'Classic' hobbies—racing, rallying, concours or clubs?

Now that you have chosen your classic car, serviced it, repaired it and maybe restored it to as-new condition, what are your plans? Surely you bought the car with something in mind?

There are some people, of course, who get carried away by the opportunity to buy an older car, and rush into purchase without really having a reason for doing so. Because it was the glamour, or the rarity, of a particular car which prompted the deal in the first place, the 'it seemed like a good idea at the time' principle often applies. Those, unfortunately, are the people for whom the entire classic car scene soon palls, and it sometimes results in a valuable car being tucked away again to carry on rotting. They have my sympathy, for they will usually have wasted a lot of their time, and money, along the way.

I doubt if many people buy a classic car to use as everyday transport these days, and in my opinion they have almost certainly been unwise to do so. Those who do have presumably convinced themselves that modern motoring, in modern cars, doesn't suit their life style, and that an older car, with older engineering and obsolete safety standards, suits the overcrowded driving conditions of daily life. I have already commented on their decision in an earlier chapter, so at this point I need only guess that they are in a tiny minority of owners, and leave them to their commuting problems.

The vast majority of classic car owners are enthusiasts, and want to use their cars as part of a hobby. As with all hobbies, that of owning and enjoying a classic car can be a pleasant pastime or an obsession, a cheap and cheerful diversion or an expensive proposition. Fortunately there is such a choice of activities that an owner can spend just as much time, and money, as he can afford.

Everything should really start with membership of the appropriate one-make club. In fact, if you have read my earlier comments on restoration and preservation, and agreed with them, you will have become a member even before the car is ready to be used. Every one-make club, of course, exists to help its members keep their cars on the road, to preserve and supply technical literature and advice, and to find, preserve, and sometimes remanufacture parts. You will probably have benefited from these services while you were at the restoration stage.

In many cases, one particular make or model of car is only served by a single one-make club, but in other cases you may be faced with a bewildering choice. That choice, in fact, is good news for you; in many cases one club will concentrate on one aspect of classic car ownership, and another so-called 'rival' club will concentrate on another.

British examples of this include the two major MG and Jaguar clubs. The MG Owners' Club concentrates on the practical side of MG ownership, features special insurance schemes, approved suppliers, and sells a whole range of MG-orientated accessories. The longer-established MG Car Club offers much more sporting activity in the form of race meetings and other competition activity, while also offering practical and technical help.

Of the two Jaguar clubs, the Jaguar Car Club was once the 'official' factory-supported organization, and is more of a sporting and social club than one for the oily-handed brigade. The Jaguar Enthusiasts' Club, on the other hand, came into existence more recently and is interested primarily in the practical and restoration side of things.

If you have enough money to spend on membership fees, by all means join every club which covers your car, at least for the first year or so, but otherwise take advice from friends and acquaintances before you sign up

If you own a Jaguar XK120, you will almost certainly become a member of one of the one-make clubs and get the opportunity for race circuit parades like this.

with any one. Apart from the obvious services on which you can draw (which, of course, should include access to historical material, and perhaps to the borrowing or hiring of rare service and repair literature), there are other, less obvious, benefits to one-make club membership.

One is that you will often be able to swop experiences, and restoration 'wrinkles', with another member, and another is that you will be able to get good advice about the best specialists or suppliers of parts. (You will also be able to find out about the cowboys who, in spite of their failings, continue to survive, and thrive, in the motoring world.) In some cases, too, a large and well-organized club has a 'self-help' system in operation, which means that if you hit trouble on the road, many miles from home, there is often a club member willing to turn out and help you get under way again.

Clearly, if you live in the UK and give your heart to a rare Pegaso, a magnificent Stutz Bearcat or something rare, old and Italian, you have less chance of joining a British-based one-make club than if you buy a Triumph, an MG or a Jaguar, but never despair. A few enquiries to the established classic car magazines will at least tell you if there is a one-make club in this country which covers your passion. If there isn't you have two choices. One is to discover the headquarters of the one-make club overseas, and join it (but if there is a language problem with bulletins and literature, can you cope?); the other is to start a one-make club yourself!

To join a one-make club and to enjoy its fellowship is a very straight-forward way to be involved in classic cars. However, even before you buy a particular car and join the club, I presume you will have taken a con-scious decision about the car, and the sort of membership it will involve. If, for instance, you join in with owners of conventional cars like Morris Minors or Triumph TR6s, you may find that major events involve camping, discos round a camp fire, and boisterous winter parties. If, on the other hand, you join the Rolls-Royce Enthusiasts' Club, the Bugatti Owners' Club or the Porsche Club, you may find things altogether more dignified, more up-market and more expensive to support. Which is for you?

Most other classic car activities involve competition of one sort or another, and I need hardly point out that these can be wildly expensive and very specialized indeed. To some classic car owners, however, to go racing, rallying, or to indulge in concours, is the most important aspect of the movement.

Concours

Thousands of owners want to get involved in motor sport, but few (if they admit it to themselves) have the appropriate skills to allow them to be successful in high-speed motoring. However, one aspect of competition in which *every* owner can win, whether young or old, male or female, is

Paul Garland's Morris Minor 1000 Traveller is one of the most successful on the British concours circuits — you don't need an exotic car to excel at this sport.

to enter the car for a concours competition. The crude way to describe a concours is as a 'car beauty contest', but really it is a much more complicated business than that.

I apologize, but I now have to burst into elementary French! Many years ago, a concours event meant a *concours d'élégance* (literally, an elegance competition), a contest in which the judges looked for the best presented, most beautiful car; style, beauty and flair were all-important, but originality was not critical. In those days, in Britain, you needed something magnificent, like a coachbuilt Rolls-Royce, a Hispano-Suiza or a Lagonda, to be in with a chance. *Concours d'élégance* is still an important pastime in the USA, where some cars have extensive and expensive preparation merely to be shown as glossy, static exhibits.

Once the classic car movement became established in the 1970s and a huge variety of cars was acknowledged, the emphasis changed. Concours became more widespread, but the idea of running to the old-style *concours d'élégance* rules was rapidly abandoned. The new fashion, which has now been established as the normal British standard, was to run a *concours d'état* (a 'competition of condition') instead.

As the translation suggests, the modern type of concours judges a car on its state of presentation and preservation rather than on its beauty. This means that the judging can concentrate on the car's state of preservation, on its originality and on the function of all its equipment, rather than on its styling. Most marking systems take into account the amount of use the car gets, and some insist that the cars are driven to and from the meetings themselves.

In theory, if not always in practice, this means that a beautifully maintained though mundane (maybe even ugly) classic car should always be marked higher than an elegant machine which is rather more scruffy. This is a principle that some classic car owners find hard to accept. For that reason, some of the most exclusive one-make clubs in the country tend to shun the modern type of concours — under modern rules it is quite possible for a Bentley to be defeated by a Morris Minor 1000, or a Ferrari by a Reliant Scimitar GTE — and the owners of the more exotic machinery feel that this is a nonsensical situation. There are arguments on both sides, but the fact is that the *concours d'état* method of judging is now here to stay, and more proud owners are interested in this sort of motoring competition than ever before.

In the initial stages, at one-make club level, it costs next to nothing to prepare your own car for a concours competition; apart from buying the necessary polishes and cleaning compounds, and laying in a supply of rags and cloths, the major expense is one of time and hard work. Even so, I should warn you right from the start that standards are very high and are rising steadily. Before you even enter your car for its first event you should attend a few concours as a spectator, and get a feel for the level of competition you will have to meet. If it is at all possible, try to find out what the judges' marking sheets look like, so that you can decide what 'weight', or importance, is put on the various aspects of the car's presentation.

It goes without saying that your car should always be very clean and smart. There are no marks — literally, and actually — for leaving dirt in the seams and rust marks on the brightwork. In theory, all that you ever need to do is to ensure that your pride and joy is in its best possible condition, clean, well-polished and smart, inside, outside, in the engine bay and underneath.

On the first occasion, no doubt you will be happy with your efforts, and with the results, but I suspect that the judges will not. Do not show your disappointment too much, but make sure that you collect the marking cards which apply to your car, and resolve to improve on the poor points which emerge.

Some years ago I was chatting to a concours specialist whose car was currently on show at an exhibition about 40 miles (64 km) from his home:

'The show closes at 9 p.m.,' I said. 'Will you take the car home tonight?'

'Oh yes, no problem', he said, 'I drive it everywhere.'

'What happens if it is raining?' I asked him.

'It doesn't matter whether it's wet *or* dry,' he replied. 'I have a cleaning routine. *Every* time I bring the car back at the end of a journey I spend four hours on it, washing, leathering down, cleaning — because if I leave it to the next day it takes twice as long to get the same result!'

He wasn't joking, and to match people like that you will eventually have to spend the same amount of time on your car. The fact of the matter

Top *Pre-judging preparation for this well-known Jensen CV8 concours car. Some owners cosset their cars all the time to make sure that they are in the best shape at any instant.*

Above *Preparation for an important concours begins days before an event. The car often travels to the venue overnight, and polishing continues for hours before and during the day's judging. This is Brian Hatson's Aston Martin DB4.*

is that by concours standards your initial idea of pre-show preparation may not be adequate.

On the other hand you must also come to terms with the face that over-restoration (chrome plate where originally there was none, bright painted castings which were originally just matt black, the wrong colour for leather or the soft top) is just as likely to see your car marked down as is under-preparation. You must also realize that there is simply no substitute for hard work and diligence in preparing a car for inspection.

To succeed in concours, you can choose to be supreme at one of three levels:

The lowest, and least expensive, level is merely to aim to have the cleanest and best-preserved car that you can prepare, yet continue to use on a semi-regular basis. You will be fighting a constant battle to keep mud, grime and salt out of every nook and cranny of the structure, and the effort it takes to prepare the car for a competition may be heart-breaking. You will certainly keep such a car under cover, perhaps even under sheets, but you don't have the time, or the commitment, to work on it every week. Incidentally, it is this sort of car which is often advertized as being 'to concours standard' — and some are better than others.

The second level, and one which is achieved by scores, if not hundreds, of British classic car owners, is to have a genuine concours car which is only driven to and from events but which is never normally used for everyday motoring. Such cars generally have a 'tender' or 'service' car in attendance at every concours, receive hours of attention most evenings of the week (especially before an important event), and are fussed over continuously while the car is on parade at an event, before *and* after the judging is complete. Without exception, such cars have an important winter rebuild programme mapped out for them, live in a dry and well-ventilated garage, and are always covered by sheets between working sessions.

The third level is achieved only by a handful of British owners (though there are more such fanatics in the United States). Such a car is a concours machine, pure and simple, which is driven as sparingly as possible. Such a car is withdrawn from an event, and does not even travel to it, where rain is likely, or where dust may be blown across the area. I known of some competitors at a national event in 1986 who complained of jet engine fuel mist being dropped by aeroplanes on their way into nearby London Heathrow Airport...

Such a car will be trailered to an event if the regulations allow it (or trailered to a nearby unloading point if they do not!), and will be parked on sheets, sometimes with display mirrors artfully arranged to show the underside without the judge having to crawl underneath. I have seen such cars arrive and have the 'slave' wheels and tyres replaced by the concours variety, have the concours carpets and seats fitted in place of temporary fittings, and have 'working' components such as batteries and ignition leads swopped over as well. I have also seen such cars having their brake pads polished, and the recessed panel welded joints cleaned out with the aid of cotton wool 'buds'.

These are the cars which have become an art form rather than working machines which can be enjoyed, and on which an almost limitless amount of time, effort and money has been expended. There seems to be

BENSON and HEDGES CONCOURS

NATIONAL CHAMPION 1986

In 1986, Britain's premier concours series was that sponsored by Benson & Hedges. All the hard work was justified for Roger Rowley, when his Reliant Scimitar GTE was acclaimed as Supreme Champion.

at least one owner in every one-make club who aspires to this sort of concours level. While I admire their dedication and obvious application to the task, I have to say that this should not be what classic car motoring is all about. Even so, if you want to get to the top, this is the standard you will have to achieve.

Racing and speed events
Even before the classic car movement boomed in the 1970s, there were several opportunities for older cars to compete against each other, whether in circuit racing, sprints or hill climbs. Many competitions were organized by the Vintage Sports Car Club and active one-make clubs (Bugatti, Aston Marton and Jaguar all spring to mind), and individual events were part of regular meetings run by large clubs like the BRSCC and the BARC. Except in rare, all-embracing events like the Pomeroy Trophy or the Brighton Speed Trials, speed events in the 1960s were mostly for vintage and post-vintage thoroughbred cars, and almost all of these were for sports cars or genuine racing cars. Owners of saloon cars or more modern cars had a thin time.

The next development was the increasing popularity of 'historic' racing, in which more and more front-engined competition cars — sports cars *and* single-seaters — were dug out of storage, renovated and raced again. Before long, and aided by smoother circuits and more modern tyre compounds and construction, some of these cars were circulating faster

If the cars were raced in the 1950s, why not in the 1980s? This shows an Alvis 3-litre dicing with a Jaguar Mk VII in the Tulip rally, at Zandvoort.

than they had ever done before. The problem was that the fastest cars were few and far between. The inevitable happened — 'replicas' appeared which were almost indistinguishable from the real thing, they started to win races, and devalued the entire currency of historic racing. Those cars, at least are well known among enthusiasts....

It was not until the 1970s, however, that classic saloon car racing was introduced, and this sport now has its own small but enthusiastic following. A saloon car racing enthusiast of the 1950s could have gone into a twenty-year sleep at the time, wakened up again, and found nothing unfamiliar on the circuits. Jaguar Mk II, MG Magnettes and Austin A35s battled it out then, and they continue to do so today. There are racing classes, too, for production sports cars of the period, which provide very exciting racing.

At first glance, all this looks like an attractive pastime for a classic car owner to take up, and so it is, but of course there are major snags (and potential expenses) to be considered first.

The most important factor is that the cars used in classic racing are by no means standard, and cannot normally be used on the roads between events. It means that, at a stroke, a classic car owner becomes a *racing* car owner — and there is a great deal of difference between the two breeds. It also means that if he is to stay in touch with the conventional classic car scene, he has to treat his classic racing car purely as a racing car — and buy another road-going classic as well!

To go classic racing is not at all a cheap and cheerful operation. Like all other racing cars, a classic saloon or sports car has to be fitted with certain items of safety equipment before being allowed to compete, and most serious competitors tune and race-modify their cars to the very limit of the regulations. For some free-spending 'enthusiasts', if that means breaking

Above *Two Volvos battling with two Sunbeam Rapiers at Crystal Palace in the 1959 RAC Rally.*

Right *An HRG was a suitable rally car in the 1940s and early 1950s — these days, perhaps, better for hill-climbs or classic trials.*

the regulations by fitting non-standard items to the engine, or constructing lightweight panels to get the weight down, then this will be done. Don't forget, too, all the other necessary expense — such as a trailer for the race car, a tow car to lug the trailer, a crash helmet, overalls and other details for the driver, and the cost of repreparing the car between events. Still interested?

Finally, there is the ever-present risk of being involved in a racing accident. It doesn't have to be your own fault, or even your own accident — burst tyres, for instance, are not unknown, and there is always the danger of being involved in someone else's shunt. I would not want to discourage anyone from going racing in the various classic categories, but please do not think that it is going to be cheap, or easy.

It probably costs less to go hillclimbing or sprinting in a classic car, but

Ian Hall's Riley Sprite is not only the smartest of a very distinguished group of such cars, but it is also raced and used in hill-climbs as well. Now that is classic car enthusiasm.

at least the contest is purely you against the clock, and if the accident happens you will only have yourself to blame. This, in fact, is probably the ideal way to start competing in a classic car, for you will soon decide if you want to get more deeply involved *before* you commit yourself to a lot of investment.

Rallies

For a classic car enthusiast, a rally can involve anything from a weekend run towards a one-make club's rendezvous, to an out-and-out high-speed classic car rally over closed roads. In most cases, however, the term 'rally' actually takes on its original pre-war meaning, where the owners can use their cars in absolutely standard condition, and where no harum-scarum driving is involved.

You could, of course, rally *at* a venue, rather than rally *to* a venue (for that is what a lot of one-make car gatherings are all about), or you could take part in a road rally, the most important British event being undoubtedly the Norwich Union RAC Classic Run. There are many examples of each event, from club up to national level (and, if you have enough time and money, even at international level), and the joy of every event is that there is often very little actual competitive motoring involved, so you will not be disgraced if you do not try to be the fastest, or the most ruthlessly competitive.

In every type of classic car motoring, however, remember that you took up this occupation as a hobby, and that the definition of a hobby is : 'a favourite subject or occupation that is not one's main business'. It should be an enthralling pleasure. Let's keep it like that, shall we?

Bibliography

The world of motoring is well covered by books in the English language, and marque histories have usually been written about cars generally accepted to be 'classics'. Some, like Ferrari and Porsche, are covered by dozens of volumes, while other worthy marques are covered by a single volume.

To list every title, past or present, would be impossible, so here is my advice on the best books covering marques and subjects. I have to be honest and point out that several of these books were written by myself, but then you wouldn't want me to be excessively modest, would you?

Note: Some excellent books are now out of print, and these are denoted in the list by an asterisk (*). Most can be found at Autojumbles, or in book shops specializing in new and 'previously owned' books.

Marque histories

There are three excellent British series of books which cover most important marques and families of cars in commendable factual detail:

Autohistories — nearly 50 titles (Osprey)
Collector's Guides — more than 30 titles (Motor Racing Publications)
Super Profiles — more than 30 titles (Haynes)
In addition:
Abarth, Pat Braden and Greg Schmidt (Osprey)
(AC) Cobra, Trevor Legat (Haynes)
Alfa Romeo: A History, Peter Hull and Roy Slater (Transport Bookman Publications)
Alfa Romeo, tutte le vetture dal 1910 (Italian *and* English text), Luigi Fusi (Emmeti Grafica)
Alfa Romeo Catalogue Raisonnée, Luigi Fusi and 'Johnny' Lurani (Automobilia)
Alfissimo, David Owen (Osprey)
Allard, the Inside Story, Tom Lush (Motor Racing Publications)*

Alvis: The Story of the Red Triangle, Kenneth Day (Gentry/Haynes)
Aston Martin V-8, Michael Bowler (Cadogan)
The Power Behind Aston Martin, Geoff Courtney (Oxford Illustrated Press)
Aston Martin, the Story of a Sports Car, Dudley Coram (Motor Racing Publications)*
Audi Quattro: The Development and Competition History, Jeremy Walton (Haynes)
The Austin, 1905-1952, Bob Wyatt (David and Charles)
Austin-Healey: The Story of the Big Healeys, Geoff Healey (Gentry/Haynes)
More Healeys, Geoff Healey (Gentry/Haynes)
Healeys and Austin-Healeys, Peter Browning and Les Needham (Haynes)
Austin Seven, Chris Harvey (Oxford Illustrated Press)
The Austin Seven: The Motor for the Million, Bob Wyatt (David and Charles)
Bentley: Cricklewood to Crewe, Michael Frostick (Osprey)
Bentley R-Type Continental, Stanley Sedgwick (Bentley Drivers' Club)
All the Pre-War Bentleys as New, Stanley Sedgwick and Hugh Young (Bentley Drivers' Club)
Twenty Years of Crewe Bentleys: 1945-1965, Stanley Sedgwick (Bentley Drivers' Club)
BMC, The Cars of, Graham Robson (Motor Racing Publications)
BMW, a History, Halwart Schrader/Ron Wakefield (Osprey)
Bristol Cars and Engines, Leonard Setright (Motor Racing Publications)
British Leyland: The Truth about the Cars, Jeff Daniels (Osprey)
Bugatti, Hugh Conway (Foulis/Haynes)
Cadillac: The Complete History, Maurice Hendry (Automobile Quarterly)
The Camaro Book: From A through Z-28, John Lamm (Lamm-Morada)
Chevrolet, 1911-1985, Richard Langworth and Jan Norbye (Consumer Guide)
The Complete History of Chrysler Corporation, Richard Langworth and Jan Norbye (Consumer Guide)
Cord: Without Tribute to Tradition, Dan Post (Post-Motor)
Corvair Affair, Mike Knepper (Motor Book International)
Corvette: America's Sports Car, Jay Koblenz (Consumer Guide)
The Daimler Tradition, Brian Smith (Transport Bookman Publications)
De Lorean: Stainless Steel Illusion, John Lamm (Newport Press)
De Tomaso Automobiles, Wally Wyss (Osprey)
Duesenberg: The Pursuit of Perfection, Fred Roe (Dalton Watson)
Ferrari, Hans Tanner and Doug Nye (Haynes)
Dino: The Little Ferrari, Doug Nye (Osprey)
The Complete Guide to the Ferrari 308 Series, Wally Wyss (Dalton Watson)
The Ferrari Legend: The Road Cars, Antoine Prunet (Patrick Stephens)*
Fiat, Michael Sedgwick (Batsford)*
Fiat Sports Cars, Graham Robson (Osprey)
Forty Years of Design with Fiat, Dante Giacosa (Automobilia)*
(Ford) Escort Mk 1, 2 & 3: The Development and Competition History, Jeremy

Walton (Haynes)
Anglia, Prefect and Popular: From Ford Eight to 105E, Michael Allen (Motor Racing Publications)
Capri: The Development and Competition History, Jeremy Walton (Haynes)
Consul, Zephyr, Zodiac: the Big Fifties Fords, Michael Allen (Motor Racing Publications)
GT40 (Ford GT40), Ronnie Spain (Osprey)
Mustang: The Complete History of America's Ponycar, Gary L. Witzenburg (Automobile Quarterly Publications)
The Thunderbird Story, Richard Langworth (Motorbooks International)
Frazer Nash, David Thirlby (Haynes)*
From Chain Drive to Turbocharger, Denis Jenkinson (Patrick Stephens)
The Complete History of General Motors, 1908-1986, Richard Langworth and Jan Norbye (Consumer Guide)
The Legendary Hispano-Suiza, Johnny Green (Dalton Watson)
HRG: The Sportsman's Ideal, Ian Dussek (Motor Racing Publications)
Jaguar Sports Cars, Paul Skilleter (Haynes)
Jaguar Saloon Cars, Paul Skilleter (Haynes)
Jaguar: The Definitive History of a Great British Car, Andrew Whyte (Patrick Stephens)
E-Type: End of an Era, Chris Harvey (Oxford Illustrated Press)
Jeep, Michael Clayton (David and Charles)*
Jensen Interceptor, Mike Taylor (Cadogan)
The Jensen Healey Stories, Peter Browning and John Blunsden (Motor Racing Publications)*
Jowett Jupiter: The Car that Leaped to Fame, Edward Nankivell (Batsford)
Lagonda, Arnold Davey and Anthony May (David and Charles)
Lamborghini: The Cars from S'Agata Bolognese, Rob Box and Richard Crump (Osprey)
Lamborghini Miura, Peter Coltrin and Jean Francois Marchet (Osprey)
La Lancia, Wim H. J. Oude Weernink (Motor Racing Publications)
Land Rover: Workhorse of the World, Graham Robson (David and Charles)
Lotus: The Elite, Elan, Europa, Chris Harvey (Oxford Illustrated Press)
The Original Lotus Elite: Racing Car for the Road, Dennis Ortenburger (Newport Press)
Legend of the Lotus Seven, Dennis Ortenburger (Osprey)
Theme Lotus 1956-86, Doug Nye (Motor Racing Publications)
The Story of Lotus: 1947-60, Ian H. Smith (Motor Racing Publications)
The Story of Lotus: 1961-71, Doug Nye (Motor Racing Publications)
Maserati: The Complete History, Luigi Orsini and Franco Zagari (LDA)
Maserati Road Cars, Richard Crump and Rob Box (Osprey)
Magnificent Mercedes, Graham Robson (Haynes)*
Three Pointed Star, David Scott-Moncrieff (Gentry/Haynes)
Mercedes-Benz Production Models (1946-86), Robert Nitske (Motor Books International)

Mercedes-Benz 300SL, Robert Nitske (Motorbooks International)
MG, Wilson McComb (Osprey)
The Mighty MGs, Graham Robson (David and Charles)
MG: The Immortal T-Series, Chris Harvey (Oxford Illustrated Press)
The MG Story, Anders Clausager (Haynes)
Mini after 25 Years, Rob Golding (Osprey)
The Mini Story, Laurence Pomeroy (Temple Press)
Metro: the Book of the Car, Graham Robson (Patrick Stephens)
Morgan: First and Last of the Real Sports Cars, Gregory Houston Bowden
(Haynes)
The Four-Wheeled Morgan — The Flat-Radiator Models, Ken Hill (Motor
Racing Publications)*
The Four-Wheeled Morgan — Cowled-Radiator Models, Ken Hill (Motor
Racing Publications)
Morris Minor: The World's Supreme Small Car, Paul Skilleter (Osprey)
The Morris Motor Car, Harry Edwards (Moorland Publishing)
The Bullnose and Flatnose Morris, Lytton P. Jarman and Robin I.
Barraclough (David and Charles)
The Fabulous Firebird, John Lamm (Lamm-Morada)
Porsche: Excellence was Expected, Karl Ludvigsen (Automobile Quarterly
Publications)
The Porsche Book: A Definitive Illustrated History, Lothar Boschen and
Jurgen Barth (Patrick Stephens)
Porsche 911 Story, Paul Frère (Patrick Stephens)
Project 928, Julius Weitmann and R. Steinemann (Patrick Stephens)
Porsche 924, 928 and 944, Jerry Sloniger (Osprey)*
Range Rover/Land-Rover, Graham Robson (David and Charles)
Riley Sports Cars, Graham Robson (Oxford Illustrated Press)
Riley: As Old as the Industry, David Styles (Styles)
The Rolls-Royce Motor Car, Anthony Bird and Ian Hallows (Batsford)
The Magic of a Name, Harold Nockolds (G. T. Foulis)*
The Rover Story, Graham Robson (Patrick Stephens)
Saab — from Two-Stroke to Turbo, Anders Tunberg (Motor Racing
Publications)
The Sonett, and All Other Saab Sports Cars, Bjorn Svallner (Allt om Hobby
AB)
Saab: The Innovator, Mark Chatterton (David and Charles)
Alpine: the Classic Sunbeam, Chris McGovern (Gentry/Haynes)
Tiger: The Making of a Sports Car, Mike Taylor (Gentry)
Tiger, Alpine, Rapier, Richard Langworth (Osprey)
Georges Roesch and the Invincible Talbot, Anthony Blight (Grenville)
The Story of Triumph Sports Cars, Graham Robson (Motor Racing
Publications)*
The Triumph TR5/TR250 and TR6 Companion, Steven Rossi and Ian Clarke
(Kimberley)

Triumph Spitfire and GT6, Graham Robson (Osprey)
Triumph Herald and Vitesse, Graham Robson (Osprey)
The Story of Volvo Cars, Graham Robson (Patrick Stephens)
The Complete Guide to the Volvo 1800 Series, Creighton (Kimberley)
The VW Story, Jerry Sloniger (Patrick Stephens)
Small Wonder: the Amazing Story of the Volkswagen, Walter Henry Nelson (Hutchinson)
VW Treasures by Karmann, Jan Norbye (Motorbooks International)
VW Golf GTi Companion, Ray Hutton, Editor (Motor Racing Publications)
The Origin and Evolution of the VW Beetle, Schuler (Automobile Quarterly)

General

American Cars, Leon Mandel (Stuart Tabori and Chang)
The Automobile: The First Century, David Burgess-Wise, William Boddy and Brian Laban (Orbis)
British Family Cars of the 1950s, Michael Allen (Haynes)
Cars 1886-1930, Nick Georgano (Beekman House)
Cars of the Fifties and Sixties, Michael Sedgwick (Nordbok)
Cars of the Thirties and Forties, Michael Sedgwick (Nordbok)
Complete Book of Collectible Cars 1930-1980, Richard Langworth and Graham Robson (Consumer Guide)
Encyclopedia of American Cars, 1930-1980, Richard Langworth (Consumer Guide)
An Encyclopedia of European Sports and GT Cars, 1945-1960, Graham Robson (Haynes)
An Encyclopedia of European Sports and GT Cars, from 1961, Graham Robson (Haynes)
The Encyclopedia of Sports Cars, Nick Georgano (Bison)
Extraordinary Automobiles, A. Martinez and J-L. Nory (Haynes)
101 Great Marques, Andrew Whyte (Octopus)
Great Marques of Germany, Jonathan Wood (Octopus)
Mid-engined Exotic Cars, Wally Wyss (Zuma Marketing)
Milestone Sports Cars, 1950 to 1965, A. Martinez and J-L. Nory (Haynes)
The New Encyclopedia of Motorcars 1885 to the Present, Nick Georgano (Editor) (Edbury Press)
Standard Catalogue of American Cars 1805-1942, (Old Cars Publications)
Standard Catalogue of American Cars 1946-1975, (Old Cars Publications)
Supercar Road Tests, Jeremy Sinek (Editor) (Hamlyn)
Ultimate Automobiles, Alberto Martinez and José Rosinski (Haynes)

Appendix 1

One-Make Clubs

Every classic car owner, no matter how wealthy or how knowledgeable, benefits from knowing as much as possible about his particular car. One way to get the best out of ownership is to enjoy the fellowship of a one-make car club, and to learn from the experience of other members. Here is a selection of the most significant one-make clubs in the UK:

Alfa Romeo Montreal Owners' Register
Bob Dalton, 52 Bennett's Close, Cobham, Surrey.

Alfa Romeo 2600/2000 Register
"Knighton". Church Close, West Runton, Norfolk.

Alfa Romeo 1900 Register *(includes 6C2500 information)*
Peter Marshall, Mariners, Courtlands Avenue, Esher, Surrey KT10 9HZ.

Allard Owners' Club
Miss P. Hulse, 1 Dalmeny Avenue, Tufnell Park. London N7 0LD.
Telephone: 01-607 3589.

Alvis Owner Club
E. W. Wimble, 82 Dorling Drive, Ewell, Surrey.

American Auto Club
PO Box 56, Redditch, Worcs.

American Auto Club, Pre '50
Hotcotmoors, Cranfield Road, Salford, Milton Keynes MK17 8ST.

Amilcar Register
Flat 3, 28 Buxton Old Road, Disley, Stockport, Cheshire SK12 2BB. Secretary: Roger Howard.

Armstrong Siddeley Owners' Club
169 Bolton Road North, Stubbins, Ramsbottom, Bolton BL0 0NA. Secretary: S. Keyte. Spares Manager: R. G. Allen, Conkwell Farm, Winsley, Bradford-on-Avon, Wiltshire BA15 2JG.

Aston Martin Owners' Club (AMOC Ltd)
Jim Whyman, Burtons Lane, Chalfont St Giles, Bucks HP8 4BL, Little Chalfont.
Telephone: (02404) 4742.

Austin A30-A35 Owners Club
John Jewison, 42 Boswell Road, Doncaster DN4 7DD.

Austin Seven Clubs Association, The
Robin Newman, Dixton Cottage, Monmouth, Gwent NP5 3SJ.

Austin Big 7 Register
R. E. Taylor, 101 Derby Road, Chellaston, Derby DE7 1SB.

Austin-Healey Club
Mrs C. S. Marks, 171 Coldharbour Road, Bristol BS6 7SX.

Vintage Austin Register
Frank Smith, The Butts House, Ashover, near Chesterfield, Derby.
Telephone: 0246 590295.

Autovia Car Club
Nigel Plant, 14 Sycamore Crescent, Barnton, Northwich, Cheshire CW8 4NS.

Bean Car Club
M. Crouch, Glaziers, Glaziers Lane, Normandy, Guildford, Surrey, GU3 2DQ.

Bentley Drivers Club
Mrs B. M. Fell, 16 Chearlsey Road, Long Crendon, Aylesbury, Bucks HP18 9AW.
Telephone: 0844 208233.

Berkeley Enthusiasts' Club
M. Rounsville-Smith, 41 Gorsewood road, St John's, Woking, Surrey GU21 1UZ.

Berkeley Register
44a London Road, Welwyn, Herts.

BMW Car Club
The Secretary, 558 London Road, Isleworth, Middlesex TW7.

BMW Drivers' Club
Judy Stewart, PO Box 8, Dereham, Norfolk.
Telephone: 0362 4459.

Bond Owners Club
Stan Carnock, 42 Beaufort Avenue, Hodge Hill, Birmingham B34 6AE.
Telephone: 021 784 4626.

Borgward Drivers' Club
David Stride, 81 Stanway Road, Earlsdon, Coventry CV5 6PH.
Telephone: 0203 74020.

Bristol Owners Club
Lou Bates, Willow Layne, Burcot, Abingdon, Oxon OX14 3DP.

British Salmson Owners' Club
General Secretary: Tim Grisdale, 36 Station Road, Ridgmont, Bedfordshire MK43 0UH.

Telephone: 052 528 548.

Brough Superior Club
A. J. Wallis, 26 Meadow Close Grove, Wantage, Oxon.

Buckler Car Register
Stan Hibberd, 62 Burwood Road, Hersham, Walton on Thames, Surrey.

Bugatti Owners' Club
Geoffrey Ward, Prescott Hill, Gotherington, Cheltenham, Glos GL52 4RD.
Telephone: 024267 3136.

Citroën Car Club
P. C. Brodie, 53 Norman Court, Nether Street, London N3 1QQ. Prestel.
Telephone: 01-349 2260.

Clan Owners Club
Robert Russell, 77 Ashby Road, Woodville, Burton-on-Trent, Staffs.
Telephone: 0283 217361.

Classic Corvette Club (UK)
Francis York, 4 Parsonage Close, Bishops Tachbrook, Warwicks.

Clyno Register
J. J. Salt, New Farm, Startley, Chippenham, Wilts.
Telephone: 0249 720271.

DAF Owners' Club
S. K. Bidwell, 56 Ridgedale Road, Bolsover, Chesterfield, Derbyshire.

Daimler and Lanchester Owners' Club Ltd
John Ridley, The Manor House, Trewyn, Abergavenny, Gwent NP7 7PC.

Datsun Z Club
Penny Coken, Woodlands, Horsham Lane, Ewhurst, Surrey.

De Tomaso Drivers' Club
Philip Stebbings, 19 Westpark, Eaton Rise, London W5.

Delage section of VSCC
F. C. Annett, 43 The Highway, Sutton, Surrey SM2 5QS.

DKW Owners' Club
Membership Secretary: Rose Cottage, Rodford, Westerleigh, Bristol. Club and Events Secretaries: 36 Swannington Road, Nr. Coalville, Leicestershire.

Dutton Owners' Club
Richard Felton, "Forgeville", Finkle Street, Stainforth, Doncaster, DN7 5AL.

Facel Vega Owners' Club
17 Crossways, Sutton, Surrey SM2 5LD.

Fairthrope Sports Car Club
R. B. B. Gibbs, Rose Cottage, Hollington, Long Crendon, Bucks HP18 9EF.
Telephone: 0844 208418.

Ferrari Owners' Club
Godfrey Eaton, 10 Whittox Lane, Frome, Somerset BA11 1BY.
Telephone: 0373 62987.

Fiat Dino Register
M. Morris, 59 Sandown Park, Tunbridge Wells, Kent.

Fiat Motor Club (GB)
Miss M. B. Berryman, 82 Addington Road, Reading Berks RG1 5PX.

Fiat Osca Register
M. Elliott, 36 Maypole Drive, Chigwell, Essex.

Fiat Register, The
Models to 1940
A. Cameron, 7 Tudor Gardens, West Wickham, Kent.
Telephone: 01-777 4729.

Fiat Twin-Cam Register, The
3 Benhurst Close, Selsden, Surrey.

Ford AVO Owners' Club
Peter Williams, 67 Rolls Park Avenue, Chingford, London E4 9DG.

Ford Cortina 1600E Enthusiasts' Club
Peter Underwood, 111 Priory Way, Haywards Heath, West Sussex RH16 3NS.

Ford Cortina 1600E Owners' Club
Alan Clarke, 22 Stonehurst Road, Braunstone, Leics LE3 2QA.

Ford Sidevalve Owners' Club
Mrs J. Myers, 25 Kellett Grove, Leeds 12.

Ford 105E Owners' Club
Mr Lewis, 81 Campton Road, North End, Portsmouth, Hants.

Ford Model T Register of Great Britain
Alan J. Meakin, 14 Breck Farm Lane, Taverham, Norwich.
Telephone: 0603 867700.

Ford V8 Pilot Owners' Club
Trevor Millard, 31 School Road, Dagenham, Essex RM10 9QB.

Ford Y and C Model Register, The
61 Gallows Hill Lane, Abbotts Langley, Herts WD5 0DD.

Frisky Register, The
John Meadows, 8 Ruston Way, Blythewood, Ascot, Berks.

Gilbern Owners Club Ltd.
B. C. Fawkes, Glyn Ebbw, 24 Mayfield, Buckden, Huntingdon, Cambs, PE18 95X.

Gorden-Keeble Owners' Club
Ann Knott, Westminster Road, Brackley, Northants NN13 5EB.
Telephone: 0280 702311.

(Hillman) Imp Club, The
R. Knight, 71 Inglesham Road, Penhill, Swindon SN2 5DJ.

Hillman Register, The *Pre 1931*
Clive Baker, 16 Parklands, Wotton-under-Edge, Glos.

Honda S800 Sports Car Club
Chris Wallwork, 664 Bradford Road, Birkenshaw, Bradford, Yorkshire.

Humber Register
H. Gregory, 176 London Road, St Albans, Herts.

Post Vintage Humber Car Club
W. Gardiner, 85 Southgate, Sutton Hill, Telford, Salop, TF7 4HF.

Jaguar Drivers' Club
Jaguar House, 18 Stuart Street, Luton, Beds LU1 2SL.
Telephone: 0582 419332.

Jaguar Enthusiasts Club
G. Searle, 37 Charterhouse Road, Ashvale, Surrey.

Jensen Owners' Club
Charles Edward House, 127/128 Brighton Road, Birmingham, West Midlands B12 8QN.

(Jowett) Jupiters Owners' Auto Club
Steve Keil, 16 Empress Avenue, Woodford Green, Essex.
Telephone: 01-505 2215.

Lagonda Club
Mrs V. May, 68 Savill Road, Lindfield, Haywards Heath, Sussex RH16 2NN.
Telephone: 0444 414674.

Lamborghini Owners' Club
Hanna Ashley, 44 Sussex Road, Haywards Heath, Sussex.

Lancia Motor Club Ltd
Mrs B. M. Rees, The Old Shire House, Aylton, Ledbury, Herefordshire HR8 2QE.
Telephone: 053 183 226.

Land-Rover Register, The *1947-51*
Langford Cottage, School Lane, Ladbroke, Warks.

Land-Rover Series One Club, The
All Series 1 Land Rovers from 1948 to 1958
David Bowyer, East Foldhay, Zeal Monachorum, Crediton, Devon EX17 6DH.
Telephone: (036 33) 666.

Lea Francis Owners' Club
R. B. Sawers, 2 St. Giles Avenue, South Mimms, Herts. EN6 3PZ.

Lincoln-Zephyr Owners' Club
Colin Spong, 22 New North Road, Hainault, Ilford, Essex.

Lotus Cortina Register
"Blades", Hornash Lane, Shadoxhurst, Ashford, Kent TN26 1HT.

Lotus Drivers' Club
Jenny Barton, 2 Charlbury Mews, Sydenham, Leamington Spa, Warwicks.
Telephone: 0926 313514.

Club Elite *1957-63*
Miles Wilkins, The Coach House, The Street, Walberton, Arundel, West Sussex.

Club Lotus (and Lotus Register)
Margaret Richards, PO Box 8, Dereham, Norfolk NR 19 1TF.
Telephone: 0362 4459.

Marendaz Special Car Register
John Shaw, 23 Vineries Close, Leckhampton, Cheltenham, Glos.

Maserati Club Michael Miles, The Paddock, Old Salisbury Road, Abbotts Ann, Andover, Hants SP11 7NT.
Telephone: 0264 710 312.

Club Matra
R. Davies, 5 Narlborough Road, Westcliff, Bournemouth.

Mazda Owners' Club
Ray Smith, 23 Redwood Glade, Leighton Buzzard, Beds.
Telephone: 0525 376608/370920.

Mercedes-Benz Club Ltd., The
A. M. Rees, Fairways, Glynher Road, Llandybie, Ammanford, Dyfed.

Metropolitan Owners' Club
W. E. Dowsing, 4 Burnham Road, Knaphill, Woking, Surrey GU21 2AE.

Telephone: 048 67 4841.

MG Car Club, The
PO Box 251, Studley Warwickshire
B80 7AT.
Telephone: 052 785 3666.

MG Owners' Club
2/4 Station Road, Swavesey, Cambs
CB4 5QJ.

MG Y Type Register, The
J. G. Lawson, 12 Nithsdale Road,
Liverpool, L15 5AX

MG Octagon Car Club *Pre-56 cars,*
i.e. TF, YB and before.
Harry Crutchley, 36 Queensville
Avenue, Stafford ST 17 4LS.
Telephone: 0785 51014.

Mini Cooper Club
Joyce Holman, 1 Weavers Cottages,
Church Hill, West Hoathly, West
Sussex RH19 4PW.

Mini Sportscar Club
Bank House, Summerhill, Chisle-
hurst, Kent, BR7 5RD.
Telephone: 01-467 6533.

Morris Minor Owners' Club
Jane Flanders, 127-129 Green Lane,
Derby DE1 1RZ.

NSU Owners' Club
Mrs Rosemarie Crowley, 58
Tadorne Road, Tadworth, Surrey
KT20 5TF.
Telephone: 073 781 2412.

Panhard et Levassor GB, Les Amis
de
Mrs Denize Polley, "La Dyna", 11
Arterial Avenue, Rainham, Essex.
RM13 9PD

Club Peugeot UK
Paul Davies, 91 Mill Road, Burgess
Hill, Sussex.

Piper Club
Clive Davies, Pipers Oak, Lopham
Road, East Harling, Norfolk.

Railton Owners' Club
B. McKenzie, Fairmiles, Barnes Hall

Road, Burncross, Sheffield S30 4RF.
Telephone: 0742 468357.

Rapier Register
Mr and Mrs D. C. H. Williams,
Smithy, Tregynon, Newtown,
Powys.
Telephone: Tregynon 396.

Reliant Sabre, Scimitar Owners'
Club
P.O. Box 67, Northampton NN1
1LR.
Telephone: 0604 24998.

Renault Owners' Club
Melvyn Gent, 22 Diamond Drive,
Irthlingborough, Northants.

Riley Motor Club Ltd.
J. S. Hall, 'Treelands', 127 Penn
Road, Wolverhampton, West Mid-
lands, WV3 0DU.

Riley Register
J. A. Clarke, 56 Cheltenham Road,
Bishops Cleeve, Cheltenham, Glos
GL52 4LY.

Ro80 Club GB
Brian Taylor, 38 Yew Tree Drive,
Oswaldtwistle, Lancs BB5 3AX.
Telephone: 0254 37187.

Rolls-Royce Enthusiasts' Club
Lt-Col E. B. Barrass, 6 Montacute
Road, Tunbridge Wells, Kent TN2
5QP.
Telephone: 0892 26072.

Rover P4 Drivers' Guild
Colin Blowers, 32 Arundel Road,
Luton, Beds.

P6 Rover Owners' Club
16 Wark St, Chester-le-Street, Co.
Durham DH3 3GP.

Rover Sports Register
C. S. Evans, 8 Hilary Close, Great
Boughton, Chester CH3 5QP.

Rover 3/3½ litre Club
107 Water Lane, Leeds L11, W.
Yorks.
Telephone: 0532 459569.

SAAB Owners' Club (GB)
16 Denewood Close, Watford, Herts WD1 3SZ.

Singer Owners' Club
Martyn Wray, 52 Waverley Gardens, Stamford, Lincs.

Singer Car Owners, Association of
Barry Paine, 41 Folly Road, Wymondham, Norfolk.
Telephone: 0953 605411.

Standard Motor Club
Flat 1, 52 Selbourne Road, Southgate, London N14 7DH.

Star, Starling, Stuart and Briton Register
D. E. A. Evans, 9 Compton Drive, Dudley, West Midlands.

Sunbeam-Talbot Alpine Register
Secretary: P. E. Shimmell, 183 Needlers End Lane, Balsall Common, West Midlands.
Telephone: 0676 33304.

Sunbeam, Talbot Darracq Register
H. Tennant, North Mill Farm, Membury, Axminster, Devon.

Sunbeam Rapier Owners' Club
Peter Meech, 12 Greenacres, Downton, Salisbury, SP5 3NG.
Telephone: 0725 21140.

Sunbeam Tiger Owners' Club
Brian Postle, Beechwood, 8 Villa Road Estate, Cousett, Co. Durham.

TR Register, The
271 High Street, Berkhampstead, Herts.
Telephone: 044 27 5906.

TR Drivers' Club
K. Webb, 21 Boncombe Ingleside, Netley Abbey, Southampton, Hants.

Trident Car Club
45 Newtown Road, Verwood, Nr. Wimborne, Dorset BH21 6EG.
Telephone: 0202 822697.

Club Triumph Ltd.
Malcolm Warren, 14 John Simpson Close, Wolston, Coventry CV8 3HX.
Telephone: 0203 544770.

Triumph Sports Six Club
121B St Marys' Road, Market Harborough, Leics LE16 7DT

Triumph Razor Edge Owners' Club
Steward Langton, 62 Seaward Avenue, Barton-on-Sea, Hants. BH25 7HP.
Telephone: 0425 618074.

Triumph Roadster Club
R. Fitsall, 11 The Park, Carshalton, Surrey.
Telephone: 01-669 3965.

Triumph Sporting Owners' Club
Richard King, 16 Windsor Road, Hazel Grove, Stockport, Cheshire SK7 4SW.

Triumph 2000/2500/2.5 Register
Mrs L. Berry, 18 Ravensmead, Chinnor, Oxon OX9 4JG.

Trojan Owners' Club
D. Graham, Troylands, 10 St. Johns, Earlswood Common, Redhill, Surrey.

Turner Register
Dave Scott, 21 Ellsworth Road, High Wycombe, Bucks HP11 2TU.

TVR Car Club Ltd.
Vic Brookes, 'Calderstones', 1 Brackenhills, Upper Poppleton, York YO2 6DH.

Unipower Owners' Club
Gerry Hulford, 8 Coppice Road, Horsham, Sussex.

Vanden Plas Owners' Club *Including Sheerlines and Princess limousines.*
C. Dawe, 10 Playses Green, Hambridge, Langport, Somerset.

Vauxhall 30/98 Register
David Marsh, The Garden House, Middleton-by-Youlgreave, Near

Bakewell, Derbyshire.

Vauxhall Droop Snoot Group
Kit Spackman, "The Point", 15 Stanford Road, Lydney, Glos. GL15 5HR.
Telephone: Office 04536 71491. Home 0594 41268.

Volkswagen Split Window Club
Roger Beasley, 2 Wickenden Road, Sevenoaks, Kent.

VW Cabriolet Owners' Club
Mark & Wendy Richie, 58 Bronwydd, Birchgrove, Swansea, West Glam. SA7 9QJ.
Telephone: 0792 817771.

Volvo Owners' Club
Mrs Suzanne Groves, 90 Down Road, Merrow, Guildford, Surrey GU1 2PZ.

Vulcan Register *(section of Bean Car Club)*
David Hales, 20 Langbourne Way,

Claygate, Esher, Surrey KT10 0DZ.
Telephone: 0372 62046.

Wartburg Owners' Club
John Everson, 43 Robertson Street, Battersea, London SW8 3TX.

Wolseley Hornet Special Club
R. Banks, Taliesin, Heath Road, Horsell, Woking, Surrey.

Wolseley 6/80 and Morris Oxford (MO) Club *(Incorporating the Wolseley 4/50, Morris Six (MS) and related commercial vehicles.)*
John Billinger, 67 Fleetgate, Barton-on-Humber, North Lincs DN18 5QD.
Telephone: 0652 635138.

Wolseley Register
Secretary: David Allen, Glenville, Glynde Road, Bexleyheath, Kent DA7 4EU.

Appendix 2

Motor museums in the British Isles

The following collections are wholly or partly devoted to the display of motor cars. In some cases, motor cycles and commercial vehicles are also displayed.

Automobilia
The Old Mill, St. Stephen, St. Austell, Cornwall.

Automobilia
Billy Lane, Old Town, Hebden Bridge, Yorkshire. Tel: 0422 844775.

Bentley Motor Museum
The Pump House, Bentley Farm, Halland, Sussex.
Telephone: 082 584 574.

Betws-y-Coed Motor Museum
Betws-y-Coed, Caerns, North Wales.
Telephone: 069 02 427.

Bonython Manor Motor Museum
Bonython Manor Farm, Cury Cross Lane, Helston, Cornwall.
Telephone: 0326 240550.

Bourton Motor Museum
The Old Mill, Bourton-on-the-water, Gloucestershire.
Telephone: 0451 21255.

British Motor Industry Heritage Trust
Heritage Collection, Syon Park, Brentford, London TW8 3JF.
Telephone: 01-560 1378.

Broughton-in-Furness Motor Museum
Old Town Hall, Broughton, Kendal, Cumbria.
Telephone: 0966 41410

Caister Castle Motor Museum
Caister-on-Sea, Great Yarmouth, Norfolk.
Telephone: 057 284 251.

Donington Collection (Racing Cars)
Donington Park, Castle Donington, Derby.
Telephone: 0332 810048

Doune Motor Museum
Carse of Cambus, Doune, Perth-shire, Scotland.
Telephone: 078 684 203.

East Anglia Transport Museum
Chapel Road, Carlton Colville, Suffolk.
Telephone: 098 683 398.

Effingham Motor Museum
Trojan Ltd, Copthorne, Sussex.
Telephone: 0342 713011

Gangbridge Collection
Gangbridge House, St. Mary Bourne, Hants.
Telephone: 026 473 220.

Grampian Transport Museum
Alford, Aberdeenshire, Scotland.
Telephone: Alford 2292.

Hatfield House Motor Museum
Hatfield, Herts.

Historic Vehicles Collection of C. M. Booth
Falstaff Antiques, High Street, Rolvenden, Kent, TN17 4LP.
Telephone: 058 084 234.

Jersey Motor Museum
St. Peter's Village, Jersey, Channel Islands.
Telephone: 0534 82966.

Lakeland Motor Museum
Holker Hall, Cark in Cartmel, Cumbria.
Telephone: 044 853 509.

The Land Rover Museum
Dunsfold Land Rovers Ltd, Alford Road, Dunsfold, Nr. Godalming, Surrey, GU8 4NP.

Lark Lane Motor Museum
1 Hesketh Street, Off Lark Lane, Liverpool L17 8XJ.

London Cab Company Museum
1-3 Brixton Road, Brixton, London SW9 6DJ.
Telephone: 01-735 7777.

Manx Motor Museum
Crosby, Isle of Man.
Telephone: 0624 851 236.

Midland Motor Museum
Stourbridge Road, Bridgnorth, Salop.
Telephone: 07462 61761.

The Motor Museum *(specializing the Jaguars)*
Mill Lane, Maldon, Essex.

The Motor Museum
Dargate, Nr. Faversham, Kent.

Mouldsworth Motor Museum
3 Hillside Road, Frodsham, Cheshire.

Museum of British Road Transport
Cook Street, Coventry CV1 1NN.
Telephone: 0203 25555 ext 2091.

Myreton Motor Museum
Aberley, East Lothian, Scotland.
Telephone: 08757 288.

National Motor Museum
Beaulieu, Hampshire SO4 7ZN.
Telephone: 0590 612345.

Newburn Hall Motor Museum
35 Townfield Avenue, Newburn, Tyne & Wear.
Telephone: 0632 642977.

Patrick Collection
Patrick House, 180 Lifford Lane, Kings Norton, Birmingham B30 3NT.
Telephone: 021 459 4471.

Peter Black Collection
Lawkholme Lane, Keighley, Yorkshire.
Telephone: 0535 61177.

Port Erin Motor Museum
Port Erin, Isle of Man.
Telephone: 0624 832964.

Ramsgate Motor Museum
The West Cliff Hall, Ramsgate, Kent.
Telephone: 0843 581948.

Sparkford Motor Museum
Sparkford Nr. Yeovil, Somerset BA22 7JJ.

Stanford Hall Motor Cycle & Car Museum
Lutterworth, Leicestershire LE17 6DH. Telephone: 0788 860250

Stratford Motor Museum
1 Shakespeare Street, Stratford-Upon-Avon, Warwicks.
Telephone: 0789 69413.

Totnes Motor Museum
Totnes, Devon.
Telephone: 080422 357.

West Wycombe Motor Museum
Cockshoot Farm, West Wycombe, High Wycombe, Bucks HP14 3AR.
Telephone: 0494 443329.

Some of the many museums which incorporate motor vehicles

Black Country Museum
Tipton Road, Dudley, Worcs.
Telephone: 0384 56321.
Bradford Industrial Museum
Moorside Mill, Moorside Road, Bradford, Yorks.
Telephone: 0273 631756.
Bristol Industrial Museum
Princes Wharf, Prince Street, Bristol BS1 4RN.
Telephone: 0272 299771.
Cothey Bottom Heritage Centre
Brading Road, Ryde, Isle of Wight.
Telephone: 0983 68431.
Easton Farm Park & Motor Cycle Collection
Easton, Wickham Market, Suffolk.
Telephone: 0728 746475.
Glasgow Museum of Transport
25 Albert Drive, Glasgow G41 2PE.
Telephone: 041 423 8000.
Hull Transport Museum
36 High Street, Kington-upon-Hull, Hull, Humberside.
Telephone: 0482 222737.
Museum of Science & Industry
Newhall Street, Birmingham B3 1RZ.
Telephone: 021 236 1022.

North of England Open Air Museum
Beamish Hall, Stanley, Co. Durham.
Telephone: 0207 31811.
Nottingham Industrial Museum
Courtyard Building, Wollaton Park, Nottingham NG8 2AE.
Telephone: 0602 284602.
Riber Castle Fauna Reserve and Wildlife Park
Riber Castle, Matlock, Derbyshire.
Telephone: Matlock 2073.
Royal Scottish Museum
Chambers Street, Edinburgh EH1 1JF.
Telephone: 031 225 7534.
Sandringham Museums *(Royal cars)*
Sandringham Estate, Norfolk.
Science Museum
Exhibition Road, London SW7 2DD.
Telephone: 01-589 3456.
Shuttleworth Collection
Old Warden Aerodrome, Biggleswade, Bucks.
Telephone: 076 727 288.
Ulster Folk & Transport Museum
Cultra Manor, Holywood, BT18 0EU Co. Down, Northern Ireland.
Telephone: Holywood 5411.

Index